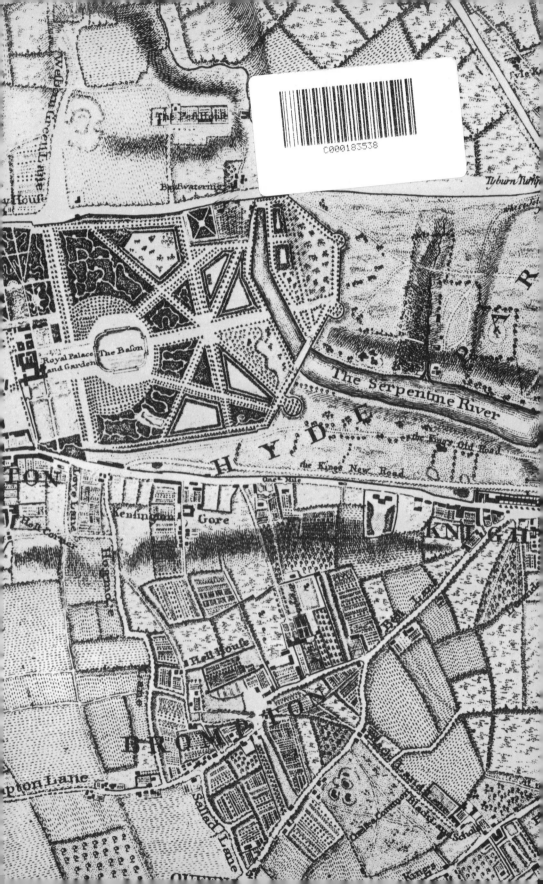

Wells in Greene Lane

The Powder House

The Watering

Tyburn Turnp

Royal Palace and Garden

The Bason

The Serpentine River

H Y D E

the Kings Old Road

the Kings New Road

One Mile

P A R K

TON

Grove Lane

Kensington Gore

Hell Corner

KNIGH

Hell House

BROMPTON

pton Lane

Salled Lane

Scholl

Kings

TWO VILLAGES

January 1974.

TWO VILLAGES

The Story of
Chelsea and Kensington

MARY CATHCART BORER

Foreword by Sir Malby S. Crofton, Bt
Leader of the council,
The Royal Borough of Kensington and Chelsea

W. H. Allen
London and New York
A division of Howard and Wyndham Ltd
1973

PRINTED AND BOUND IN GREAT BRITAIN BY RICHARD CLAY (THE CHAUCER PRESS) LTD,

BUNGAY, SUFFOLK

FOR THE PUBLISHERS W. H. ALLEN & CO. LTD,

44 HILL STREET, LONDON WIX 8LB

ISBN 0 491 01061 3

Contents

There are four sections of illustrations falling between
pages 52–53, 84–85, 148–149, 212–213

Acknowledgements

I should like to thank the Editor of the *Sunday Times* for permission to quote from articles appearing in the *Sunday Times* of 17 August, 1969 and 9 November, 1969, Aerofilms Ltd and Radio Times Hulton Picture Library for permission to reproduce photographs, John Murray (Publishers) Ltd for the quotation from *1851 and the Crystal Palace* by Christopher Hobhouse, Hamish Hamilton Ltd for the quotation from *My Grandmothers and I* by Diana Holman Hunt, Warne and Co. Ltd for the quotation from Beatrix Potter's *Journal*, Sir John Rothenstein for the quotation from *Men and Memories* by William Rothenstein.

I should also like to express my gratitude to the Committee of the Chelsea Physic Garden, the Curator, W. G. Mackenzie, Brian Hubbard of the Chelsea Pottery, Frederick Brill, the Principal of the Chelsea School of Art, the Reverend C. E. Leighton Thomson, M.A., Vicar of Chelsea Old Church, A. Stansfield, Secretary of the Chelsea Arts Club and Mrs Orde, Honorary Secretary of the Chelsea Society, for all their kindness and help in the writing of this book and the members of the staff of the Kensington and Chelsea Libraries who were so cooperative and helpful in the task of choosing the illustrations.

M.C.B.

Foreword

I AM very glad to have the opportunity of writing the Foreword to this history of the Royal Borough of Kensington and Chelsea. I remember that nearly twenty-five years ago when I bought my present home in Kensington how fascinated I was to learn that the house, dating from 1870, had been built on market garden land which was still undeveloped when George Bernard Shaw was a young man living round the corner in one of the older houses of Victoria Grove. I discovered then that modern Kensington and Chelsea consists of a string of ancient villages knitted together by Victorian infill.

Would there had been Amenity Societies in those days, as powerful as the Chelsea or Kensington Societies now are, to control the speculative building which ran up terrace after terrace of six-storied homes to house the expanding middle classes of the Victorian Industrial Revolution.

Yet much of the present character of the area springs from this speculative building, which produced many handsome squares and the quirkiness, for example, of Dutch Gothic in Queensgate or Courtfield.

I also remember talking to a Miss Alexander, who lived until only a few years ago at Aubrey House at the top of Campden Hill. She told me that she remembered as a girl going down on Sunday afternoons to see the cows being milked on the Ilchester Estate at the bottom of Holland Park. I was fascinated, too, to discover that there had been a race-course in Ladbroke, in use until relatively recent times, and that Portobello Road, now a world-wide tourist attraction, was a fashionable country walk in the early part of the last century. In that area, too, there was a flourishing pottery industry, now long gone, much less well known than its counterpart in Chelsea.

The present Royal Borough now finds itself athwart the path of the economic gale which arises from ever rising land values in modern city centres and, more particularly in the last few years, from the tourist boom. As many visitors now come to London in the course of the year as there are people in the Greater London Area, i.e. about seven million. Many come on cheap package tours in charabancs and many are young people, particularly students. They consider the King's Road and Kensington High Street to be major shopping areas, and to cater for them there has been an invasion of restaurants and boutiques which has pushed out many of the small service shop-keepers. In addition there has been a wholesale conversion of houses into hotels to accommodate the tourists.

Apart from tourists, the Borough has inevitably attracted the attention of big property developers while the demands of traffic have created a great arterial road through the middle of the Borough and the notorious West Way in the North.

In the face of all these challenges the Borough Council, vocifer-ously urged on by the numerous Amenity Societies, has fought a desperate struggle to maintain the residential character of this unique part of London. Half the Borough has now been declared a conserva-tion area: Kensington and Chelsea Corporation Act stands upon the statute books to prevent any more hotel conversions: a permanent litter patrol watches the streets, while parking meters contain the traffic.

Yet, we have to learn to live with change, for without change any community dies and becomes an odalisque. Neither I, nor I believe any of my fellow residents, really want our historic and beautiful Borough to become like, for instance, Cordoba in Southern Spain, or other cities where preservation itself has become the prime pur-pose of existence.

Buildings must change for they wear out and so many of them in the Borough are unworthy, particularly in the North, where they give rise to severe housing stress. Dealing with buildings is relatively easy, for we can conserve what is good and scrap what is bad. The preservation of a balanced community of all classes, colours and creeds is far more difficult. At the top end, the lovely houses and luxury flats in so much of what is still London's best residential quarter have attracted more and more embassies, diplomats and international executives. At the bottom end, the lower income groups are catered for by an ever-increasing pool of Council or Housing Trust accommodation. In the middle, older or retired folk and others living on modest incomes have found themselves steadily pushed out. Rents have risen alarmingly and ruthless landlords have found it worthwhile to cajole, or even harass existing tenants so that they may re-let their rooms on a furnished, short-stay basis.

Yet, despite these swirling tides of economic force and social change, the Royal Borough goes forward today confidently and vigorously. This book, whose publication I greatly welcome, will remind all who read it of the tremendous trust which is placed in the hands of those who are fortunate enough to live and work and serve in this unique community, which has, I believe, no parallel anywhere else in the whole world.

I

The Early Villages

IN 1963 the London Government Act combined the boroughs of Kensington and Chelsea into the Royal Borough of Kensington and Chelsea. It was the most recent chapter in a thousand-year-old story of two villages which, though so close together, developed independently through the centuries and still, though legally joined to form a civic entity, with a common civic administration, preserve their individualities.

Today the Royal Borough is an L-shaped area running approximately north-west to south-east, from the Harrow Road and North Kensington to Holland Park and Central Kensington. Southwards it broadens into Earls Court, South Kensington and Knightsbridge, and south again is Chelsea, forming the base of the L, divided by the King's Road and running down to the river.

It contains some of the most attractive parts of London and much of its charm lies in the survivals from the colourful past of the two remote little hamlets from which the new borough has evolved, for both have romantic stories and have been the homes of kings and queens, artists and writers, and men and women both famous and infamous.

Until the end of the fifteenth century, Chelsea was a little fishing village, but two hundred years later Defoe was to call it a 'town of palaces'. Sir Thomas More was the first famous resident, and after his execution Henry VIII took possession of his house and built a palace for his children close by. Here Prince Edward and Princess Elizabeth spent much of their childhood and both Anne of Cleves and Catharine Parr ended their days.

With the Restoration, Charles II built the Royal Hospital and the disreputable Lord Ranelagh the sumptuous Ranelagh House adjoining it. Charles Cheyne became Lord of the Manor and leased land to the Society of Apothecaries for the Physic Garden.

Chelsea's tradition of beautiful gardens had begun. Pepys enjoyed them on his river jaunts to the taverns on the water-front. John Evelyn visited them as a connoisseur.

By the eighteenth century the palaces were disappearing, but the first riverside houses of Cheyne Walk were built and behind them the terraces of delightful smaller houses, many of which still survive.

Writers and artists came to live there, enchanted by the river and the peace. Addison lived at Sandford Manor; Steele in Cheyne Walk; Swift lodged in Church Street; Sir Robert Walpole's house was next to the hospital.

The Ranelagh gardens were opened, outrivalling Vauxhall in splendour, and remained high fashion throughout the middle years of the eighteenth century. They were closed in 1805 and forty years later the Cremorne Gardens opened, at the other end of Chelsea.

Turner painted his glorious sunsets from the roof of his cottage in Cheyne Walk. Leigh Hunt and his tribe of noisy children lived in Upper Cheyne Row, Thomas and Jane Carlyle just round the corner in Cheyne Row. At the Queen's House in Cheyne Walk, Rossetti lived out his strange, lonely life, killing himself with chloral. Whistler built the White House for himself in Tite Street. At his home in the same street Oscar Wilde rose to fame, while during the early years of the present century Chelsea was the home of Henry James and a score of distinguished artists, including Walter Sickert, Wilson Steer and John Sargent.

In Tudor times, Kensington, like Chelsea, was a small village clustered round its church. The first mansion was built by Sir Walter Cope and his Cope Castle became the beautiful Holland House, which was to be a social stronghold of the Whig party. Nottingham House near by was bought by William III and renamed Kensington Palace. And after Kensington became a royal suburb the village grew quickly, Kensington Square becoming the home of many members of the nobility attending the Court.

It was at Kensington Palace that Queen Mary II and then William

III died. Queen Anne spent much of her time there and a good deal
of the intrigue of her reign, the quarrels of Sarah Churchill and Abigail Hill and the scheming of Harley and St John, took place in its
dark little rooms. George I lived there with his mistress and then
George II with his long-suffering Queen Caroline.

Later it was to be the home of several of George III's children,
including the Duke of Kent, father of Princess Victoria: and the
princess lived there with her widowed mother until her accession in
1837.

During the nineteenth century and the early part of the twentieth
century there were as many artists and writers living in Kensington
as in Chelsea. Leigh Hunt moved there from Upper Cheyne Row.
Thackeray lived in Young Street, John Stuart Mill and Burne-Jones
in Kensington Square. Millais lived luxuriously in Palace Gate,
Holman Hunt more simply in Melbury Road, a near neighbour of
G. F. Watts, Lord Leighton and a dozen or more of the late Victorian
artists.

The Royal Borough suffered grievous losses during the bombing
of the Second World War, including the destruction of Chelsea Old
Church and Holland House, though the Church has been rebuilt and
the façade of Holland House preserved. More has gone with post-
war reconstruction and the Chelsea and Kensington Societies have to
fight hard to preserve what is left of the two old towns, for cherished
corners of the borough are constantly threatened. Yet they are part
of an irreplaceable heritage and no excuse of expediency can justify
their destruction.

Walk across Kensington Gardens at sunset on an October evening,
when even the Round Pond is deserted, and the autumn mists dim
the sound of the distant traffic, and you will feel remote enough to
lose yourself in time. From the shadows that surround you Edwin
the Saxon trudged across this historic ground to his home in the
solitary hamlet of Chenesiton, a huddle of rough huts built in a clearing of the great Middlesex forest, on land which today forms the
heart of Kensington. The settlement was on rising ground, just above
the tidal swamps of the Thames – a few smallholdings, some cattle
pastures, one or two vineyards and a little wooden church, just large
enough for the hundred or so Saxon villagers.

A mile or two to the east lay the even smaller hamlet of Knightsbridge and two miles farther on, beyond the village of Charing, the
walled city of London. Alongside Chenesiton ran the neglected

remains of the Roman road from London to the west. A mile or two
to the south was the little riverside fishing village of Chelsea. To the
south-west and the west the land sank away to the lonely, reedy
marshes of the winding Thames, where the silence was hardly ever
broken, except by the boom of the bittern and the haunting croak of
the heron, but northwards rose the forest-covered slopes of Notting
Hill and Campden Hill, and far beyond them the heights of Hampstead and Highgate.

How the hamlet of Kensington came by its name no one can say. It
may once have belonged to the family called Chenesi, but no records
of their history have survived and it was soon to be known as
Kensington.

   With the coming of the Normans, Edwin, the Saxon thane of
Kensington, was unceremoniously dispossessed and nothing was ever
heard of him again. The fields and forests and wild heaths of the
manor of Kensington were granted to William's counsellor, the
Bishop of Courtances, who in turn gave the tenure to Earl Aubrey de
Vere, for his services during the Conquest. On the death of the
Bishop, in 1093, the de Vere family became the absolute owners of
Kensington and Earl Aubrey was appointed the Grand Justiciary of
England.

   The manor of Kensington was a roughly rectangular tract of land,
lying north-west to south-east. The south-eastern boundary was
where the Fulham Road now runs, so that it included the hamlets
where later West Brompton and Little Chelsea were to arise. Its
western boundary ran to the west of the Brompton cemetery and
parallel with Warwick Road to Shepherd's Bush and then continued,
still north-westwards, to the northernmost part of the Kensal Green
cemetery. Here the boundary turned sharply south-eastwards,
following the line of the Harrow Road for about a mile, and then
dropped south to the Bayswater Road and Kensington Gardens. It
did not extend farther eastwards than the Broad Walk, for this was
land belonging to the Abbots of Westminster, but went on southwards, down Queen's Gate and then north-east along the Brompton
Road to meet the Fulham Road.

   The land to the east of medieval Kensington, belonging to St
Peter's Abbey, Westminster, comprised the manor of Eia, and this
was divided into the three manors of Neyte, Eabury and Hyde.

   Aubrey de Vere's eldest son, Geoffrey, died before him. In his
youth, Geoffrey had been cured of a serious illness by the Abbots of

Abingdon, a kindness for which he was eternally grateful, for on his deathbed he persuaded his father to grant the church of St Mary, which had been built in 1100, and 270 acres of land surrounding it, to the Abbots of Abingdon. Aubrey kept his promise and St Mary's, the parish church of Kensington, became known as St Mary Abbots, while the land which went with it was made into a separate parish known as Abbots Kensington.

The de Vere family held their manorial court at Earls Court and although they never lived in Kensington, except perhaps for brief visits, they held the manor for the next five hundred years, it being ultimately divided into the four manors of Earls Court, Abbots Manor, West Town and Knotting Barns or Notting Hill.

With the death of Geoffrey, his younger brother, Aubrey the Grim, became the heir and ultimately succeeded to the manor, as well as the hereditary office of Lord Great Chamberlain. He also became Lord Chief Justice and during the civil war of Stephen's reign Henry I's daughter, Maud, created him Earl of Oxford, the first of a long line.

The history of the de Vere family throughout medieval times was a record of high office and honourable service to the King, during which they played a valiant part in all the wars. There were occasional backslidings, of course. Richard, the ninth Earl, a young man 'full of vivacity', was a great favourite of Richard II, and the King's uncle, the Duke of Gloucester, with the rest of the opposition party, became so infuriated with all the honours which were bestowed on him, his 'youthful sallies' and other impertinences, that, despite the King's protests, they insisted on his being packed off to Ireland, where he was already Marquis of Dublin and Duke of Ireland. As soon as Parliament had dispersed, however, the young King recalled his friend to England. But trouble soon broke out again, for the Earl divorced his wife, Philippa, a member of the Royal Family, in order to marry a low-born Bohemian, who was one of the Queen's maids-of-honour. The Duke of Gloucester, who had recently survived an attempt on his life by the King's party, took Philippa's divorce as a further insult to his family and decided that the time had come to deal more firmly with the impudent young Earl of Oxford. He mustered his private army and did battle with Earl Richard near Burford. The Earl was soundly beaten, 'with the loss of all his baggage', but by swimming across a river managed to escape with his life. Parliament accused him of high treason, his estates were confiscated and he was banished. He retired to the Low Countries, but shortly afterwards was injured during a wild boar hunt and died 'in great distress and penury'.

His seventeen-year-old son succeeded to the title and the de Veres remained Lords of the Manor of Kensington.

During the Wars of the Roses, John, the thirteenth Earl, joined the Lancastrians, but after the Battle of Tewkesbury he managed to escape to France. He returned to fight at Bosworth, after which his honours and estates were restored to him. He settled down in all his former pomp and glory and was unwise enough to flout the King's new law and retain his private army. When Henry VII visited him, shortly after his accession, he found 'two long lines of liveried retainers drawn up to receive him' and on his departure he said to the Earl: 'I thank you for your good cheer, my Lord, but I may not endure to have my laws broken in my sight. My attorney must speak to you.'

The Earl was fined £10,000, which he duly paid, and with the accession of Henry VIII he was confirmed in his office of Lord Great Chancellor and was also made Lord High Admiral.

While these events were shaping England's history, little change was taking place in Kensington. It remained a small rural hamlet, on the westerly route from London, by which it was approached by the Knights' bridge over the West Bourne river.

Who these knights were and why they wanted to cross the bridge no one knows for certain. The most attractive legend is that a company of Crusading knights, 'light in heart, if heavy in arms', passed through this district on their way to receive the blessing of the Bishop of London at Fulham, before setting off on their journey to the East. A bitter quarrel broke out between two of the knights, which they decided to settle by combat. They fought on the bridge while their companions watched from the banks of the river. Unfortunately, both the knights fell into the river and were drowned, and 'the place was for ever after called Knightsbridge, in remembrance of their fatal feud'.

Knightsbridge was a lonely place and the ale houses which had grown up around its ancient stone bridge had already earned an evil reputation as the resorts of footpads and robbers, who made the journey from London to the west a hazard which few travellers would attempt alone.

At the beginning of the sixteenth century there were no important buildings in Kensington. The Norman church of St Mary Abbots still stood among the farmhouses and labourers' cottages. The small manor-house, where the Earls of Oxford probably stayed during their brief visits, was in the West Town manor, near where Addison road now runs and conveniently close to the Earl's Court. Kensington at this time was known mainly for its springs of mineral waters. There was one at Notting Hill, another at Earls Court and a third close to the village, where Palace Green now stands.

It was Chelsea which was becoming better known. In early Tudor times, when the population of the whole of England was less than four million souls, the Thames above the walled city of London flowed slowly through the marshes and reeds, the loosestrife and yellow flags which bordered the fields of Middlesex and the lonely wooded hills of Surrey. Between London and Westminster was the village of Charing and two miles above Westminster was another little settlement – a handful of cottages clustered round a small church and manor-house – which was called Chesilsey or Chelsey, because of the shelf of pebbles and sand along the river strand where it was built.

In medieval times the manor of Chelsea had belonged to St Peter's Abbey of Westminster, but there was little of value in its desolate woods and unreclaimed marshes, and in the early days it seems to have changed hands several times. By early Tudor times Sir Reginald Bray, the architect who designed the lovely Henry VII chapel at Westminster Abbey, was living in the manor-house with its wonderful fan-vaulting, as well as St George's chapel at Windsor. The tomb of his son and heir, Edmund, the first Lord Bray, stands today in Chelsea Old Church, and from the Bray family the manor of Chelsea descended to Sir William Sandys, who held it until 1536.

Little is known about Chelsea before this time. The boundaries of the fields and woods which comprised the manor were very similar to those of modern Chelsea, defined by river courses which have long since disappeared. People talked of a few small orchards at Chelsea and also a vineyard, but most of the villagers probably earned their living from the abundant fish in the Thames, for there were many fast-days in the Church calendar and the demand for fish was high. By the sixteenth century the river was producing half London's fish supply, most of which was marketed at the ancient wharf and market at Billingsgate.

'What should I speak of the fat and sweet salmons daily taken in this stream, and that in such plenty (after the time of the smelt is past) as no river in Europe is able to exceed it?', wrote Stow rapturously. 'But what store of barbels, trouts, chevens, perches, smelts, breams, roaches, daces, gudgeons, flounders, shrimps, eels . . . are commonly to be had therein.'

In early medieval times many members of the nobility had their town houses in London, but as the city increased in importance, both commercially and socially, more people came flocking into it. By the beginning of Tudor times the population of London was not far short of 100,000. Over the pleasant gardens and shaded courts spread narrow lanes and twisting alleys, crowded with the houses of trades- men and artisans, and before long the city, with its open drains and piles of refuse, became so congested that the peers and gentry began to move out to the west, where the air was cleaner and the water purer, leaving their mansions to the rich city merchants, who moved in from their houses and warehouses along Thames Street and the busy London quays.

Just outside the city boundary was the Temple Church, surrounded by the Inns of the Templars, which by Tudor times had been taken over by the lawyers, and along the south side of the rough, muddy track, already known as the Strand, which ran between the Temple and Westminster where in the thirteenth century Peter of Savoy built the Savoy Palace, arose Essex House, Arundel House, Somerset House, Durham House, and, at Charing, York House, the palace of Cardinal Wolsey. This Ann Boleyn admired so much that, on the Cardinal's downfall, Henry VIII turned it into the Royal Whitehall Palace. These mansions were set in large gardens with lawns sloping down to the water steps, alongside which were the boat-houses where the household barges were moored.

Sir Thomas More, in search of peace and fresh air, decided to go farther afield than the Strand, and bought a plot of land in the heart of the country, on the river-front at Chelsea, close to the home of his friend Sir William Sandys. He built his house facing the river, a few hundred yards to the west of the church, about where Beaufort Street now runs, and its gardens reached northwards to where the King's Road was eventually to be made.

More was a Londoner, the son of a justice of the King's Bench, and was born in 1478, in Milk Street, off Cheapside. He was sent to St Anthony's school in Threadneedle Street, the school which invari- ably won in the debates with the scholars of Christ's Hospital and was constantly at war with the boys of St Paul's. He became a page in the household of the Archbishop of Canterbury and then went to Oxford, which at this time was astir with the new learning of the Renaissance. After Oxford, he spent four years at the Inns of Court, but from boyhood he had been deeply religious, and from 1499 to 1503 he lived the life of a solitary, devoting himself to study and prayer, thinking to become a Franciscan priest. However, his plans changed, and in 1504 he was returned to Parliament. After the death of Henry VII, Wolsey introduced him to the new king, Henry VIII, and, somewhat unwillingly, More was drawn into public life. Honours and high office came to him quickly, but he never lost his scholarly humility and ascetism. He endured self-imposed fasts, scourged himself in secret and to the day of his death wore a hair shirt beneath his robes.

The King loved the gentle and witty Sir Thomas More, knowing him for a man of rare integrity who would give him wise and honest counsel.

While still in his twenties and early thirties, More had published several books of historical biography, written in impeccable classical English prose, but his most famous work, the sociological romance *Utopia*, first printed in 1516, was written in Latin.

Utopia was not unlike Plato's *Republic*, and the work shows More's remarkable liberalism. He preached a system of communal living, whereby people could obtain the utmost happiness from life, although he was sufficiently realistic to doubt men's capacity to attain this blessed state. In *Utopia* all are contented with the bare essentials of life and everyone works for a living, but as wants are few, no one need work for more than six hours a day. In these conditions, avarice and temptation to crime disappear, and there are no aggressive wars, nor is there a death penalty, the punishment for the worst crimes being slavery.

Most important of all, in that intolerant age, no one is punished for his religious views, 'it being a fundamental opinion among them, that a man cannot make himself believe anything he pleases; nor do they drive any to dissemble their thoughts by threatening, so that men are not tempted to lie or disguise their opinions among them; which, being a sort of fraud, is abhorred by Utopians'.

'The most and wiser part of Utopians believe that there is a certain godly power, unknown, everlasting, incomprehensible, inexplicable, far above the capacity of man's wit,' wrote More, and he pleaded for tolerance in all matters of religion. Not only was he in favour of the marriage of priests, but advocated cremation, and euthanasia for those who were incurably ill and desired it. He was also an advocate of education for women, and his favourite daughter, the cherished Margaret Roper, was herself an accomplished classical scholar, as well educated as the erudite Lady Jane Grey and the Princess Elizabeth.

It was in 1520, when he was made Chancellor of the Exchequer, that More moved his household from their home in Bishopsgate to Chelsea. His greatly loved first wife had died, but his second wife, Dame Alice, though reputed to be sharp-tongued, was a kind mother to his four children, Margaret, Elizabeth, Cicely and John.

The house at Chelsea, said Erasmus, was 'neither mean nor subject to envy, yet magnificent and commodious enough'. It was a spacious, red-brick mansion with mullioned windows, facing the river but set back a little and approached by two courts, the inner one being protected by two gate-houses. Inside were the characteristic stone-flagged hall and long gallery. The walls were hung with tapestries, the floors strewn with rushes, for warmth and comfort, and the sparse furniture – the settles, stools, chairs, chests, tables and beds – were of carved oak.

This first important Chelsea household was idyllically happy in its simplicity, for More ordered it in accordance with his Utopian ideals. It was large, for it included his father, Margaret's husband, William Roper, the two younger daughters and their husbands, John and his child wife Anne, eleven grandchildren, the poor orphaned relative, Mercy Griggs, tutors, secretaries, attendants servants and his jester, Henry Patterson, as well as an assortment of pets, including a monkey, a fox, ferrets, weasels and a variety of birds.

'There is no man living so affectionate to his children as he,' wrote Erasmus, 'and he loveth his old wife as well as if she were a young maid.'

There was no high living. More preferred simple food and drink – milk, fruit and eggs with beer, rather than elaborate dishes and choice wines. Family prayers were held night and morning and they attended the parish church close by, where More built a private chapel on the south side of the chancel, and regularly took part in the services. 'The Duke of Norfolk, coming on a time to Chelsey to dine with him, fortuned to finde him in the quier, with a surplis on his backe, singinge, to whome, after service, as they homeward came arme in arme, the Duke said: "God's bodie! God's bodie! my Lord Chancellor, what a parish clerke, a parishe clerke!"'

The garden was a constant delight to More and here he built a small chapel, library and gallery for his private devotions and study. 'Being one day at dinner with Sir Thomas More,' wrote Ellis Heywood, 'we afterwards descended about two stones' throws into the

garden, walked on a little lawn in the middle and up a green hillock.
... It was an enchanting spot, as well from the convenience of the
situation – from one side almost all the noble city of London being
visible, and from the other the lovely Thames, surrounded with
green fields and wooded hills – as for its own beauty . . .'

At Chelsea, among their books and music, the virginals, clavi-
chords, lutes and flutes in which they all delighted, life was peaceful
and gay, for More, with all his piety, was a wit, yet 'his wit never
wounds, but is open, sweet and anything but bitter. For he only jests
inside his teeth', wrote Beatus Rhenatus.

In 1529, after the downfall of Wolsey, More was appointed Lord
Chancellor of England. It was now part of his duty to pass judgement
on all men who questioned the tenets of the Roman Catholic Church.
There was undoubtedly a streak of fanaticism in More, and in these
later years it was said to have manifested itself in a cruelty to heretics
which is hard to reconcile with his earlier writings. John Tewkesbury
is only one of several men who, according to Foxe, was taken to
Chelsea, after publicly denying the doctrines of purgatory and tran-
substantiation, kept in the stocks at the porter's lodge for six days and
then carried into the garden and mercilessly flogged. Afterwards he
was returned to the Tower, where he was tortured on the rack and
ultimately burned at Smithfield.

How much truth there is in these stories no one can now say.
Erasmus described Sir Thomas More as the mildest and kindest of
men, and many contemporaries denied that he ever condemned men
to death for their religious views. Later writers have taken the opposite view and Froude called him a 'merciless bigot'. Yet More himself denied that he had ever administered corporal punishment for
heresy to any but two people, one a lunatic and the other a child.

As well as Henry VIII, many distinguished men visited the Mores
at Chelsea, including the saintly Bishop Fisher of Rochester, Linacre,
Thomas Heywood, the poet and playwright, and the young German
wood-engraver and painter, Hans Holbein. Erasmus had met Holbein in Basle, where he was seeking refuge not only from the European wars but also from an unhappy marriage. Erasmus gave him an
introduction to the Chelsea household and here Holbein arrived in
1526. He stayed with the Mores until 1529, and his enchanting picture *The Household of Sir Thomas More* is a precious record of those
happy years.

Holbein returned to Basle, but within two years he was back in
England, setting up a studio in London, where he earned his living by

painting portraits, in the newly devised oil paint, of the rich German merchants of the Steelyard in Thames Street. His portraits became high fashion and by 1536 he had been appointed Court painter to Henry VIII, with rooms allotted to him in the palace of Whitehall.

Up till this time the only English painting had been 'water work' murals in churches and private houses. Now the fashion changed. The medieval murals and pictorial tapestries disappeared as carved oak wall panelling came into use, and in palaces and mansions the panelling was hung with Holbein portraits. Many English artists tried to copy him but his first worthy successor was Rubens.

But while Holbein was rising to fame, his friends in Chelsea were suffering grievously. As Henry VIII grappled with the increasing problems of his divorce from Queen Katharine, More saw, with grave misgivings, the widening breach with Rome. In 1532, no longer able to support the King's policy, he resigned the Chancellorship. It was a financial sacrifice, for he had little private money. He gave his barge and its crew of eight watermen to his successor, his fool to the Mayor of London. With these and other stringent economies, he hoped to live on at Chelsea in peaceful retirement, but it was not to be.

In 1534 he was summoned to Lambeth to take the oath of supremacy. Although he well knew the consequences if he refused, More could not accept a layman as head of his Church. That morning he went early to the Chelsea parish church to make his confession and receive the sacrament from his friend Dr Lark, the rector; and then 'whereas, whenever at other times before he departed from his wife and children, they used to bring him to his boat, and then kissing them, bid them farewell; at this time he suffered none of them to follow him to his gate, but pulled the wicket after him, and with a heavy heart, as by his countenance appeared, he took boat with his son Roper'.

At Lambeth, after refusing to take the oath, he was arrested and committed to the Tower. He spent the next fifteen months enduring terrible privations in a small damp cell. Dame Alice, distraught and uncomprehending, pleaded with him to accommodate his conscience, be practical and return to his family in Chelsea, but he sadly refused. At his trial he was found guilty of high treason and condemned to execution on Tower Hill. The day before his death, calm and courageous, he wrote a last letter to Margaret, who had already bade him a heart-broken farewell. 'I never liked your manner toward me better than when you kissed me last,' he wrote, 'for I love when daughterly love and dear charity hath no leisure to look to worldly courtesy.'

After the execution, More's head was displayed on a pole on London Bridge, until his family were able to rescue it for Christian burial. Even the King was troubled by the brutality of his old friend's punishment, for the story goes that when the news of the execution was brought to him, he turned to Ann Boleyn and exclaimed bitterly, if unreasonably: 'Thou hast been the cause of this man's death.' However, his remorse was only transitory, for shortly afterwards Dr Lark met the same fate. John More was taken prisoner, and although he was later released, died shortly afterwards.

The King took possession of the Chelsea house, turned out Dame Alice and presented it to the Marquis of Winchester. Dame Alice protested that she was homeless and penniless and was granted a small pension and a cottage near by: and Margaret and William Roper also continued to live in Chelsea, as tenants of the manor.

King Henry, having a fondness for Chelsea and a short memory for past tragedies, now decided to build a palace there for himself and his family. He made a proposal to Lord Sandys to exchange the manor of Chelsea for an estate in Hampshire, and the King not being a man with whom one could argue, Lord Sandys had little option but to agree. The manor-house was small and the King sold it to Richard Jervoise, a connection by marriage of the Sandys family. For his new palace he chose a site on the river-front, less than a quarter of a mile from More's house, just to the east of where Oakley Street now runs. The two-storeyed, red-brick Chelsea Place, or Palace, set in five acres of garden, was magnificent, consisting of 'three cellars, three halls, three parlours, three kitchens . . . larders and nine other rooms with a large staircase in the first story: three drawing-rooms, seventeen chambers and four closets, in the second, with garrets over part of them, and summer rooms with a bedroom'. The water supply came from a conduit which he built in Kensington, tapping one of its mineral springs.

Building began in 1536 and was finished the following year. Henry had married Ann Boleyn in 1533 and their daughter Elizabeth was born a few months later, but by the time the foundations of the palace at Chelsea were laid, Ann had been led through the sinister, terrible traitors' gate, on the water-front of the Tower, to the execution block, wearing 'a beautiful nightrobe of grey damask trimmed with fur, showing a crimson kirtle beneath' and a pearl head-dress, which she removed before placing her head on the block. And, by

the time the Chelsea palace was completed, Henry's third wife, Jane
Seymour, had died in childbirth, leaving the infant who was to become Edward VI. The marriage to Anne of Cleves was quickly an-
nulled and her successor, the lovely Catharine Howard, was beheaded in 1542.

During these troubled years Henry paid frequent visits to the
palace, for it was here, in the clear, country air of Chelsea, believed
to be so good for both asthma and consumption, that his two young
children, Elizabeth and Edward, lived. They were in the care of Lady
Bryan, who seems to have been chronically short of funds.

Elizabeth was only four years old when her mother was executed
and Lady Bryan wrote to the King's Chamberlain, complaining that
the princess 'hath neither gown nor kirtle, nor petticoat, nor no
manner of linen, nor foresmocks, nor kerchiefs, nor rails, nor body
stitchets, nor handkerchiefs, nor sleeves, nor mufflers, nor biggens'.
In 1538, when Prince Edward was scarcely a year old, the King complained, after a visit, that his son was not suitably dressed for his high
station, whereupon Lady Bryan promptly replied that 'the best coat
my Lord Prince has is tinsel, and that he shall have on at the time. He
hath never a good jewel to set in his cap. But I shall order all for my
lord's honour the best I can, and Master Vice-Chamberlain and
Master Cofferer will do their best'.

Henry's sixth wife, Catharine Parr, survived him and after his
death, in 1547, she made her home at the Chelsea palace with the two
children, Elizabeth being by now fourteen and Edward ten: and they
were often joined by their cousin, the precocious little Lady Jane
Grey, who was a granddaughter of King Henry's younger sister
Mary. Though only eleven years old at this time, she was already,
under the tutorship of Roger Ascham, able to read and write Greek,
Latin, French and Italian, and within the next few years was to study
both Hebrew and Arabic.

The Duke of Somerset, Jane Seymour's brother, had become Lord
Protector during Edward's minority, and his younger brother, Tom
Seymour, the Lord High Admiral, was looking for a wife sufficiently
rich and influential for his family's exalted position. He aspired to
Princess Elizabeth but the Council rejected the idea. The young King
Edward suggested he marry either his step-mother Anne of Cleves
or his half-sister Mary Tudor, but neither was attractive enough for
the Admiral. In the end, fearing another rebuff from the Council, he
secretly wooed and married Catharine Parr and came to live in the
palace. But to the mortification of poor Catharine, he soon made it

abundantly clear that it was the young Princess whom he preferred and, although old enough to be her father, he pursued her scandalously.

When the matter came to be examined, Elizabeth's nurse, Mrs Ashley, declared: 'At Chelsea, the Lord Admiral, incontinent after he was married to the Queen, would come many mornings into the Lady Elizabeth's chamber before she was ready, and sometimes before she rose. And if she were up would bid her good morrow, and ask how she did, and strike her upon the back, or buttocks familiarly, and so go forth through her lodgings; and sometimes go through to the maidens, and play with them and so forth; and if she were in bed, he would put open the curtains and bid her good morrow, and make as though he would come at her; and she would go farther in the bed, so that he could not come at her. One morning he strave to have kissed her in her bed, and this examinate was there, and bade him go away for shame.'

It is not at all certain that Elizabeth found the overtures of the Lord Admiral entirely unwelcome, but she was removed from Chelsea to Cheshunt and shortly afterwards Queen Catharine died. The scandalmongers even whispered that Tom Seymour had poisoned her. Their life together was certainly very unhappy and even her dying words to him were a whispered reproof. 'You have given me many shrewd taunts,' she sighed sadly.

Tom Seymour was subsequently attainted for other misdemeanours and, like his brother Somerset, executed. With the death of the Duke of Somerset, in 1552, the Duke of Northumberland became Lord Protector. He was given the manor of Chelsea and moved into the palace. He had already married his fourth son, Lord Guildford, to Lady Jane Grey, and it was at Chelsea that his fifth son, who was to become the Earl of Leicester and husband of the ill-starred Amy Robsart, spent part of his boyhood.

A few months after Northumberland's appointment, in the summer of 1553, young King Edward, sixteen years old and now living at Greenwich, died of consumption. Henry VIII had named Mary Tudor as the next in succession, but Northumberland, fearing for the future of the Protestant party in England, as well as for his own fortune, tried to put Lady Jane Grey on the throne. The plot failed and after nine days as Queen, the seventeen-year-old Jane and her young husband were committed to the Tower and executed, along with the Duke. The Northumberland family was hated in England and the country supported the proclamation of Mary Tudor as Queen. The

Northumberland estates were confiscated and the Queen even laid claim to the Duchess' magnificent wardrobe – dresses of satin and wrought velvet, black, crimson and purple – embroidery of 'love laces of gold and silver' and lengths of costly cloth of gold – but the Duchess was a sick woman. She was allowed to live on in the Chelsea palace, where she died only a few months later, in 1554. She was buried at Chelsea with regal splendour. Two heralds attended the funeral procession and seventy-two torches were carried. On her bier rested her waxen effigy, under a canopy, and her tomb still stands, in the north-eastern corner of the More Chapel.

Katharine of Aragon had died soon after the divorce, and before Henry's marriage to Jane Seymour, but Anne of Cleves still survived, a sweet-tempered, gentle soul, for all her lack of physical attractions, and she was now moved into the Chelsea palace for her last years. She never learned to speak English and spent her days in a state of mild and mute incomprehension, inoffensively sewing, but she was always treated with dignity, and when she died, in 1557, her body was carried in state from Chelsea to Westminster for burial.

The palace and manor of Chelsea were now bestowed for life on the widow of the late Protector, the Duchess of Somerset, and after she died, in 1588, Lord Howard of Effingham, the Lord High Admiral and hero of the Armada and Cadiz, later to become the Earl of Nottingham, moved in. Queen Elizabeth had a great affection for her admiral and visited him, at her childhood home in Chelsea, nearly every year, until her death in 1603.

With the end of the Tudors, more than ninety years had passed since Sir Thomas More had first made Chelsea famous. Many changes had taken place in his old home. Lord Winchester had lived there until his death in 1572, when it passed to his step-daughter and her husband, Lord and Lady Dacre. Lady Dacre survived her husband for only a few months, leaving the Chelsea house to Lord Burleigh, who himself died a year later, so that by 1596 the house became the property of his son, Sir Robert Cecil, Queen Elizabeth's Secretary of State.

At the old manor-house, Sir Richard Jervoise had died and some time during the later part of the sixteenth century the house had been acquired by Sir Thomas Lawrence, goldsmith and merchant adventurer of the City of London. He too built a chapel in the parish church and his memorial there is dated 1593, but his family was to live on in Chelsea until the end of the seventeenth century.

On the river-front, not far from the palace, the Earl of Shrewsbury had built a mansion. It was in his care that, for many years, Elizabeth entrusted Mary Queen of Scots. The Earl treated her with so much consideration that his Countess, who had already buried three extremely rich husbands, became jealous. Between Mary's endless scheming and his wife's angry reproaches, the unfortunate Earl had such an unhappy time that, when Elizabeth posted him to a command in Lancashire, he thanked her for relieving him of two 'she-devils'.

The Earl died in 1590, leaving the Countess, who was the grandmother of Arabella Stuart, in possession of the house in Chelsea, as well as her magnificent seats at Chatsworth, Hardwick and Oldcotes, all of which passed, at her death, to William, Earl of Devonshire.

There was another large mansion in Chelsea, just west of Sir Thomas More's house, built by Sir Arthur Gorges. Sir Arthur's son ultimately became owner of Sir Thomas More's house, while Gorges House passed to Sir Robert Stanley, after he had married Sir Arthur Gorges' daughter.

Chelsea was growing, but only very slowly. These five noble mansions dominated the riverside. There are references in the records to several smaller houses which were built here in Tudor times, but all traces of them have long since vanished, and by the end of the sixteenth century there were probably not more than thirty households in the whole manor, apart from the cottages of the peasants. In fact so quickly was the population of London growing and the suburbs spreading, that at the end of Elizabeth's reign a proclamation was published, forbidding the building of any new houses within three miles of the city.

With the dissolution of the monasteries and the appropriation of the Church lands, Abbots Kensington had gone to the Crown and King Henry also came into possession of Westminster Abbey's manor of Hyde, which he converted into a private deer park. It stretched over the whole area now occupied by Hyde Park and Kensington Gardens, St James' Park and Regent's Park and its western boundary was the land of the de Veres. This gave the King an uninterrupted stretch of hunting-ground from Westminster to Hampstead Heath, where deer abounded as well as hare, partridge and pheasant, and herons fished in the chain of pools, which were fed from the Bourne on its course from Hampstead southwards across the Royal Park to Knightsbridge and the Thames at Millbank, just east of Chelsea.

One unexpected effect of the dissolution of the monasteries was a

decline in English agriculture and horticulture. The monks had been
skilful farmers and gardeners. They had exchanged knowledge with
visiting monks from Europe and also had access, in their libraries, to
the agricultural works of the classical writers. With the end of the
monasteries, much of this knowledge was lost. To add to the trouble,
thousands of acres of monastic lands were sold, not as arable ground
but as pasture, for sheep-rearing had become more profitable than
arable farming and entailed less labour. During the next few generations, therefore, English agriculture tended to become less efficient
and the old kitchen-gardens, with their herbs and vegetables and
fruit trees, began to disappear.

The population of the country was increasing but the production
of food was declining. Food prices rose, and although the diet of most
people was bread and cheese, with meat or fish when they could
afford it, and a few peas, beans and root vegetables, cultivated on
their own plots, such ordinary vegetables as cabbages and onions had
to be imported from Holland. Katharine of Aragon is said to have
complained that she could not obtain even a simple salad in England.

At the beginning of Queen Elizabeth's reign, the English wool
trade suffered a reverse, when Spain blocked the European markets,
but England's fortunes rose again when she found markets for her
wool farther afield, and by the end of the century she had attained a
period of relative prosperity and security. Moreover, the price of
food had increased sufficiently for arable farming to be as profitable
as sheep-rearing. The result was a revival of interest in agriculture
and horticulture. Cabbage, onion, carrot, parsnip, turnip, cauli-
flower, melon, pumpkin, cucumber, radish and lettuce seeds were
imported from Holland and the taste for them quickly grew. Fruit
trees, ornamental shrubs and flowers soon followed, brought from
Europe and also by travellers from America, the West Indies and
the East.

Market gardens were laid out in the suburbs of London to supply
the growing demand, particularly in the fields of Fulham, Kensington and Chelsea. The old convent garden of the monks of St Peter's
Abbey of Westminster, in the fields north of the Strand, which had
come into the possession of the Russell family, was re-established.
Soon Covent Garden, as it came to be called, was a popular market
for fruit and vegetables, and at one time more than half its supplies
came from the orchards and market gardens of Chelsea and Kensington.

By the beginning of the seventeenth century, many more new

plants had been introduced. Sir Walter Raleigh's potato did not gain favour for many years but apricot, almond, peach, fig, orange and lemon trees arrived and, as the art of grafting was studied, many improved strains of our native apple, pear, cherry, walnut and filbert trees were developed. Strawberries, raspberries, gooseberries and currants were cultivated and a wide variety of herbs, which were used not only for cooking, but medicinally and also in the preparation of cosmetics.

In 1563 the first English gardening book appeared, Thomas Hill's *Profitable Art of Gardening*, and in 1597 Gerard published his famous *Herbal*.

Every house of any pretensions now had its flower garden and among the English roses, daffodils, pansies, wallflowers, marigolds, stocks and carnations, the exotic tulips, nasturtiums, honesty, larkspur, love-in-the-mist, Christmas roses, passion flowers and dahlias began to appear.

Early in his reign, James I ordered the planting of a mulberry garden in Chelsea, for the promotion of an English silk-weaving industry. A large mulberry garden certainly existed during the seventeenth century, but it was not until the early years of the eighteenth century that there is any evidence of a small silk-weaving industry in Chelsea.

At this time the population of London was already nearly two hundred thousand and at holiday times the citizens would sometimes escape from the heat of the overcrowded city and stroll westwards to Kensington and Chelsea to buy fresh fruit and vegetables and sample the burgundy which was still being made at the Kensington vineyard.

The de Vere Kensington property passed, through a succession of married sisters, to the seventh Earl of Argyll, who had more interests in Scotland than in the south. In 1591 Walter Cope, a wealthy landowner by inheritance and a merchant of the City of London, 'a gentleman of rare and excellent parts', decided to move from the Strand to the fresh, invigorating air of Kensington. He bought the manor of West Town and lived in the old manor-house for a time, and within the next few years he bought the rest of the Argyll property, Earls Court and Notting Hill, and Abbots Manor from the Crown. He disposed of Notting Hill and 200 acres of Abbots Manor, but kept the rest and in 1605 set about building a grand manor for himself, which he called Cope Castle. It was the first important mansion in Kensington.

II

*Kensington in the Early
Seventeenth Century*

WALTER COPE was a man of culture and taste and he attained
high office. In 1603 he was knighted by King James and made
Gentleman of the Privy Chamber. His beautiful new house, set in a
park of natural woodland, was a proper setting for his honours. The
original building comprised the main body of the house and the
architect was probably John Thorpe, who designed Audley End.
Like so many Jacobean mansions, it was of red brick with stone
facings, in a style which was a mixture of Gothic and Renaissance.
The entrance porch on the south front, approached by a shallow
flight of steps, was open, each of the sides forming a rounded arch,
and the rooms on the two floors above it had deep bay windows
extending over the porch, the upper floor being surmounted by a
cupola. The rooms on either side of the porch had large mullioned
windows, the upper floor being surmounted by Dutch gables. Beyond them, in perfect symmetry, were arched colonnades with a
stone balustrade above, each baluster being carved in the form
of a fleur-de-lis, which was the family emblem. The rooms on
the first floor above the colonnades had large oriel windows,
those on the second floor flat casements with Dutch gables above.
On either side of the house rose small brick towers surmounted by
cupolas.

The entrance hall was over 40 feet long and 18 feet wide and the
staircase and first-floor State rooms – the dining-room, red drawing-

room, yellow drawing-room and other entertaining rooms – were on the same scale of elegant grandeur.

Sir Walter moved into Cope Castle with his family in 1606, by which time more mansions were being built in Kensington. In 1604 Sir George Coppins had bought some thirty-six acres of land from Sir Walter which lay to the east of the Cope estate and adjoined the boundary of Hyde Park. On this land, which included Henry VIII's bath and conduit for supplying water to the palace at Chelsea, he built a red-brick house, much smaller and plainer than Cope Castle, though it may well have been designed by the same architect, John Thorpe.

The original house had an entrance porch facing south, approached by a short flight of steps, which led to an entrance hall with screens, thereby retaining the medieval pattern of domestic building. Beyond them, at the northern end, was a dais, with a large bay window behind it and smaller windows on either side. On either side of the hall were large rooms with bow windows, that to the east, looking over Hyde Park, being the parlour, the one to the west being used very probably as a chapel. The wide staircase led from the north-east corner of the hall, to the gallery and 'great chamber' and there were more rooms on the second floor.

Between these two mansions Sir Baptist Hicks, a wealthy silk-mercer of Cheapside, who had also been knighted by James I, was soon building a third house, on land which he had bought from Sir Walter Cope, or, as legend has it, had won from him during a game of chance. Hicks' house was a smaller version of Cope Castle, a beautiful Jacobean mansion of red brick and stone, with a wide entrance porch, oriel windows and Dutch gables, and it stood on the west side of the lane running north from St Mary Abbots church and the village high street, which came to be known as Church Lane and later as Church Street.

Sir Walter spent a vast amount of money on his castle and as his honours increased, so did his spending. He became Chamberlain of the Exchequer, joint Keeper, with his patron Sir Robert Cecil, of Hyde Park and eventually Master of the Court of Wards and Liveries. Not only was Cope Castle furnished luxuriously but it housed Sir Walter's magnificent library. However, it had its drawbacks, for it proved to be extremely cold.

King James was frequently in Hyde Park, following his favourite sport, hunting the deer 'in a doublet green as the grass he stood on, with a feather in his cap and a horn by his side', and he often dined there, at the little pavilion built among the trees. In 1612 he was a visitor at Cope Castle, but he found it too draughty for his comfort. 'He was quickly weary of Kensington, because he said the wind blew through the walls, that he could not lie warm in his bed.'

Sir Walter did not live long to enjoy his proud castle, for he died in 1614, leaving debts of £27,000. Other properties had to be sold to meet them, but Lady Cope inherited the castle, provided she did not marry again. However, she did, so the property descended to their daughter Isabella, who was already married to Sir Henry Rich, a son of the Earl of Warwick. Sir Henry was a very beautiful and attractive young man, but not particularly well off at this time, being, as Lord Clarendon put it, 'the younger son of a noble house, and a very fruitful bed'.

As a youth he had soldiered in the Dutch campaigns for a time, but when he returned to England and attended Court he soon caught the attention of King James who, ever fond of beautiful young men, bestowed upon him 'unpleasing caresses'. The Duke of Buckingham also took a great fancy to young Henry who, always mindful of his own interests, was wise enough to be circumspect with the King and 'took all ways he could to endear himself to the Duke', though his real affections were with the Earl of Carlisle. His plan paid handsome dividends, for the King 'scarce made more haste to advance the Duke, than the Duke did to promote Henry', who was said to have 'preferred the Duke to his wife'. He was appointed a Gentleman of the Bedchamber of Charles, the Prince of Wales. By 1623 he was made Baron Kensington and the following year the Earl of Holland. After plans for Prince Charles' marriage to the Infanta of Spain had broken down, Henry was sent to Paris to negotiate the Prince's marriage to Henrietta Maria, and he wooed her so successfully that she always retained a special fondness for him.

In 1625, soon after the accession of Charles I and Henrietta Maria, the Duke of Buckingham was murdered by a madman, but Henry, Lord Holland, continued to prosper from the increasing number of high offices bestowed on him, largely through the affection of the Queen. He was made Groom of the Stole and First Lord of the Bedchamber, General of the Horse and Captain-General North of the Trent. He became immensely rich and during these years made many additions to Cope Castle, which had now come to be called Kensington House and was soon to be known as Holland House.

Henry added two wings, each with colonnaded walks and rooms above with beautiful oriel windows surmounted by Dutch gables, to match the main part of the house. These wings with the house thus formed three sides of a courtyard, the fourth side being a low stone balustrade broken by a flight of shallow steps leading to a formal garden.

On the first floor of the west wing the Long Gallery, which was later to become the library, ran the entire length of a hundred feet. He added the beautiful plaster ceiling to the entrance hall, which was later to become the breakfast-room; and the decoration of the 'Gilt room', on the first floor, above the entrance hall, with its superb panelling divided by fluted Ionic pilasters, was designed by Henry and Isabella for the ball they gave to celebrate the marriage of Charles and Henrietta Maria. They also employed the most fashionable architect of the day, Inigo Jones, to design an impressive gateway, approached by a double stairway, with stone piers surmounted by heraldic beasts.

In 1628 Elizabeth Preston, the thirteen-year-old daughter of the self-styled eleventh Earl of Ormonde, was left an orphan. Her father had been drowned while crossing from Ireland and her mother had died three weeks later. Charles I committed her to the wardship of Henry Holland and his wife, who kept her closely guarded at Holland House. Though the wardship was highly profitable to the Hollands, they treated her almost as a prisoner, allowing her neither tutor nor governess nor any means of education, but Elizabeth was a girl of spirit and managed to teach herself quite adequately.

A large fortune awaited her, but much litigation was involved. The claim of Walter Butler, the rightful eleventh Earl, had been disputed by Elizabeth's father, a cousin by marriage. Preston had been a favourite of King James and the Duke of Buckingham and, when the case had come before the Court of Justice, King James had shamefully declared for Preston. Walter Butler had refused to accept the ruling and declined to pay the enormous fine which the refusal had entailed. He had therefore been clapped into the Fleet prison and kept there for the next eight years, until the death of James and the accession of Charles. During these years of his imprisonment his son had died and his grandson James, who was to become the first Duke of Ormonde, was living as a royal ward in the care of the Archbishop of Canterbury, in conditions of deprivation and penury which were little better than those of his cousin Elizabeth.

By the time old Sir Walter was released, James was fifteen and he and his grandfather were allowed to live together. They were very poor and took a lodging in Drury Lane, from where the tenacious old Sir Walter began a long campaign to recover his Irish estates and his rightful fortune.

Elizabeth's mother had always wanted Elizabeth to marry her cousin James, in order to heal the family feud, and to young James, although he had never met Elizabeth, the same idea had occurred, as an obvious solution to the bleak state of his finances. In secret he attended a service at St Mary Abbots, where he knew she was taken each Sunday by the Hollands, and he was delighted with what he was able to see of her. The Hollands were bitterly opposed to the marriage, determined to hold on to Elizabeth's great wealth for as long as possible. So James began a secret courtship, on one occasion visiting her at Holland House in disguise. Very soon the nineteen-year-old James and the fourteen-year-old Elizabeth Preston were deeply in love and they were helped by Isabella, the Hollands' daughter, who acted as a willing messenger for their love letters.

Unfortunately, in the course of this clandestine romance, James also made love to Isabella, and she had to be spirited away to France to have a son. James was now writing to both girls and in his confusion sent a letter to Elizabeth which had been intended for Isabella, but Elizabeth was an accommodating girl and when she thus learnt of Isabella's predicament she seems to have entertained no hard feelings. At last, after extracting a payment of £15,000, the Hollands allowed Elizabeth and James to marry, and all ended happily. Walter Butler was finally judged the legal heir to the Earldom of Ormonde and James succeeded him, he and Elizabeth becoming enormously wealthy and living in princely style. During the troubled years of the Civil War and the Commonwealth they remained unswervingly loyal to King Charles and the royalist cause, and for the rest of their long lives they were happily devoted, James' brief affair with Isabella being soon forgotten, for she had quickly recovered her health and spirits and before long became Lady Thynne.

With the passing years, Henry Holland grew increasingly irritable and pompous. In 1633 he was confined to Holland House for a time, after a quarrel with Lord Weston, during which he had challenged him to a duel. Five years later he retired from Court, to sulk at Holland House, because he had not been given the office of Lord High Admiral, after which he had hankered, but he was soon back again.

About 1620 Sir George Coppins had sold his house to Sir Heneage Finch, the Recorder of London, who became Speaker of the House of Commons in Charles I's first parliament, and here he remained for many years, a melancholy man living in a rather gloomy house, surrounded by a formal garden with clipped yew hedges and neat flower beds.

In 1628 Sir Baptist Hicks had been created Lord Campden, taking the title from his estates at Chipping Campden, and his house became known as Campden House.

By the middle of the seventeenth century, therefore, Kensington had three large mansions, Holland House, in its beautifully wooded park, Campden House and Finch's house. The little village, centred round its parish church of St Mary Abbots, was busy and prosperous with its market gardening, the gardens stretching down into the fields of Brompton, while to the west of Holland Park was the ancient vineyard, which had been in existence since Norman times and was still producing burgundy. Cottages and inns lined the main street of the village and building was slowly spreading along Church Street, but the way to Knightsbridge, alongside the Royal deer park, was still lonely and dangerous for solitary travellers, and Knightsbridge was still notorious for the cut-throats and footpads who haunted its inns.

When the troubles began which led to the Civil War, Henry Holland took part in the Scottish campaign, as General of the Horse, but it was a failure. It was an excessively hot summer and nothing went right. After the retreat, his army was disbanded and 'the Earl of Holland, in great pomp, returned to his house in Kensington'. He was to prove himself a fair-weather friend to King Charles and Queen Henrietta Maria, for he now suffered a change of heart and declared himself for Parliament.

By August 1647, Members of Parliament were meeting with General Fairfax and Lord Holland at Holland House and many skirmishes took place between Kensington and Knightsbridge. Holland continued to support Cromwell until the Royalists' cause was clearly hopeless and he realised at last that the King's life was in mortal danger. Then, remembering all the benefits he had received from Charles and the enduring trust and affection of the Queen, the unpredictable Earl seems to have been overcome with remorse. He made a last-minute, desperate but forlorn attempt to go to their rescue. With the young Duke of Buckingham, he led an insurrection at Kingston, but the army he had hastily gathered was pitiably small compared with the forces ranged against him. He was defeated and taken prisoner, being held first at Warwick Castle and then in the splendour of his own beautiful home at Kensington, from where he was brought to trial and condemned to death.

On 9 March 1649, less than six weeks after the execution of Charles I, he suffered the same fate. On the scaffold he made an hour-long speech and then 'pulled off his gown and doublet, having next to him a white satin waistcoat, put on a white satin cap with silver lace and prepared himself for the block, took his leave, and embraced with much affection Mr Hodges, Mr Bolton, his servants and others on the scaffold, forgave his executioner, gave him money, thought to be ten pounds in gold, and laid himself down on the block, and prayed awhile, then gave the sign by stretching forth his arms, upon which the executioner severed his head from his body at one blow...'

So ended the life of the 'gay, beautiful, gallant Lord of Holland, whom neither the honours showered on him by his Prince, nor his former more tender connection with the Queen, could preserve from betraying and engaging against both'.

General Fairfax used Holland House for his own residence for a time. 'The Lord General is removed from Queen Street to the late Earl of Holland's house at Kensington, where he intends to reside', announced a current journal. And here both Cromwell and Ireton came to confer with him from time to time, but before long the house was restored to the widowed Isabella, who lived there until her death, with her eldest son Robert, the second Earl Holland and his family.

During the Commonwealth, play acting was forbidden and most of the London theatres were destroyed, but the old Cock Pit in Drury Lane survived and here William Davenant, Shakespeare's godson – perhaps his natural son – and his company of actors sometimes, at great risk, gave secret performances to carefully selected audiences. One day, however, the news leaked and soldiers broke in. They cleared the auditorium, broke up the stage and took all the players off to prison for a few weeks. After that they were more circumspect and gave their performances in the houses of the nobility. Robert, the second Earl Holland, often asked them to Holland House, where a small audience was invited to watch them and contribute to their expenses, notice of the show being given in advance, with great discretion, by Alexander Goffe, the actor who was so brilliant in the women's parts.

Lord Campden had died in 1629 and the house had passed to his son-in-law, Lord Noël, who played an infinitely more gallant part during the Civil War than Henry Holland. He died in the King's garrison at Oxford, but his son Baptist, the third Lord Campden, raised his own troop of horse and a company of foot to fight for the

King. His father-in-law was the gallant Earl of Lindsey, one of the four noblemen who at King Charles' trial declared that they had advised the King wrongly and caused his downfall: and they had offered themselves for execution if the King's life were spared.

At the end of the Civil War, Lord Campden's house was confiscated and Commonwealth officials occupied it for a time, but it was eventually restored to him and, at the Restoration, Charles II, who never forgot a loyal friend, paid him special honour. The old Earl of Lindsey came to live with his son-in-law during his last years and on more than one occasion the King had supper with them both at Campden House.

The dour Sir Heneage Finch was dead. He had left his home to his five-year-old younger son, but the year after the Restoration the boy's elder brother, another Sir Heneage Finch, who later became the Earl of Nottingham, bought it from him. The first Sir Heneage had been dismal but his elder son and grandson, the first and second Earls, were of even more sombre temperament, and became known as the 'black, funereal Finches'.

'The first Earl suffered under a long depression of spirits before he died', wrote Leigh Hunt. 'The second was a man of so atrabilarious a complexion, and such formal and dreary manners, that he was nicknamed Dismal; and Dismal's son, from the swarthy appearance, and the way in which he neglected his dress, was called the Chimney-sweep.'

During the Civil War and the Commonwealth there was little new building in Kensington, but with the Restoration came many changes.

III

Chelsea and the Stuarts

AT the beginning of Stuart times gardens were as formal as they had been during the sixteenth century, with neat little flower-beds, cut square, triangular or in symmetrically curved 'knots'. They were bordered with low hedges of clipped box, lavender, rosemary, marjoram, thyme or thrift and divided by trim gravel paths. The boundary hedges of these gardens were usually of yew, clipped at the corners into pyramids, globes or whatever flight of fancy happened to take possession of the topiarist at the time, a peacock with outspread tail being considered the most stylish.

'A garden,' wrote Sir Francis Bacon, 'is the purest of human pleasures,' but he was scornful of the excessive formality of some of the Elizabethan gardens, which were 'but toys: you may see as good signs many times in tarts'.

When Thomas Hill wrote his *Profitable Art of Gardening*, he included advice on the siting of gardens, the best times to dig and plant and the most effective manures to use, much of which information he had borrowed from the Italians.

The first English garden in the grand Italian manner, with statues, fountains, sundials and arbours, canopied with roses and clematis, built into the recesses of great yew hedges, was made by Sir John Danvers, early in the seventeenth century, at his house in Chelsea. Danvers House was built to the east of Sir Thomas More's house. The nucleus may have been the chapel and library which Sir Thomas had built in his garden, and here, in the Danvers' time, Orlando Gibbons came to play on the organ, in the 'stately room' above the hall.

Sir John had expensive tastes and overspent wildly, becoming hopelessly but cheerfully in debt, but his lovely garden, now buried under the bricks and mortar of Paulton's Square, perhaps began Chelsea's long tradition of beautiful gardens. And Paulton's Square, built in the 1830s, is today one of Chelsea's most attractive corners, with its trim white houses, surrounding the pleasant garden, and the magnificent plane tree at the northern end, soaring over the rooftops of the King's Road.

Aubrey tells us: 'The Pleasure and Use of Gardens were unknown to our great Grandfathers: they were contented with Pot-herbs: and did mind chiefly their stables. But in the time of King Charles II Gardening was much improved, and became common. 'Twas Sir John Danvers of Chelsey . . . who first taught us the way of Italian gardens . . . He had a very fine Fancy, which lay (chiefly) for Gardens, and Architecture. The Garden at Chelsey in Middlesex (as likewise the House there) doe remaine Monuments of his Ingenuity. He was a great acquaintance and Favourite of the Lord Chancellor Bacon, who took much delight in that elegant garden.'

And Aubrey adds the delightful note: 'Sir John, being my Relation and faithfull Friend, was wont in fair mornings in the Summer to brush his Beaver-hatt on the Hysop and Thyme, which did perfume it with its naturall Spirit; and would last a morning or longer.'

Sir John's first wife was a widow, the mother of Lord Herbert of Cherbury, and several years older than her second husband. In fact, Aubrey says she was old enough to have been his mother and he married her for 'love of her Witt'. She was greatly loved in Chelsea, for her kindness and charity, and was a close friend of Dr Donne, who often visited her, for he had a close connection with Chelsea, being a descendant of both Sir Thomas More and John Heywood.

In 1627, when Lady Danvers died, he conducted her funeral at Chelsea Old Church, and in the congregation was his close friend, Isaak Walton, who wrote of the deep emotion with which Donne preached the funeral sermon. Donne, he said, 'preached like an angel . . . carrying some to heaven in holy rapture, and inticing others by a sacred art and courtship'.

Donne was also an intellectual and it was his skill in theological controversy which attracted him to King James. The King delighted in logic and debate, and early in his reign had favoured the idea, probably suggested to him in the first place by Dr Matthew Sutcliffe, Dean of Exeter, of founding a theological college. The purpose of the college was to confute the doctrines of the Church of Rome, the terms of its statute laying down that it was for 'the defence of true religion now established within the realm of England and for the refuting of errors and heresies repugnant unto the same.'

A site was chosen at the eastern end of Chelsea, where the Royal Hospital now stands. Six acres of land were leased, at a yearly rent of £7 10s from old Admiral Howard, the Lord of the Manor, and the King presented the college with twenty-two adjoining acres, which were Crown property. Plans were drawn for a large building in the form of a quadrangle which partially enclosed a smaller, cloistered quadrangle. It faced north, on to the road which now ran from Westminster to Chelsea, and in the fields at the back of the building an avenue of elms was planned, to reach down to the river.

But the building was never completed, for there were not sufficient funds available. King James laid the first stone in 1609 and Dr Sutcliffe, to whom the project was very dear, paid for the building of the southern side of the main quadrangle out of his own pocket, to the tune of £3,000. King James sent oak from Windsor Park for the timber work, but thereafter he contributed nothing but goodwill.

The Foundation provided for a Provost and nineteen Fellows. Seventeen of the Fellows were to be in holy orders and the other two were to work as historians. The King appointed Sutcliffe as the first Provost and one of the first historians was the distinguished Camden. The other Fellows were also chosen by the King, but as vacancies fell due, their successors were appointed by the Chancellors of Oxford and Cambridge, the Archbishop of Canterbury and the Bishop of London.

Sutcliffe's brick building was 'one hundred and thirty feet long and thirty-three broad, containing on the ground floor a kitchen, two butteries, two larders, a hall and two large parlours; on the first floor were four "fair chambers", two withdrawing-rooms, and four closets; the same on the next floor; and on the third a very large gallery, having at each end a little room with turrets, covered with slate'.

Each Fellow was allotted a room, but as none of them was ever paid they were not often in residence. It was hoped to derive an income for the College by supplying the City of London and its suburbs with fresh water, piped underground from the River Lea and the Hackney marshes, and the King gave permission for the college to build waterworks at Hackney, but in 1616, when Sir Hugh Myddleton founded the New River Company, which carried fresh water from the hills of Hertfordshire to the great reservoir at Islington, the College income disappeared.

Appeals for money were launched but few people were interested and there was little response. The Catholics ridiculed the place and even Laud dubbed it 'Controversy College'. Sutcliffe impoverished himself by giving more of his private fortune to support it, but in the end 'he was deserted, Uriah-like, and left to fight alone'. It was apparent that the College filled no real need, although Fellows were still appointed, and when Sutcliffe died, early in the reign of Charles I, a second Provost, Dr Featly, was installed.

Although Dr Featly was a staunch Protestant, the College was associated with the High Church party, and during the Civil War he was cruelly persecuted for allowing the Book of Common Prayer to be used at his church at Lambeth. He was dispossessed of his livings but, being a sick man, was allowed to live at the College for a short spell, until his death in 1644. Dr Slater was elected to succeed him but lasted only a few months, and the fourth and last Provost was Dr Samuel Wilkinson, the Royalist rector of Chelsea. This was the last year that the College functioned, for as Cromwell's armies gained ascendancy, no Fellows dared put in an appearance there.

Lord Monson, a descendant of Admiral Howard and now Lord of the Manor and ground landlord of the College, was a Roundhead and, being hard-pressed for money, brought a suit against Wilkinson for possession of the College, probably because the rent had not been paid. A disreputable and destitute young nephew of Dr Sutcliffe also arrived on the scene and claimed a right to live in the College, on the grounds that his uncle had paid for it. Lord Monson admitted him, but Wilkinson eventually succeeded in evicting him, whereupon young Sutcliffe brought a petition for permission to pull down the building and sell the materials. The wrangling continued until the days of the Commonwealth, when it faded away in frustration and Cromwell's government used the College to house Scottish prisoners.

At the Restoration, an enthusiastic divine petitioned Charles II to re-establish Chelsea College, which had become 'a cage of unclean beasts, a stable for horses, and a resort of loose women', but the King was not interested. Lord Monson could make no further claim, for he had been an accessory to the execution of Charles I and was now sentenced to be drawn on a sledge from the Tower to Tyburn and back and then imprisoned for life.

As the Roundheads fell, the Royalists returned from exile to assume their former glory and power, and among them was the Duke of Newcastle, a grandson of the Countess of Shrewsbury. He had fought gallantly for Charles but in the end had been forced to seek refuge in Holland. On his return from Rotterdam, his wife said that, when he saw the smoke of London, he asked someone 'to jog him and awaken him, as he had been sixteen years asleep, and was not yet quite awake'. His daughter, Lady Jane, had remained in England during his long years of exile, living at first in poverty, among the ruins of the family seat at Bolsover Castle; but during the Commonwealth she had married Charles Cheyne, and by the time her parents returned to England she and her husband were living at Blacklands House in Little Chelsea, a village to the north of Chelsea, which has now been engulfed in Fulham. When the Newcastle family recovered their wealth and estates, Lady Jane received a considerable fortune, with which she and Charles Cheyne bought the palace and manor of Chelsea.

Young Sutcliffe once more petitioned for possession of Chelsea College but had no success. By 1665 it was being used to house prisoners captured during the Dutch wars, many of whom succumbed to the plague that year and were buried in the forecourt.

John Evelyn had been appointed one of the four Commissioners for the Sick, Wounded and Prisoners of War, and on 8 February 1665 he wrote in his diary: 'I visited our prisoners at Chelsea College, and to examine how the marshal and sutlers behaved. These were prisoners taken in the war; they only complained that their bread was too fine.' Two months later he was asking the King's advice on the treatment of a fresh batch of prisoners. Very soon, however, conditions deteriorated, for despite all his entreaties, Evelyn was kept so short of funds that the prisoners were near to starvation. In desperation, he wrote to the Duke of York's secretary: 'I beseech your honour, let us not be reputed barbarians, or if at last we must be so, let me not be the executor of so much inhumanity.'

By September 1667, when the war was over and the prisoners freed, King Charles offered the College to the newly-formed Royal Society, and on 24 September Evelyn wrote: 'Returned to London, where I had orders to deliver the possession of Chelsea College (used as my prison during the war with Holland for such as were sent from the fleet to London) to our Society, as a gift of his Majesty our founder.'

But by this time, the building was so dilapidated that it was of little value. It proved an expensive white elephant to the Royal Society, which continued for many years to hold its meetings at Gresham College, Sir Thomas Gresham's former mansion in Bishopsgate.

The little parish church of Chelsea village had been standing since at least the thirteenth century and probably longer. It was too small for the growing population of the village and the ancient tower was crumbling. In 1667, therefore, John Bowack, writing in 1706, says that 'the shattered tower and west end of the church were pulled down, and the north and south aisles carried several yards towards the west, by two brick walls, being in all about eighty feet from the ground. The walls of the church were raised, the windows enlarged, the old parts beautified, the inside new paved, the churchyard considerably raised and enclosed with a high wall of brick, and most of this done at the voluntary charge of the inhabitants, and the whole roof, lead, timber etc., at the sole cost of Lady Jane Cheyne.'

Charles Cheyne was an enthusiastic gardener and transformed the gardens of Chelsea Palace, though Evelyn, a great and knowledgeable lover of gardens himself, was reserved in his comment on the fountains, which were, he said: 'very surprising and extraordinary'. He was more enthusiastic about his visit to the Countess of Bristol's Chelsea garden and the 'rare collection of orange trees, of which she was pleased to bestow some upon me', and to Henry Wise's nursery garden at Brompton, where Evelyn's companion, a young botanist, 'was in admiration of the stores of rare plants and the method he found in the noble nursery, and how well it was cultivated'.

Although it was to be another century before Linnæus produced his classification of plants which founded the modern science of botany, the study of plants was taken very seriously during the Restoration years. In 1673, while the Royal Society was still wondering what to do with the crumbling Chelsea College, Charles Cheyne leased a plot of land of between three and four acres, a few yards to the west of the College and fronting the river, to the Society of Apothecaries, for the creation of a Botanical or Physic Garden. The garden was stocked with a variety of medicinal plants, both English and foreign, and by 1680 the botanist John Watt (or Watts) was appointed Curator.

Evelyn, visiting the garden in 1683, wrote in his diary: 'I went to see Mr Watts, keeper of the Apothecaries' garden of simples at Chelsea, where there is a collection of innumerable rarities of that sort particularly, besides many rare annuals, the tree bearing Jesuit's bark, which had done such wonders in quartan agues. What was very ingenious was the subterranean heat, conveyed by a stove under the conservatory, all vaulted with brick, so as he had the doors and windows open in the hardest frosts, secluding only the snow.'

However, a few years later a visitor wrote that 'Chelsea Physick Garden had great variety of plants, both in and out of green houses: their perennial hedges and rows of different coloured herbs are very pretty, and so are the banks set with shades of herbs in the Irish stitchway, but many plants of the garden were not in so good order as might be expected, and as would have been answerable to other things in it. After I had been there, I learned that Mr Watts, the keeper of it, was blamed for his neglect, and that he would be removed.'

It was not until the early years of the next century, when the garden came under the patronage of Sir Hans Sloane, that it reached its full importance.

The Royal Society decided to try and sell Chelsea College, but Prince Rupert had established a laboratory close by, to experiment with his drops and other inventions, and prospective customers objected to the smell. The Society spent £30 on repairs, but in 1678 the roof collapsed and Christopher Wren advised the Society to demolish it. There remained the land, a valuable site overlooking the river, and it was here that Charles II at last decided to build his hospital.

Up till the time of the Restoration there had been no standing army in England, but Charles, while ostensibly disbanding Cromwell's New Model army, took the precaution of retaining some five thousand cavalry and infantry for his personal protection, whom he called the Guards. The Opposition strongly disapproved and at one time declared the army illegal, but it became the foundation of the regular army and the numbers soon increased to about nine thousand, so that within a few years the Grenadier Guards, the Coldstream Guards and the Royal Horse Guards were all established. The problem soon arose of how to care for the wounded, sick and aged soldiers. In 1670, Louis XIV had founded the Hotel Royal des Invalides in Paris. Ten years later, the Duke of Ormonde, Lord Lieutenant of Ireland, had established a military hospital at Kilmainham, near Dublin, the money for its maintenance being raised from a sixpence in the pound levy on the troops' pay.

King Charles was anxious to fulfil the pledge he had made in 1661 to the soldiers who had fought for him during the troubles at Tangiers. 'They shall always be in my particular care and protection', he declared. But he was prevented from founding a hospital, partly from political considerations and partly from lack of funds, for the Treasury, grappling with the disasters of the Plague, followed by the Great Fire of London, would not countenance the expense. Eventually, however, as the King's popularity throughout the country increased and the Opposition became less obstructive, he made his plans. The army paymaster was Sir Stephen Fox. Up till his time the army had been paid only twice or, at the most, three times a year, which meant that the men were always short of ready cash. Stephen Fox, by borrowing from the banks, where his credit was good, and advancing money to the men at weekly or monthly intervals, charging them a shilling in the pound for his services, managed to please the men and amass a large fortune for himself at the same time. 'The continual turning thus of money, and the souldiers moderate allowance to him for his keeping touch with them, did so inrich him that he is believ'd to be worth at least £200,000, honestly gotten and unenvied, which is next to a miracle', wrote Evelyn. 'With all this he continues as humble and ready to do a courtesie as ever he was. He is generous and lives very honourably, of a sweete nature, well spoken, well bred, and is so highly in his Majestie's esteeme and so usefull, that being long since made a knight, he is also advanc'd to be one of the Lords Commissioners of the Treasurie . . .'

Fox, who had already given much of his fortune to charity, now drew up a scheme for a military hospital, which he discussed first with Evelyn, who had favoured the proposition for many years, and then with the King. King Charles at last felt ready to agree and decided to buy back Chelsea College from the Royal Society, in order to build the hospital on the site.

On 14 September 1681, Evelyn recorded: 'Din'd with Sir Stephen Fox, who propos'd to me the purchasing of Chelsea College, which His Majesty had sometime since given to our Society, and would now purchase it again to build an hospital, or infirmary for soldiers there, in which he desired my assistance as one of the Council of the Royal Society.'

In the end, it was Sir Stephen Fox who found the £1,300 to buy back the College, and after several delays over the surrender of the lease of the surrounding land, Sir Christopher Wren, by this time President of the Royal Society, was asked to make his plans. On 16

February 1682, King Charles laid the foundation stone. Money was
still short and a public fund had to be opened, for, although both the
King and Stephen Fox contributed generously, the Treasury still
refused to help. However, when the King visited the hospital in 1685,
a few weeks before his death, he was pleased with the progress, for
the main court was complete, except for the portico, colonnade and
cupola.

The story that Nell Gwynn urged Charles to build the hospital,
after her kind heart had been wrung by the sight of a crippled soldier,
who told her he had been wounded during the Civil War, appears to
have been nothing but a romantic Victorian myth, and her only
connection with Chelsea that has any solid proof is that her mother,
Mary Gwynn, lived in a house somewhere to the east of the hospital,
with a garden which ran down so abruptly to the river that she fell in
one day and was drowned!

During his brief reign, James II also contributed to the hospital, as
well as providing pensions for the men who had suffered on his be-
half during the Monmouth rebellion, which were to be paid until
such time as the hospital should be ready to receive them.

Charles Fox had succeeded his father as Paymaster-General in
1682, but Sir Stephen still took an active interest in the hospital,
raising funds from a levy on soldiers' pay and also from the flourishing business of the sale of officers' commissions. King James more
than doubled the standing army and it soon became clear that the
hospital must be enlarged. Wren, with Sir Stephen Fox's advice,
made the additional plans, but Charles Fox, disapproving of the
King's persecution of the Monmouth party, resigned on a matter of
principle. The King appointed Lord Ranelagh as Paymaster-General
and the connection of Charles Fox with the hospital ended.

Lord Ranelagh's appointment was much to his satisfaction, for he
had been on the verge of bankruptcy. The building of the two additional quadrangles proceeded. In 1687 work began on the formal
gardens and the following year Wren gave the contract for the planting to George London and Henry Wise.

Lord Ranelagh kept his position during the Revolution of 1689
and was soon on friendly terms with King William, who 'upon his
coming to the Crown visited the said Hospital and renewed the
former direction for the speedy finishing and furnishing of it'.

While this work was under way, Lord Ranelagh – a 'young man
of great parts and great vices', 'a person who loved his ease and belly,
and all sorts of Pleasures, and most profuse therein', supervised the

building of his own residence, Ranelagh House, in the grounds of the hospital, and by ingenious chicanery amply restored his fortunes. Ranelagh House was a magnificent red-brick mansion, 'very fine within, all the rooms being Wainscoted with Norway oak, and all the chimneys adorned with carving, as in the council-chamber in Chelsea College,' while of the garden, a visitor wrote, in 1691, 'being but lately made, the plants are but small; but the plots, borders and walks are curiously kept and elegantly designed, having the advantage of opening into Chelsea College Walks. The kitchen garden there lies very fine, with walks and seats, one of which being large and covered, was then under the hands of a curious painter.'

By 1689 the Royal Hospital was nearly ready for occupation, but it was another two and a half years before its completion, during which time Lord Ranelagh was busy embellishing his own house and garden at the hospital's expense. But by August 1691 he could delay no longer. A Royal Warrant transferred the management of the Royal Hospital from Lord Ranelagh to a committee of three, composed of himself, Sir Stephen Fox and Sir Christopher Wren, and they were instructed to bring the buildings into use as quickly as possible. Staff were engaged and in March 1692 Wren's beautiful building was opened, majestic in size, impressive in its simple elegance. The building has changed very little since those days. The domed vestibule leading from Figure Court, the main courtyard, the great hall, the chapel and the four-storeyed wings for the men's cubicles are as Wren conceived them. The additional accommodation was in the form of four pavilions built round smaller courts. A century later, however, when Robert Adam was Clerk of Works at the hospital, he made certain alterations and embellishments, which included changing the casement windows of the Council Chamber to mahogany sashes and installing a marble chimney-piece.

During its first year, five hundred pensioners were admitted to the hospital and more than a hundred more were quartered nearby, living as out-pensioners. But all too often, during Lord Ranelagh's time, these men were not paid their pensions and 'lived in a miserable way upon credit in shops and lodging houses'.

Even while Lord Ranelagh was coming under suspicion he managed to persuade Charles Montague, the head of the Treasury Board, that he had built Ranelagh House at his own expense and that it was his private property. He was also granted in perpetuity all the ground he had appropriated in Chelsea, which amounted to nearly one-third of the hospital's land.

Lord Ranelagh was eventually called to account. By 1702 he was accused of gross fraud, being in default of £72,000. He was forced to resign, but the house and land remained his property. He was unable to sell them, however, as people assumed that the Crown would eventually seize them to help settle his debts. This did not happen. His only punishment was poverty and ignominy and he was plausible enough to be able to borrow money for his last years. Swift called him the vainest old fool he'd ever met, but, in the end, as Swift said, 'he died hard'.

By this time Queen Anne was on the throne. There were many reforms in the army and a tighter control of the finances of the hospital. Grants were now made by the Exchequer and the old abuses disappeared. The Royal Hospital at Chelsea became a home for which thousands of war veterans during the ensuing years were to be supremely thankful.

London was growing very quickly. In 1600 its population was about two hundred thousand and by the time of William and Mary it had increased to more than half a million, a rate of growth far greater than that of the population of the country as a whole, which was probably not more than five and a half million in 1700, as compared with four million a century earlier.

The ancient Roman wall of London still stood and as an ever-increasing number of houses was built, both inside the city and in its immediate suburbs, it became ever more noisy and congested. In summer it was hot and airless. In winter the smoke of its thousands of coal fires mingled with the mists from the river to produce a heavy pall of fog.

Chelsea, so close at hand, was still only a country village, with gardens, farms and the great houses spread among its fields and along the water-front, and it soon became a favourite pleasure resort for Londoners seeking fresh air and diversion. They came mainly by boat, to fish or stroll along the sandy shore, to admire the sunsets on the broad stretch of the river, which Turner was to love so well, to buy fresh fruit and vegetables from the market gardens, or asparagus from the Battersea gardens on the south bank, and to amuse themselves at the waterside taverns which were beginning to appear in increasing numbers.

Soon after his accession, James I issued an edict, similar to the one made by Elizabeth, forbidding the building of any new houses within three miles of the city, and during the Commonwealth an Act of Parliament was passed prohibiting new building within ten miles, for the 'great and excessive number of houses, edifices, out-houses and cottages erected and new-built in and about the suburbs of the City of London and the parts adjoining' was found to be 'very mischievous and inconvenient, and a great annoyance and nuisance to the commonwealth'.

This was the kind of law which could never be kept for long and in Chelsea, as elsewhere near London, more houses were built – mansions for the rich, houses for the gentry and upper middle classes, cottages for those catering for their needs and for the gardeners. By the Restoration, the population of Chelsea was probably about a thousand, and the most popular tavern was the Swan, at the eastern end of Chelsea Reach.

In April 1666, Pepys, with Mrs Pierce and Knipp, the actress of whom Elizabeth Pepys was so jealous, went by coach to Chelsea, thinking to 'have been merry', but when they reached the Swan, 'a gentleman walking by called to us to tell us that the house was shut up by sickness. So we with great affright turned back.' The illness was almost certainly another outbreak of the Plague and Pepys confessed that, for his part, he retreated 'in great disorder'.

The great houses of Chelsea were maintained in all their aristocratic splendour. Thomas More's house had been rebuilt in 1597 by Sir Robert Cecil and subsequently came into the hands of the first Duke of Buckingham. After the Commonwealth, his son recovered it and it was known as Buckingham House, but he was forced to sell it to pay his debts, and it became the property of the Earl of Bristol, whose widow sold it in 1682 to the Beaufort family, after which time it became known as Beaufort House.

Gorges House, the garden of which adjoined the grounds of Beaufort House, was sold in about 1664 and became a school for a few years, but at the end of the century the Milman family bought it and it remained in their hands for the next sixty years.

In 1674 the Earl of Lindsey rebuilt an old house just to the west of Beaufort House and Lindsey House, though much altered, still survives.

The old manor-house, for long the home of the Lawrences, was sold by the widow of Sir Thomas Lawrence to the Duchess of Monmouth, after the death of the Duke, and it became known as Monmouth House.

In 1663 the Bishop of Winchester bought a house which had recently been built by the Duke of Manchester, adjoining the old palace, and as Winchester House it became the residence of the

Bishops of Winchester, surviving, like Shrewsbury House, until the beginning of the nineteenth century.

The Cheyne family were still living in the palace, but towards the end of the century they sold some of their land, on which, a few years later, the first little houses in Cheyne Row were built.

Lord Ranelagh was still enjoying himself at Ranelagh House, which Defoe described as 'a little palace, I had almost called it a paradise'.

From 1660 until his death in 1685 John, Lord Robartes, who became the Earl of Radnor, lived in Danvers House with his beautiful young wife, Laetitia. He was 'a staunch Presbyterian, sour and cynical', and proved himself a 'troublesome and intractable husband', particularly after it had become clear that the Duke of York had become greatly enamoured of Laetitia and that she was 'inclined to be grateful'.

To get rid of him, the Earl was offered appointments as far from London as possible, during which time it was hoped that Laetitia would take office at the Court, but he was not to be shifted and sent his wife 'on a pilgrimage to Saint Winifred, the virgin and martyr, who was said to cure women of barrenness' and he 'did not rest until the highest mountains in Wales were between her and the person who had designed to perform this miracle in London, after his own departure'.

So Laetitia remained with her husband and bore him four sons and five daughters: and after his death she married her neighbour Lord Cheyne, and lived with him until his death in 1689.

Early in the century the King's Road was a narrow lane through the Chelsea fields and market gardens, but at the Restoration it was made into a serviceable coach road for the King, on his journeys from Whitehall or St James' to Hampton Court. Not until 1713 was it officially called the King's Road, and it remained a private road for royalty until the reign of George III. People who wished to use it were issued with pass tickets.

North of the King's Road and the nursery gardens which lined it was Chelsea Common, where the City train bands used to exercise, and north again, where the Fulham Road now runs, was the hamlet of Little Chelsea. Here, at the time of the Restoration, lived Robert Boyle, the chemist, son of the Earl of Cork. He received many distinguished visitors, among them Monsieur de Monconys, who travelled from London in a stage-coach, at a cost of five shillings, to inspect the 'very fine laboratory, where he makes all his extracts and other preparations' and Evelyn, who watched his 'pneumatic engine perform divers experiments'.

During the 1670s the young Hans Sloane, who was later to have such a close association with Chelsea, arrived from Ireland to study medicine in London, and he too visited his fellow Irishman in the house 'where glasses, potts, cymicals and mathematical instruments, books and bundles of papers did so fill and crowd his bed-chamber, that there was but just room for a few chairs'. Sloane also visited the Physic garden to study botany, but after he had qualified he went abroad for several years, and it was not until the early years of the eighteenth century that he returned to Chelsea.

It was at this time that Chelsea began to develop. Danvers House was one of the first great mansions to go. After the death of the Earl of Radnor, it had passed into the possession of the Marquis of Wharton. It was pulled down in 1720 but the first houses in Danvers Street were built in 1696. The Cheyne family sold the manor to Hans Sloane in 1712. He did not move into the old palace until 1742, but several years before this he sold some of the land along the river-front, for the building of the houses which became known as Cheyne Walk, after the first Lady Cheyne. The Beaufort family left Beaufort House about 1730 and it stood empty until 1737, when Hans Sloane bought and ultimately demolished it, Beaufort Street being laid out on the site about 1766.

After the death of the Duchess of Monmouth, Monmouth House was divided into two, and between 1704 and 1750 the first little houses in Lawrence Street were built.*

Gorges House remained in the Milman family until 1726, when it was pulled down to make way for Milman Street.

Running south-westerly from the front of the Royal Hospital to the river was a road which came to be called Paradise Row. Houses had been built there during Stuart times and it was in the most westerly of these that Laetitia settled, after the death of her second husband, Lord Cheyne. During the 1690s Thomas Hill built more houses here and a few years later Thomas Franklyn, who had lost most of his farmland when the ground for the Royal Hospital was being acquired, turned to speculative building and built four houses in Franklin's Row, where Burton Court mansions now stand, as well

---

* Monmouth House, on the west side of Lawrence Street, was pulled down in the 1830s. On the east side, an early eighteenth-century house still stands, with a double entrance surmounted by a fine old portico. The two parts of the house have been called *The Duke's House* and *Monmouth House*.

as the first tavern in this part of Chelsea, the *Angel and Soldiers*, which was later called the *Angel and Fortune of War*. Early in the eighteenth century George Norris built another group of charming little terraced houses in Paradise Row, which were not pulled down until 1906. About twenty-five years before they were demolished L'Estrange described them as covered with climbing plants and having pretty parterres.

'... With their handsome entrance gates in front, and large gardens at the back, (they) might then have seemed Paradisiacal. They are low, but have generally five windows at the first floor and contain good rooms, wainscoted to the ceilings. Altogether they have an air of old-fashioned gentility, and the sides of the hall doors are ornamented with wood carving.'

During the late seventeenth and early eighteenth centuries, some fascinating characters lived in Paradise Row, including two women whose lives were in complete contrast, the Duchess of Mazarin and Mary Astell.

The Duchess of Mazarin was the beautiful, warm-hearted, feckless Hortensia Mancini, niece of Cardinal Mazarin and heiress of his immense fortune. She was born in Rome in 1647 and spent most of her girlhood at the French Court. At one time Charles II had fallen in love with her, but as an exiled prince Mazarin would not countenance the match, and after the Restoration the King's ministers considered her unsuitable. So she was married to the Duc de la Meilleraye, a dour, religious fanatic, who 'went about the country in the cause of virtue, preaching to the farmers that they should not allow their daughters to witness the common sights of the farm-yard, and maintaining that even the milking of a cow was an indelicate act.'

He was no husband for the brilliant Hortensia, but having appropriated her vast fortune, she seemed to be irrevocably tied to him. After four years, however, by which time she was twenty-seven years old, she could stand his canting austerity and harsh perversity no longer. 'If it was love for me that made him treat me in this fantastical fashion,' she said, 'it were to be wished for both our sakes that he had honoured me with a little more of his indifference.'

Disguised as a boy, she ran away, and after many adventures reached England, arriving at the Court of St James' in 1675. She was an immediate success and her beauty, culture and gaiety made her a host of friends and admirers. Charles II gave her an allowance of £4,000 a year, and it seemed at one time as though she would supplant the Duchess of Portsmouth. 'She would have succeeded entirely in gaining the King's affections', wrote Faulkner, 'could she have kept herself secluded from the vice and follies of that dissipated age.'

Her principal fault seems to have been an obsession for gambling. She had a short-lived but passionate love affair with the Prince of Monaco, followed by a liaison with a Swedish baron, which ended in tragedy. They were devoted, but the Duchess' nephew, Prince Philip of Savoy, thought fit to challenge him to a duel and killed him. For a long time she was inconsolable, draped her rooms in black and talked of entering a convent. When she had recovered, she took to gambling again and would sometimes play basset all through the night, until dawn, undeterred by her heavy losses.

Most summers she would spend in the country air of Chelsea, and in 1694, when her debts were becoming a serious embarrassment, she retired permanently to her house in Paradise Row. By this time King Charles was dead and James II no doubt reduced her allowance, as he had Nell Gwynn's. After his flight, it seems to have been discontinued altogether. Yet for the first year or two the Duchess managed to live very comfortably in Chelsea. She established a salon where she entertained dukes and peers, including her neighbours, the Duke of St Albans, Charles II's son by Nell Gwynn, and Lord Ranelagh. Her household was ordered with 'great freedom and a greater discretion'. 'All her equipages were in the best taste, and her cuisine was exquisite. . . . There you will find whatever delicacy is brought from France, and whatever is curious from the Indies. Even the commonest meats have the rarest relishes imparted to them. There is neither a plenty which gives a notion of extravagance, nor a frugality which discovers penury or meanness.'

The Duchess' constant friend was another exile from France, the elderly Seigneur de Saint-Evremond, thirty-seven years her senior and a political refugee. Charles II had welcomed him and given him a small Court appointment. St Evremond loved the Duchess dearly and was always giving her advice which she seldom heeded. This did not shake his devotion, and apart from writing many poems in her honour, he lent her what little money he could spare, as her debts mounted, knowing full well that there was little prospect of ever seeing it again.

The Duchess kept a brave face long after her means had almost vanished. Every week she gave an entertainment in the form of a drama set to music. Evremond sometimes wrote the words and occasionally the music, but most of the music was composed by

Paisible, the composer for the flute, and the singers were hired from the theatres.

In her salon, she and her friends discussed the possibility of introducing Italian opera to England and it was probably after attending one of her entertainments that Sir John Vanbrugh opened his small opera house in the Haymarket, in 1705.

The Duchess' affairs went from bad to worse. Only once was she ever able to pay her rates and she lived in constant dread of being arrested and imprisoned for debt. Friends did what they could and guests would leave money for her under their plates, but the time came when she was obliged to drink beer instead of wine and could no longer afford a carriage. On one occasion, when she had visited Evremond and returned to Chelsea on foot, he wrote begging her never again to go abroad by herself at night-time, 'exposing herself to robbers, drunken and rude people'.

Only five years after coming to live in Paradise Row, she died, at the age of fifty-one, killed by illness and worry. Her sanctimonious old husband then paid her debts, recovered her body, had it embalmed and carried it about with him until the day of his death, while poor old Evremond, stricken with grief, lived on for another three or four years, dying in 1703, by which time he was well into his nineties.

Living only a few doors away from the Duchess was Mary Astell, a pious, stern, but lovable and very intelligent spinster. She was born in 1666, the only daughter of a rich merchant of Newcastle-upon-Tyne, and when she was twenty-two she came to London and settled in Paradise Row, where she lived until her death in 1731.

Mary Astell was one of the first protagonists of education for women since Sir Thomas More, and was bitter in her condemnation of arranged marriages, which at this time were usual at almost every level of society.

In early Tudor times there had been educational opportunities for girls in the monastic institutions and later they had been admitted to some of the grammar schools, but when the Puritans came to power, the status of women sank. Education in the grammar schools, though it had been 'a common and usual course', was now forbidden, as it was 'by many conceived very uncomely and not decent'. For the next century, education for girls was considered unnecessary and the majority grew up quite illiterate. Some were taught at home and there were a few boarding-schools scattered through the country, teaching little more than needlework, dancing, music and such crafts as would fit them for their only recognized purpose in life, an early and prosperous marriage.

'I have often thought it as one of the most barbarous customs in the world,' said Defoe, 'considering we are a civilized and Christian country, that we deny the advantages of learning to women.'

Mary Astell planned to found a college for the higher education of women and in 1694, the year that the Duchess of Mazarin became her neighbour, she published *A serious proposal to the Ladies for the advancement of their true and great interest.* The first part was dedicated to Lady Mary Wortley Montague and the second part, which appeared three years later, to Princess Anne.

Mary Astell argued that education would protect women from fortune-hunters, would make married women better wives and mothers, able to teach their children, and would alleviate the unhappy tedium of the lives of upper-class spinsters, by providing them with mental resources. The purpose of her seminary was to 'stock the Kingdom with pious and prudent Ladies'.

No Dissenters would be allowed, and the college would be only for gentlewomen, for Mary Astell accepted social distinctions as preordained, asserting that 'unless we have very strange Notions of the Divine wisdom, we must needs allow that everyone is placed in such a station as they are fitted for'. And even in Heaven, though all who had led Christian lives would, she was sure, be admitted, she could not help feeling that people of quality would probably have a better time than the lower orders. Nevertheless, she was vehement in her condemnation of both men and women who misused their God-given advantages of birth and status.

In her seminary, ladies would have that which so many lacked – the leisure to study and reflect. 'Here will be no importunate visits. No foolish Amours. In Dressing, the great Devourer and its Concomitants, very little time will be spent . . . so that here's a huge treasure gain'd. . . . She will not be inveigled and impos'd on and will neither be bought or sold.'

Mary Astell regarded marriage as a state of joyless subjection for women, part of a Divine purpose which they must endure with patience and fortitude, thereby ensuring themselves a safe entry into Heaven. It would be immodest, she considered, for a woman to love before marriage, but she should 'make choice of one whom she can love hereafter; she who has but innocent affections being easily able to fix them where Duty requires'. And to marry beneath one's class, she considered as 'ill-mannered to Heaven'.

She planned the college for a double purpose, a place for temporary studies or a permanent refuge for those women who did not marry, either because they did not wish to or because their families had 'fallen into decay' and could no longer afford the dowry for a suitable husband. For a sum of between £500 and £600 she offered them a home, where 'seraphic celibacy' would become 'popular and honourable among English ladies'.

Some of these residents would probably become teachers, she suggested, giving instruction in such subjects as logic, mathematics, philosophy and the sciences, which had hitherto been considered beyond a woman's comprehension, and also in the writing of the English language, on which she gave much advice. In regard to spelling, however, her comments are unorthodox, if practical. 'And as to Spelling which they are said to be defective in', she wrote, 'if they don't believe as they are usually told, that it's fit for 'em to be so, and that to write exactly is too Pedantic, they may soon correct that fault, by pronouncing their words aright and Spelling 'em accordingly.'

Mary Astell published several more essays, and of her beautiful neighbour, the tragic Duchess, she wrote charitably: 'She who was capable of being a great Ornament to her Family and Blessing to the Age she lived in, should only serve . . . as an unhappy Shipwrack to point out the dangers of an ill-Education and unequal Marriage. . . . Had Madame Mazarin's Education made a right improvement of her Wit and Sense, we should not have found her seeking Relief by such impudent, not to say scandalous methods.'

So sympathetic were many intelligent women to Mary Astell's proposal for a seminary, that she is said to have been promised £10,000 towards its foundation by 'a great lady', who was probably Lady Elizabeth Hastings but may have been Princess Anne. But the great Bishop Burnett, who was living close by, in Church Lane, viewed the project with alarm. Mary Astell had said that 'Piety shall not be roughly impos'd, but wisely insinuated. . . . And since inclinations can't be forced . . . there shall be no Vows or irrevocable Obligations, not so much as the fear of Reproach to keep Our Ladies here any longer than they desire.' She even suggested that men who were in no financial need of a large dowry and were attracted to the idea of an educated and serious-minded wife would be free to come and make their choice from among her ladies. Nevertheless, the Bishop declared that the seminary savoured of a Popish nunnery and, to Mary's great disappointment, the 'great lady' withdrew her support.

Yet her writings, which were very courageous for the mood of the times, were widely discussed and aired a growing grievance. Bishop Burnett, who conceded many of her points, complained that she had not 'the decent manner of insinuating what she means, but is now and then a little offensive and shocking in her expressions' but they were always good friends.

Towards the end of her life, Mary Astell helped her friends Lady Elizabeth Hastings and Lady Jones, the unmarried daughter of the Earl of Ranelagh, to found a school for the daughters of the pensioners of Chelsea Hospital. This existed until 1862, and when it was closed the endowment was used to support three of the pensioners' daughters at a boarding school.

By 1731 Mary knew she was dying of cancer and towards the end she ordered her shroud and coffin to be placed by her bedside, so that she might be constantly prepared for her death. She was buried in Chelsea Old Church and in the rebuilt church her name appears to-day on the plaque of distinguished Chelsea women, which was placed there by the Federation of University Women.

At the north-eastern end of Paradise Row stood Ormonde House, which was built towards the end of the seventeenth century and occupied by several members of the Butler family. The old Duke who had served the Stuart cause so well in Ireland and in exile, seems also to have lived in Chelsea from time to time, before his death in 1688, and from 1730 to 1733 the wife of the second Duke lived in Ormonde House, while her husband languished in exile, for suspected Jacobite sympathies.

The later years of the seventeenth century saw the introduction of coffee houses in England, much to the consternation of the brewers and vintners and also to the Government, who viewed them as possible breeding-grounds for dissension. There was a coffee house in Paradise Row, as well as the Five Bells tavern, but Chelsea's most famous coffee house was Don Saltero's, first in Danvers Street and finally at number 18 Cheyne Walk.

John Salter had been a servant of Hans Sloane and accompanied him on some of his travels, in the course of which Sir Hans had given him many curios from foreign parts. Salter opened his coffee house in the 1690s and decorated it with the trophies of his journeys abroad. Visitors were soon adding to the heterogeneous collection and it developed into a museum. One of his customers dubbed him 'Don Saltero' and his 'Coffee Room and Curiosities' became a favourite Chelsea meeting-house. Coffee was not the only beverage served, for the Don was also famous for his excellent punch.

The main exhibition was arranged in glass cases on the tables of a first-floor front-room, but the walls of the coffee room were also hung with strange exhibits and in the entrance passage an alligator hung from the ceiling, flanked by an armoury of ancient weapons.

'When I came into the room,' wrote Steele, 'I had not time to salute the company before my eye was diverted by ten thousand gimcracks, round the room and on the ceiling.'

Among the display were several pieces of the holy cross, dice of the Knights Templars, painted ribbands from Jerusalem, with a pillar to which Our Saviour was tied when scourged, a petrified crabfish from China, a piece of rotten wood not to be consumed by fire, a large worm that eats into the ships in the West Indies, a piece of Solomon's temple, an Indian machete used by them before 'iron was invented', Job's tears that grow on trees, wherewith they make anodyne necklaces, a young frog in a tobacco stopper, the Pope's infallible candle, a curious flea-trap, the jaws of a wild boar that was starved to death by its tusks growing inward, manna from Canaan and Mary Queen of Scots' pin-cushion.

Salter described it as a knackatory and himself as a gimcrack-whim collector, but the enthusiasm many visitors showed for the collection is an interesting reflection of their naïveté in matters of science and religion, oddly at variance with the heights of splendour attained in the arts during the seventeenth century.

After the Don died, his daughter carried on the coffee house and museum until the 1760s and it was not until the end of the century that the collection was sold by auction, fetching £50. The coffee house became a public house until it was demolished in 1867.

IV

Kensington and the Stuarts

DESPITE the disasters which beset the early years of the Restoration – the Plague of London, the Great Fire and the war with Holland – the people of England had a wonderful capacity for enjoying themselves, if we can judge from the evidence left by the bewigged and elegantly dressed diarists and essayists of the late seventeenth century.

Though Chelsea, like Kensington, was still only a country village of farms and cottages and riverside inns, with its great houses set in beautiful gardens, Londoners had been making it a pleasure resort for many years, usually coming up river by boat. As coaches and humbler kinds of wheeled transport slowly improved, they began to come by road, to the dismay and indignation of the Thames watermen: and now they took to visiting Kensington as well, to stroll in the fields, enjoy the fresh, clear air, buy fruit and vegetables from the nursery gardens, and eat and drink at the village inns.

In the summer of 1664 Pepys went to Kensington by coach to visit Lady Sandwich, who was staying with the Vicar of St Mary Abbots, and later in the day met a number of friends. That evening they visited Sir Heneage Finch's garden, 'seeing the fountayne, and singing there with the ladies, and a mighty fine cool place it is, with a great laver of water in the middle and the bravest place for music I ever heard'.

Sir Heneage Finch was fast rising to eminence. By 1670 he was

Attorney-General, by 1673 Lord Keeper of the Seals, and in 1674 he was made Lord Chancellor. As soon as he moved into his house, in 1661, he had set about improving the gardens. He acquired from Charles II a strip of land 10 feet wide on the east of his grounds, adjoining the Park, which stretched 'from the south highway, lead-ing to the town of Kensington, and from thence crossing to the north highway, leading to the town of Acton'. Here he planted an avenue of trees and made a ha-ha, while on the south side of the house he planted an ornamental garden, with a fountain and later a grotto.

When in April 1666, Pepys and his friends had been warned that there was sickness at the Swan at Chelsea they drove to Kensington, 'and there I spent about 30s. upon the ladies with great pleasure, and we sang finally and staied till about eight at night . . .'

A week later he took Mrs Pierce and her children to the same Kensington inn, 'where we were the other day, and with great pleasure stayed till night, and were mighty late getting home, the horses tiring and stopping at every twenty steps'.

He does not mention the name of this inn, but it was clearly one of his favourite haunts, for in April of 1668 he took Knipp out 'and to Kensington; and there walked in the garden, and then supped, and mighty merry, there being also in the house Sir Philip Howard, and some company, and had a dear reckoning, but merry, and away, it being quite night . . . and in my coming had the opportunity the first time in my life to be bold with Knipp . . .'

That same month he went to Drury Lane to see her in Robert Howard's play *The Surprizell*. She came to visit him in the pit 'and there, oranges 2s. After the play, she and I, and Rolt, by coach, 6s 6d to Kensington, and there at the Grotto, and had admirable pleasure with their singing, and fine ladies listening to us; with infinite pleasure, I enjoyed myself: so to the tavern there, and did spend 16s 6d, and the gardener 2s. Mighty merry, and sang all the way to the town, a most pleasant evening, moonshine, and set them at her house in Covent Garden, and I home and to bed.'

A week or two later he went with a party of friends to a perform-ance of Sir Charles Sedley's *The Mulberry Garden*, but they found the play so dull and tiresome that yet again he carried them off 'for a country drive to Kensington, to the Grotto, and there we sang, having great content'.

Evelyn was greatly interested in the nursery gardens of Kensing-ton, particularly those of the Court gardeners, George London and his partner Henry Wise at Brompton, who had the best stock of plants and trees in the country, which they supplied to 'most of the nobility and gentlemen of England'.

'They have,' wrote Evelyn, 'a very large and noble assembly of the flowering and other trees, perennial and variegated evergreens and shrubs, hardy, and fittest for our climate; and understand what best to plant, the humble boscage, wilderness, or taller groves with; where, and how to disperse and govern them according as ground and situation of the place requires both for shelter and ornament; for which purpose, and for walks and avenues, they have store of elms, limes, platans, Constantinople chestnuts, and black cherry trees. Nor are they, I perceive, less knowing in that most useful, though less pompous part of horticulture, the potagerie, melonerie, culinarie garden. Where they should most properly be placed for the use of the family; how to be planted, furnished, and cultivated, so as to afford great pleasure to the eye, as well as profit to the master. And they have also seeds, bulbs, roots, slips for the flowering garden, and shew how they ought to be ordered and maintained . . . one needs no more than to take a walk to Brompton Park, upon a fair morning, to behold, and admire what a magazine those industrious men have provided, fit for age, and choice in their several classes, and all within one enclosure; such an assembly, I believe, as is no where else to be met with in this kingdom, nor in any other that I know of.'

At Holland House, Robert, the second Earl, succeeded to the title of Earl of Warwick in 1673. His first wife and their children all died young, but by his second marriage he had a son, Edward Rich. Shortly afterwards Robert died, leaving Edward, at the age of two, the third Earl of Holland and the sixth Earl of Warwick. During his childhood Holland House was let from time to time, and there is a legend that William Penn lived there for a while, though there is no real evidence for this.

When Edward married Charlotte Myddelton he returned to Holland House, but he died young, in 1701, leaving the widowed Charlotte, Countess of Warwick, alone at Holland House with a small son, her estate stretching from Holland Walk in the east to Addison Road in the west, from Holland Park Avenue and the Uxbridge Road in the north to Kensington High Street in the south, a wide stretch of garden and wooded parkland, surrounded by fields and farms.

In 1681 Dismal Heneage had been made Earl of Nottingham and his house was thereafter called Nottingham House, and the Noël family were still living at Campden House.

Although James I had used Hyde Park as a hunting-ground and the game was strictly preserved, the public were allowed to walk there and often enjoyed watching the hunting parties. By the time of Charles I it had become a favourite haunt of fashionable London and, although most of the park was still wild, in the north of the central part was a clearing known as the Ring or the Tour, where people liked to ride or drive in their new coaches. Even before the Restoration, the Puritans were beginning to criticise the 'most shameful powder'd men: and painted and spotted women who paraded in Hyde Park.'

During the Commonwealth the 621 acres of Hyde Park were sequestered, along with other Crown property, and sold to private owners, who posted porters with staves at the entrances and charged for admission.

Evelyn in 1653 wrote in disgust: 'I went to take the aire in Hide Park, when every coach was made to pay a shilling, and horse sixpence, by the sordid fellow who had purchased it of the State . . .'

The park grew shabby and neglected, but with the Restoration the sale to private ownership was declared null and void and it was restored to the Crown. Charles II made it free to the public again, as well as St James's Park, which had become separated from Hyde Park by buildings and houses put up during the Commonwealth.

Much of it was still wild but it was now restocked with deer and the ancient fence replaced by a wall. The Ring was refenced and became high fashion again, a place to ride or parade in one's carriage and to watch both foot and horse races. Within a few years of the Restoration, Grammont was writing: 'Hyde Park, every one knows it is the promenade of London: nothing so much in fashion, during fine weather, as that promenade, which was the rendezvous of magnificence and beauty: every one, therefore, who had either sparkling eyes, or a splendid equipage, constantly repaired thither, and the king seemed pleased with the place.'

Pepys was often there, though he frequently complained of the dust. In 1660 he watched a fine foot race, run three times round the Ring, between an Irishman and a man called Crow. Watching that race, in the dust of the Ring, was thirsty work and when it was over the spectators welcomed the cry of the milkmaid, calling 'Milk from a red cow' and gathered round to buy from her, but those with more sophisticated taste walked over to the Lodge, which had once been James' hunting pavilion, and took a quick syllabub laced with sack, before returning to the next event, a horse race on which the ladies

Leigh Hunt's house, Upper Cheyne Row

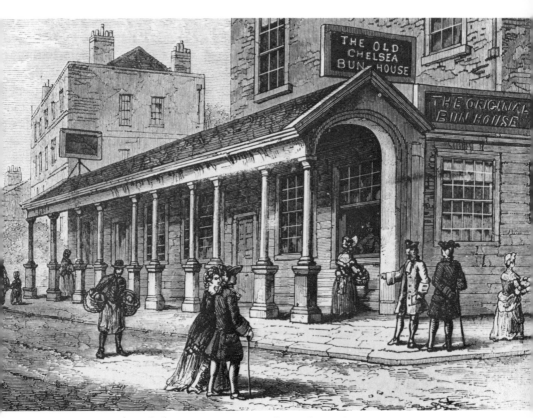

The Chelsea Bun House in the eighteenth century

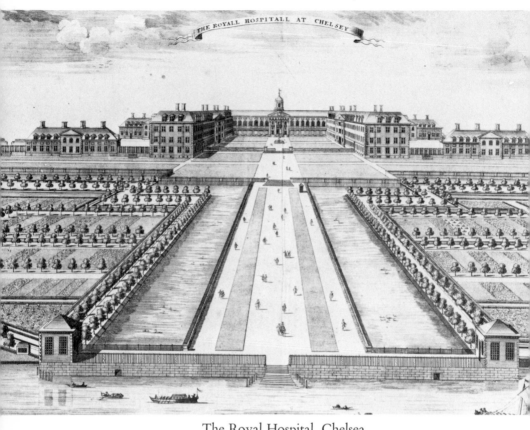

The Royal Hospital, Chelsea

Kensington Palace in the early eighteenth century

The Royal Hospital, Chelsea, from the south-east

Kensington Palace in 1753

John Hunter's house at Earls Court, Kensington

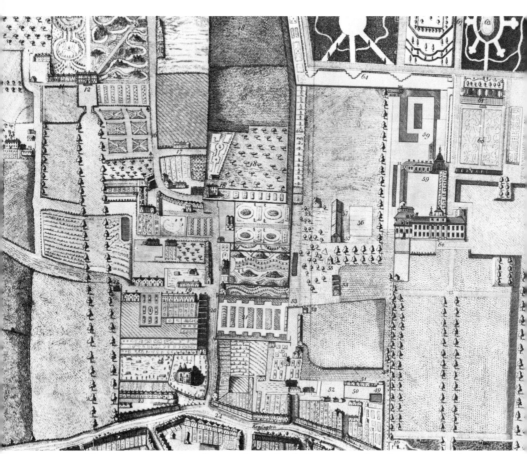

Kensington; section from John Rhodes' topographical survey of the
Parish of Kensington, 1766

Cheyne Walk, Chelsea, *c.* 1790

A View at CHELSEA 1784.

Chelsea, 1784

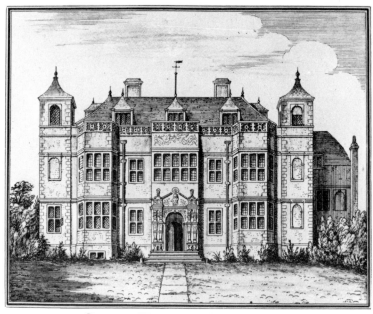

Campsea House, Kensington, in 1793

King's Road, Chelsea, *c.* 1906

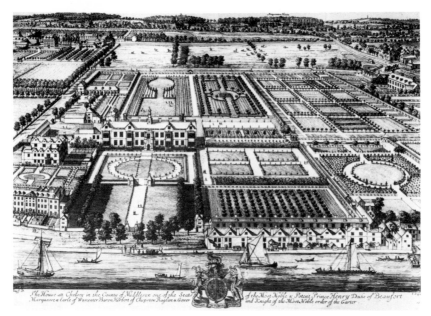

Beaufort House, Chelsea. Beaufort Street now runs over this site

Gore House, Kensington, at the time of the Great Exhibition

Cheyne Walk in 1817

Holland House in 1812

were wagering scarlet stockings and scented gloves of Spanish leather.

Pepys was in the Park to watch a muster of the guards, when the Duke of Monmouth, 'in mighty rich clothes', took over the command. He was there to see the display of fireworks on the King's birthday and often went just to enjoy 'the sight of the very fine ladies'. He took Knipp there after the play and found it very fine after some rain, 'but the company was going away most, so I took her to the Lodge, and there treated her and had a deal of good talk, and now and then did baiser la, and that was all, and that as much or more than I had much mind to, because of her paint.'

Sometimes he took Elizabeth there and they would drive to the Lodge and take a tankard of milk and a cheesecake. In 1664 he was there with Mr Povy, 'being the first day of the tour there, where many brave ladies; among others Castlemayne lay impudently upon her back in her coach asleep, with her mouth open'.

He and Elizabeth went there to display their new coach, but nothing went right that day. Elizabeth was in a bad temper, it was very dusty and windy, and then it began to rain on her new dress. There were too many common hackney coaches about too, which also seemed to annoy her, but they both cheered up when they met some friends. Samuel bought syllabubs for them all, and even though they cost him twelve shillings he ended his day as usual, pretty merry.

Away to the west of the Park, Kensington lay among its trees and fields, still a country village, and the road to Knightsbridge was still lonely and dangerous. Knightsbridge by now had its weekly cattle market and a number of inns which still had a doubtful reputation. In 1687 Thomas Ridge of Portsmouth was buried in Kensington, having been killed by thieves almost at Knightsbridge, and in 1699 John Evelyn recorded that 'this week robberies were committed between the many lights which were fixed between London and Kensington on both sides, and while coaches and travellers were passing'.

One of the worst inns was the Swan. ''Tis a bad house, that Swan; the Swan at Knightsbridge is a counfounded house,' declared Sir David Dance in Otway's *Soldier of Fortune*. Just east of where Sloane Street now runs were the Spring Gardens, pleasure gardens which had been formed in the grounds of an ancient mansion. The tavern attached to the gardens was the World's End, where Pepys sometimes ate and drank, and its reputation was little better than that of the World's End at Chelsea.

Close by, at the western end of the bridge, was the Fox and Bull, where Queen Elizabeth is said to have visited, during her journey to meet Lord Burleigh when he was living at Brompton.

There was also a lazar-house at Knightsbridge, an Elizabethan foundation attached to the Trinity Chapel, with accommodation for thirty-five sick and homeless wayfarers. During the Plague of 1665 it was used as a hospital and the dead were buried on Knightsbridge Green, a small, triangular patch of which still survives.

Trinity Chapel was a rare place for secret or runaway marriages. They were marked in the register with the words 'private' or 'secret' and the really shady ones were safeguarded with the sinister words 'secret for fourteen years' or even 'secrecy for life'. Sir Samuel Morland, who was Master of Mechanics to Charles II, was tricked into marriage here when he took Mrs Mary Ayliss for his fourth wife, thinking her to be an heiress. A week or two later he was writing bitterly: 'I was about a fortnight since, led as a fool to the stocks, and married a coachman's daughter, not worth a shilling.'

Other secret brides and bridegrooms at the Chapel included Storey, keeper of the aviary of Charles II, whose name has been immortalised in Storey's Gate, a young woman who called herself Lady Mary Tudor and was actually the daughter of Charles II by Moll Davis, and, oddly enough, the illustrious Sir Robert Walpole.

The largest inn in the village, overlooking the green, was the *Oliver Cromwell*, the name of which was later changed to the *Rose and Crown*. At one time Cromwell's arms were emblazoned in plaster work on the front of the inn and when the Parliamentary army was encamped near by and Fairfax had his headquarters at Holland House, Cromwell's bodyguard were quartered here.

Knightsbridge, for all its bad reputation, was good to look at, with its maypole on the wide green, its well, over which stood a figure of St George, the stream and the old stone bridge, with its battlemented tower, the hospital and the chapel. Close to the *Oliver Cromwell*, with its twisting chimneys, low, dark panelled rooms, large stable yards and outside galleries and staircases were the *Rising Sun*, with its beautifully panelled rooms and carved staircase, and the *Nag's Head*, which later became the *Life Guardsman*.

V

The Court at Kensington

THE plans for Kensington Square were drawn up during the brief reign of James II and the first houses built, but it was not until the accession of William III and Mary that Kensington became the Royal Court suburb.

William was a strange, dour character, obsessed with the desire to conquer France. He was an intellectual, a man of taste and a brave soldier, but he was no courtier. Princess Mary had wept bitterly for nearly two days when, at the age of fifteen, she was told that, to the dismay of her father, the future James II, and Louis XIV, her uncle Charles II had arranged for her marriage to the Calvinist William to take place in a fortnight's time. But after a few years in Holland Mary came to dote on him. Unfortunately William showed no signs of returning her affection and even his chaplain, Bishop Burnet, found cause to remonstrate with him over his treatment of her at times.

William had no intention of being a Prince Consort in England. He insisted on sharing the Crown and ensuring that, if Mary died before him, the succession should go to himself before Princess Anne.

He had little taste for the English nobility and except among his small circle of Dutch intimates he was, for the most part, unsociable. He disliked the untidy labyrinth of Whitehall Palace and even more the custom of dining in public, which had been practised by the Stuarts and their predecessors and was still expected of him. He suffered chronically from asthma, and the dampness of the old

Thames-side palace and the fogs which rolled in from the river made
him ill. He decided to move to Hampton Court, which by the late
1680s was fast falling into ruinous neglect. He and Mary met there
with Sir Christopher Wren and made plans for rebuilding the old
Tudor palace in the grand manner, after the style of the palaces of
Germany and the Low Countries, which had been modelled on pale
imitations of Louis XIV's fabulous Versailles.

However, the Government disliked not only the vast cost which
it would have involved, but also the fact that the new King would be
a long way from Westminster and his ministers.

King William was persuaded to compromise. Most of Wren's
plans for the new Hampton Court were abandoned, although certain
necessary steps for its preservation were made and a few rooms redecorated, where Queen Mary was able to arrange her fine collection
of Oriental porcelain and Delftware and introduce the chintz hangings of which she was so fond. The King contemplated making an
offer for Holland House, but after having a look round he decided
that he did not care for it. The first Lord Nottingham had died in
1682 and his son, the second Lord, had become Lord of the Admiralty. Although he still owned Nottingham House, it seems that he was
not actually living in it at this time. King William inspected it,
decided that it could be adapted to suit his purpose admirably, and on
18 June 1689, Narcissus Luttrell recorded in his diary: 'The King hath
bought the Earl of Nottingham's house in Kensington for 18,000
guineas and designs it for his seat in the winter, being near Whitehall.'

Within a fortnight Wren had made plans for the first alterations
and enlargements to Nottingham House, which was now to be
known as Kensington Palace. They involved adding new blocks at
each corner. The entrance was planned on the west side of the building, facing on to Palace Green, with an archway surmounted by a
clock tower and cupola, giving on to the courtyard of Clock Court.
The north and south side of the court were two new wings, each of
three storeys, the first two with flat, casement windows, the attic
floors with pedimented dormers. The north wing contained the
palace kitchens and beyond were to be more kitchens and offices,
built round two courtyards, Grass Cloth Court and Pump Court.

In the south wing Wren planned the long Stone Gallery, with
rooms behind for the courtiers, the gallery being approached from
Palace Green by a simple, austere, colonnaded porch, just south of the
main entrance into Clock Court.

The eastern end of the Stone Gallery led to the King's Gallery and staircase and to his apartments, while beyond them, to the north, were the Queen's apartments, including the Queen's Gallery, her closet, dining-room and drawing-room, all looking eastwards over the gardens.

By the end of the year, the rebuilding was sufficiently advanced for the Court to be able to move in, but on 25 February 1690, Evelyn recorded: 'I went to Kensington, which King William has bought of Lord Nottingham and altered, but was yet a patched building, but with the garden however, it is a very neat villa, having to it the Park and a straight new way through the Park.' This was the Route de Roi, which before very long was to be known as Rotten Row.

As the palace took shape, it proved to be too plain for many tastes, visitors from the Continent being sometimes shocked by its unpretentiousness, but its Dutch simplicity was very attractive, and although there was trouble with dampness for many years to come, its very lack of ostentation made it comfortable and homely.

King William was abroad during most of the early years of his reign, first in Ireland and then on the Continent, fighting Louis XIV, and while he was away Queen Mary, still in her twenties, attended competently to affairs of state, kept an eye on the alterations to Kensington Palace, supervised the furnishing, with the velvet and damask hangings, and also superintended the planting of an excessively formal Dutch garden along the south front.

The land to the west of the palace, a meadow known as the moor, which is now Palace Green, was left much as it was, with Henry VIII's conduit, supplying water to the old palace at Chelsea, still standing. It was used as a parade-ground, the cottages and stables on the south side being barracks, while King William's Dutch cavalry were quartered in the Life Guards House, which fronted on the high road.

Princess Anne was living in the westerly extension of the Whitehall Palace at this time, in a range of buildings alongside the cockpit, on the site of which Downing Street was later to be built. In 1683, when she was eighteen, she had married the dull but amiable Prince George of Denmark, who, on the accession of William and Mary, was created Duke of Cumberland. Anne had already had a still-born daughter, a daughter who had lived for only eighteen months, another who had lived for seven months, three subsequent miscarriages and then, on 24 July 1689, a son William, Duke of Gloucester, a frail but gallant little boy who was to live until 1700, dying, it is thought, of hydrocephaly.

In childhood Anne and Mary had been devoted but, after Mary returned from Holland, to become Queen, there were frequent misunderstandings and estrangements, the situation made more difficult by the constant shadow of the Jacobites and the claims and reproaches of their father, the Catholic James II, living in exile in France, with his young son, James Francis Edward, the warming-pan baby who became the Old Pretender.

Anne disliked William and William treated Prince George with ill-concealed contempt, yet Anne loved her husband dearly. He was a Lutheran, 'a simple normal man without envy or ambition and disposed by remarkable appetite and thirst for all the pleasures of the table . . . He had homely virtues and unfailing good humour.'*

Though contented to stay always in the background, he probably had more horse-sense and gave Anne better advice than has ever been credited to him.

In 1691, already corpulent with child-bearing and crippled with gout, Princess Anne took a lease of Campden House and moved there with the two-year-old Prince William and the ailing asthmatic Prince George, in the hope that the clean, fresh air of Kensington would bring an improvement in the health of all of them, after the dampness of Whitehall.

They lived there for the next five years and built Little Campden House in the grounds, for their suite and household.

The work on the palace continued. Wren built the Queen's Gallery and the beautiful Queen's staircase, which today visitors still mount to see the State apartments, and adjoining it the Maids of Honour rooms, but in 1691 the south wing was destroyed by fire.

'This South Wing was burnt down by Accident,' wrote Defoe in his *Tour thro' the whole island of Great Britain*, 'the King and Queen being both there, the Queen was a little surprised at first, apprehending some Treason, but King William a Stranger to Fears smil'd at the Suggestion, chear'd Her Majesty up, and being soon dress'd, they both walked out into the Garden, and stood there some Hours till they perceived the Fire by the help that came in, and by the Diligence of the Foot Guards, was gotten under Foot.'

After the fire, the King's staircase was enlarged and the Chapel Royal refurnished.

Queen Mary did not live long to enjoy her new palace for in 1694 at the age of thirty-two, she succumbed to an attack of smallpox. Though William, struggling against ill-health and preoccupied with

* Churchill, *Marlborough, His Life and Times*, Vol. I, p. 169.

his European campaigns, had been a difficult husband and given her little happiness, he had always kept his mistress, Elizabeth Villiers, discreetly in the background. He appeared to be desolate when she died and for the remaining eight years of his life spent less time than ever with London society.

However, Wren continued his work on the palace, and the 96-feet long King's Gallery was completed, with its windows, fireplaces and door-surrounds carved by Grinling Gibbons.

William's court was small and almost exclusively male. His personal favourites were his Dutch friends, Bentinck, who became the Earl of Portland and managed the royal parks and gardens for William, and Arnold Keppel, who was created the Earl of Albemarle: and other attendants included the Earl of Dorset, the witty Matthew Prior, whom the King appointed a Gentleman of the Bedchamber, Congreve, Lord Halifax, Sir William Temple, Swift, Bishop Burnet, the Duke of Devonshire, Lord Monmouth, the friend of Swift and Pope, who, at the age of seventy, became the lover of Lady Suffolk, and the Duke of Buckinghamshire, who at one time had aspired to the hand of Princess Anne.

Another visitor to Kensington Palace was Peter the Great, who had come to England to study the art of ship-building, with a view to introducing the business to Russia. He stayed in England for five months, spending three of them at John Evelyn's mansion, Sayes Court, at Deptford, close to the dockyard. 'The Czar of Muscovy, being come to England, and having a mind to see the building of ships, hir'd my house at Saye's Court, and made it his Court and Palace, new furnished for him by the king,' wrote Evelyn in April 1698.

A few weeks later, Evelyn's servant was writing to him: 'There is a house full of people and right nasty . . . The king is expected here this day; the best parlour is pretty clean for him to be entertained in.'

Evelyn had a favourite holly hedge in his garden, which he had tended with great care, but to his horror the Czar, in the course of his daily exercise, used to trundle a wheelbarrow straight through it, and by 5 June, Evelyn was writing despondently: 'I went to Deptford to see how miserably the Czar had left my house after three months' making it his court. I got Sir Christopher Wren, the king's surveyor, and Mr Loudon, his gardener, to go and estimate the repairs, for which they allowed £150 in their report to the Lords of the, Treasury.'

But the Czar, no doubt completely unaware that he had been a bad tenant, got on famously with the King, with whom he frequently dined at Kensington Palace. These were lengthy and convivial occasions, for they were both hard drinkers, William keeping to his Dutch gin and Peter to his brandy, which he laced with pepper.

It was in this year of Peter the Great's visit, 1698, that the Whitehall Palace was destroyed by fire. At the time, some people suggested that it had been a deliberate act of arson by the Roman Catholics, though it is hard to see what good it could have done them. The carelessness of a Dutch maidservant in leaving clothes to dry in front of an open fire is the more likely explanation.

Princess Anne and her family had left Campden House by now and in 1700, while they were at Windsor, the little Duke of Gloucester died. Anne was now thirty-five and since 1689 had had two children who lived for only an hour or so and eight more miscarriages.

In the early spring of 1702, King William was thrown from his horse while riding in the park at Hampton Court. His injuries were not serious and he was able to return to Kensington Palace, but he developed pneumonia and a few days later he was dead.

Two days after his funeral, Queen Anne and Prince George moved into Kensington Palace, which Bishop Burnet thought 'scarce decent', but Anne loved Kensington, and throughout her reign, although her time was divided between Windsor and Hampton Court in the summer and Kensington and St James's during the winter, Kensington Palace remained her favourite home.

Anne was already a sick woman, her health impaired by her seventeen pregnancies, and so crippled with gout that, at her coronation, she had to be carried in a specially constructed chair, while Prince George's asthma and hard drinking were perceptibly sapping what little vitality he had left. But Anne had tremendous courage, and in the little spare time left her by her eternally quarrelling and scheming ministers, set about making improvements to Kensington Palace and the gardens.

In May 1702, she was writing to Sarah Churchill, her beloved Mrs Morley: 'I went to Kensington to walk in the garden which would be a very pretty place if it were well kept, but nothing can be worse. It is a great deal of pity and indeed a great shame that there should be no better use made of so great an allowance, for I have been told the King allowed £400 a year for that one garden . . .'

Lord Portland was removed from his office of Keeper of the Royal

Parks and Gardens and Henry Wise was soon made responsible for them. He was the younger partner of George London, who had been Bishop Compton's gardener until he set up on his own at the Brompton Park nurseries: and while he toured the country, giving advice to the owners of noble estates on their gardens, Henry Wise looked after 'the magazine of cut greens' at Brompton, and here the orange trees and myrtles and other tender plants from the palace were safely housed during the winter.

Anne had a great love of gardens but she disliked William and Mary's box – particularly its smell – and 'her first works', wrote Switzer,★ 'were the rooting up the box and giving an English model to the old-made gardens at Kensington'.

Anne vowed to keep down the cost of her gardens but, as Switzer said: 'her love to gardening was not a little', and during the first four years of her reign she had spent £26,000 on them.

Henry Wise drew up plans to link the pools along the course of the West Bourne, which was ultimately to result in the formation of the Serpentine, and designed a small pool which one day was to become the Round Pond, but neither of these ideas materialised during Anne's time. However, to the east of the palace, as far as Lord Nottingham's ha-ha, on thirty acres of the estate which had hitherto been left as rough parkland, he created a garden which was ultimately to become the much-loved Kensington Gardens. Wise also planted a garden to the north of the palace, stretching as far as the Bayswater road, part of which he converted from one of the disused gravel-pits, but all traces of it have now vanished.

A year or so later Queen Anne ordered the beautiful orangery to be built, on the north side of the palace. Vanbrugh finished this in 1705 and it still survives. Originally it comprised three rooms, a drawing-room, music-room and ballroom, all small and, as today, painted white: and on summer evenings Queen Anne and Prince George gave small, intimate banquets here, surrounded by the orange trees and myrtles of the gardens, while musicians played and the nightingales sang.

Anne was no intellectual, but she had integrity and a sincere devotion to duty, which helped to steer her through the web of political intrigue, Whigs against Tories, Jacobites against anti-Jacobites, war parties against anti-war parties, which tangled itself about her unceasingly and gave her no peace.

Her Mistress of the Robes and First Lady of the Bedchamber was

★ Switzer, *Nobleman, Gentleman and Gardener's Recreation.*

her childhood friend, Sarah Jennings, who married John Churchill and was to become the Duchess of Marlborough. For years Anne had been passionately devoted to her and, in the name of Mrs Morley, maintained a rather one-sided correspondence with her dear 'Mrs Freeman'. Sarah was the dominant personality and in the early years was a great help to Anne, but she by no means returned the depth of Anne's affection. Secretly Anne bored her to distraction, but she grasped the opportunity offered by Anne's love to wield enormous influence, while John Churchill was winning his victories on the battlefields of Europe. At the Battle of Blenheim, in 1704, he drove the French from Germany; at Ramillies, in 1706, he chased them from the Netherlands. In gratitude, Anne granted him the manor of Woodstock, where later Vanbrugh was to build for him the mighty Blenheim Palace, though it cost so much and took so long in the building, that it was hardly completed before his death.

Anne's chief minister was Godolphin, a professed Tory at the head of a coalition government, but the war party were the Whigs. After Ramillies, most of the country were anxious for peace, particularly the Tories and Queen Anne herself, but as the prestige and wealth of Sarah's husband rose, with each victory, Sarah became a fervent Whig and Godolphin turned with her.

Robert Harley, later Lord Oxford, the leader of the Tory party, determined on a palace intrigue to undermine Sarah's power over the Queen, and used for his purpose Abigail Hill, a Bedchamber woman. She was a poor relation of the Jennings family whom Sarah had introduced to the palace, to take a minor court post, and she was also a distant relative of Harley's.

Abigail, who married Samuel Masham, a page of Prince George, and eventually became Lady Masham, was plain and unattractive but astute. She served Harley's purpose well and gradually insinuated herself into Anne's good graces. In 1707, by which time Sarah had already caused Anne much unhappiness by her long absences from Court, she first noticed a change in the Queen's treatment of her and began to suspect the influence of Abigail. At the news of the victory of Oudenarde the following year, Anne, though later writing in gratitude to Marlborough, exclaimed: 'Oh Lord, when will all this dreadful bloodshed cease?' The long drawn-out slaughter sickened her, and by this time she knew that Prince George was dying.

Sarah was a termagant and spared Anne nothing of her wrath. She stormed against Abigail, seeing in her increasing influence the rise to power of Harley and the Tories, the danger of a return of the Stuarts, the end of her schemes for the Whigs and the risk to the Hanoverian succession.

Anne bore her frightful scenes with remarkable dignity and restraint, ill as she was herself, with her chronic gout, and worn out with nursing the Prince. All that summer and autumn she sat up, night after night, with him at Kensington. For the last few days Sarah returned to the palace to be with Anne, but by then it was too late and she had gone too far in her vilifications. The Prince died on 28 October 1708, but it was Abigail to whom Anne now turned and shortly afterwards Abigail moved into Sarah's lodgings at Kensington for her lying-in.

It provoked yet another stormy interview with the Queen but it was not until April 1710 that Anne and Sarah finally parted, Sarah being dismissed and forced to give up her keys of office.

Lord Godolphin was also dismissed and the Marlboroughs disgraced, having been accused of deliberately prolonging the war for their own ends. The Tories were returned to power but the war dragged on until 1713, and during these years Anne was ceaselessly beset by the quarrelling factions of the Government, all fencing for position. They watched her steady decline in health and vigour. Several times it was rumoured that she was dying. For months on end she could not walk a step. She was pressed to acknowledge her successor and to invite the Electress Sophia of Hanover or her son, Prince George, to England. Yet she felt a duty to her step-brother, the Old Pretender. For Anne, devoted to the Anglican Church, it was a choice between the Hanoverians, whom she hated, and James and the Catholics, whom she had been brought up to fear.

Beset by doubts, trusting no one, least of all Abigail at the end, for she knew that nearly all the Court and Government were ready to change to the flag of whoever succeeded her, she kept her counsel and maintained a proud façade.

At Kensington Palace she continued to touch for the King's Evil. A few years earlier she had written to Sarah: 'I do that business now in the Banqueting House, which I like very well, that being a very cool room, and the doing of it there keeps my own house sweet and free from crowds.'

And she still found solace in the sunken garden beside the Banqueting House, which Henry Wise had made for her from the gravel-pit.

In July 1714 she dismissed Oxford. A day or two later he was present at the Council meeting at Kensington Palace, when the arguments, recriminations and quarrelling went on until two o'clock in the morning. When the Queen at last retired to her own apartments, she told one of her doctors, Dr Arbuthnot, 'she would hardly outlive it'. She quickly grew worse and early on the morning of 1 August, her small bedroom crowded with ladies-in-waiting, her old nurse, Mrs Danvers, Abigail, the Bishop of London and seven doctors, Queen Anne died, at the age of forty-nine.

James Stuart, by now twenty-six, waited hopefully in France for a summons to the throne, but none came. The Electress Sophia had died a few weeks earlier and the succession went to her son, James I's great grandson, the fifty-four-year-old Prince George of Hanover.

As soon as Royalty was established at Kensington, the village became fashionable and more building began, either for permanent residents or to house the many visitors who came to the Court.

In 1705 Bowack wrote of Kensington: 'This town standing in a wholesome air, not above three miles from London, has ever been resorted to by persons of quality and citizens, and for many years past honoured with several fine seats belonging to the Earls of Nottingham, and Warwick. We cannot find it was ever taken notice of in history, except for the great Western Road through it, nor hath anything occurred in it, that might perpetuate its name, till his late Majesty King William was pleased to ennoble it with his court and royal presence. Since which time it has flourished even almost beyond belief; and is inhabited by gentry and persons of note; there is also abundance of shop-keepers, and all sorts of artificers in it, which make it appear rather like part of London, than a country village.

'It is, with dependencies, about three times as big as Chelsea, in number of houses, and in summer time extremely filled with lodgers, for the pleasure of the air, walks and gardens round it, to the great advantage of the inhabitants.

'The buildings are chiefly of brick, regular, and built into streets; the largest is that through which the road lies, reclining from the Queen's House, a considerable way beyond the Church. From the Church runs a row of buildings towards the north, called Church Lane, but the most beautiful part of it is the Square south of the road; which for beauty of building, and worthy inhabitants, exceed several noted squares in London.'

Kensington Square had first been called King's Square, after James II, and the first houses built there were quite small. Near by lived Thomas Young, who seems to have been one of Sir Christopher Wren's builders. With the arrival of the Court at Kensington, Young set about building more houses, on a grander scale, and completing the square, round its small plot of grass and trees. The terraced houses, each with its small paved courtyard in front, are delightful and varied, consisting mostly of three narrow storeys above a basement, and they all have interesting fan-lights over the arched doorways.

Sir Robert Hamilton came to live in the square, after he had been released from the Tower, where William III had consigned him as a suspected Jacobite. Sir Hele Hooke was another early resident and also Charles Talbot, Duke of Shrewsbury, John Hough, created Bishop of Worcester by King William, and the royal physician, Sir Richard Blackmore: and by 1708 Richard Steele was living there.

The unfortunate Duchess of Mazarin, according to the parish books, was living there in 1692, but the investigations of Lord Ponsonby have led to the conclusion that the entry was a mistake and that it was one of her ladies, Claudine de Bragelone, who died there in 1692. This was at a time when the Duchess's fortunes were at their lowest ebb, so she may very well have stayed there for a time, to elude her creditors.

There must have been cottages and shops surrounding the square but no traces of them remain. Beyond them were fields and market gardens and to the east stood an old house, on the site of which Kensington House was later built. Here the Duchess of Portsmouth came to live for a time. She had first come to England as one of the entourage of Henrietta, Duchess of Orleans, King Charles II's sister, who had been sent to Dover by Louis XIV, to arrange the secret Treaty of Dover. Charles was at once attracted by Louise de Kérouaille's pretty baby face, and although she returned to France with Henrietta, she was soon back in England, alleged by some to have been a spy for Louis XIV.

As mistress of the King she became the Duchess of Portsmouth and their son was given the title of Duke of Richmond. Things went well for Louise for a time, but on the King's death her star quickly waned. She returned to France, but during King William's and Queen Anne's reigns she was back again, living in the old Kensington House and applying, with more optimism than justification, for a State pension.

Some fifty years after her death, the house became a French Jesuit college, where many sons of French aristocrat refugees were boarded, and Richard Sheil recalls being taken there as a boy, by his tutor, during the late eighteenth century. 'Accordingly, we set off for Kensington House,' he wrote, 'which is situated exactly opposite the avenue leading to the Palace, and has the beautiful garden attached to it in front. A large iron gate, wrought into rusty flowers, and other fantastic forms, showed that the Jesuit school had once been the residence of some person of distinction; and I afterwards understood that a mistress of Charles the Second lived in the spot which was now converted into one of the sanctuaries of Ignatius. It was a large, old-fashioned house, with many remains of decayed splendour.' He wrote of the 'beautiful walk of trees, which ran down from the rear of the building' and of a room 'covered with faded gilding, and which had once been richly tapestried'.

In Louise's time there were probably no other houses of note to the east of Kensington House, along the Gore towards Knightsbridge, for Kingston House and Gore House had not yet been built and the nursery gardens of Henry Wise and his successors stretched from the Kensington Road down to Brompton Park.

Apart from the great houses and the square, there are not many remains of the Kensington of the late seventeenth and early eighteenth centuries, just as there are none at all of the Tudor village, but just behind the church is a little cul-de-sac, Gordon Place, with rows of little three-storeyed, terrace houses on each side of a paved pathway. Each has its front courtyard with paving-stones, flowers and creepers, the front doors their attractive fan-lights, the first-floor sash-windows their small wrought-iron balconies. They were not built till the early part of the nineteenth century, but the rural atmosphere of the eighteenth century is still here. A short distance away, the Old House, which became the home of Walter Crane, is another relic of old Kensington.

Of other houses which existed at this time, Wells House, with its mineral spring, standing amidst fields and orchards, close to Notting Hill Gate and the north-eastern boundary of Holland Park, was rebuilt and became Aubrey House. Cromwell House, a mansion which was thought to have been the residence of Henry Cromwell at one time, was pulled down when Queensberry Place was built.

Brompton Hall, the home of Lord Burleigh near Earls Court, retained some of its ancient splendour into the early nineteenth century, for Faulkner, writing in 1829, said that: 'There was till lately a grand porch at the entrance. The hall, or salon, is a step lower than the rooms upon the same floor. The dining-room has a richly carved ceiling of oak, displaying in the centre the rose and crown, and in its other compartments the fleur-de-lys and portcullis; and on taking down some ancient tapestry a few years since, the arms of Queen Elizabeth, carved in oak, and curiously inlaid with gold, were discovered above the chimney-piece.'

Just to the west of old Kensington House was the elegantly appointed Colby House, built by Sir John Colby about 1720. He was very rich but also very mean, and he is said to have met his death 'by getting up from his warm bed on a winter night to fetch the key of his cellar, which he had forgotten, for fear his servant might help himself to a bottle of wine'.

In Bullingham House, which had been built in 1700, between Church Street and Pitt Street, Sir Isaac Newton came to spend the last years of his life, but two years later, in 1727, he died, at the age of eighty-five.

The medieval church of St Mary Abbots was very small. In 1685 and in 1695 new aisles were added to the north and south, but they were only temporary measures, to accommodate the increasing congregation, and by the end of the century the old church was pulled down, except for the tower, and a new, square red-brick one built, somewhat after the style of Wren, although he was not the architect. There was a Dutch gable over the western entrance and the large, arched windows gave it light and grace. There were galleries along the north and south aisles and the pulpit was presented by King William. It was described at the time as 'very large and spacious, built of brick . . . very regular and convenient . . . paved handsomely with purbeck stone . . . and the pulpit and chancel handsomely adorned with carving and painting', but later generations were to deplore its ugliness.

The pulpit still survives in the present church of St Mary Abbots, but the seventeenth-century church was to last for less than two hundred years.

VI

George I and Kensington

GEORGE I was not particularly pleased at the prospect of becoming King of England. He disliked leaving his comfortable palace at Herrenhausen and returned there as often as possible during the thirteen years of his reign. He knew nothing of English politics and spoke not a word of the language, speaking French to such ministers as understood it and Latin to the rest, including Sir Robert Walpole, to whom he left all the affairs of State.

The majority of people in England were prepared to welcome him, as a preferable alternative to the Catholic line of Stuarts, but he disappointed them and soon became unpopular: and they never forgot his treatment of his wife, Sophia Dorothea of Celles. After neglecting her for several years, he had divorced her for her romantic love affair with the handsome Count Koenigsmark. She was committed to the lonely castle of Ahlden, where she was kept a virtual prisoner for the rest of her life, forbidden even to see her son, who was to become George II. Count Koenigsmark disappeared suddenly and his fate remained a mystery for many years until the remains of his murdered body were found buried under the floorboards of a room in the palace where he had been discovered with Sophia Dorothea.

King George brought to England, his mistress, Frau von Schulenberg whom he created the Duchess of Kendal. He also brought an entourage of about a hundred Germans, which included his Master of Horse, the Baron von Kielmansegge and his wife, who was probably the King's illegitimate half-sister, for on the death of the Baron she was created the Countess of Darlington and lived at Court, a close companion of the King and the Duchess of Kendal. The King's personal attendants were two Turks, Mustapha and Mahomet, whom he had taken prisoner in Hungary. They had tended him with great skill and devotion when he was wounded during the siege of Vienna, in 1685, and in gratitude he had offered them the chance of becoming his servants and accompanying him to England, where the other servants treated them with wary respect, for they became useful palace spies and acquired considerable back-stairs power.

Royal Kensington waited eagerly to see what events and changes the new Court would bring. The village was growing busy, for the coaching days were dawning and it lay on the important western approach to London. Stage-coaches were still cumbersome and extremely uncomfortable, with no springs yet, and the roads were deplorable, for it was nobody's business to maintain them and turnpikes had not yet been installed, but the coach traffic through Kensington was enough to keep the Red Lion in a bustle. This inn, at the corner of the High Street and Church Street, was the most important coaching inn in the village at the beginning of the eighteenth century, and from its windows visitors could see the palace and its green.

In *Esmond*, Thackeray described the scene in Kensington when George I arrived in England. 'With some delays in procuring horses we go to Hammersmith about four o'clock on Sunday morning, the 1st of August (1714), and half an hour later, it then being bright day, we rode by my Lady Warwick's house and so down the street of Kensington. Early as the hour was, there was a bustle in the street, and many people moving to and fro. Round the gate leading to the palace, where the guard is, there was specially a great crowd; and the coach ahead of us stopped, and the bishop's man got down, to know what the concourse meant. Then presently came out from the gate horse-guards with their trumpets, and a company of heralds with their tabards. The trumpets blew, and the herald-at-arms came forward, and proclaimed "George, by the grace of God, of Great Britain, France, and Ireland, King, Defender of the Faith." And the people shouted "God Save the King".'

King George and the Court divided their time between St James' Palace, Windsor and Kensington, but the King preferred Kensington to any of the other royal residences and lived there as much as possible, making many important alterations and additions.

Nicholas Hawksmoor, a pupil of Wren's, made a survey of the palace and it was decided to remove the old nucleus of Nottingham House completely and build new state rooms on the first floor of the site where it had stood, including the drawing-room, Privy Chamber and the Cupola room, which was intended for the chief reception room. Sir Christopher Wren, who by this time was an old man, was removed from the office of Court Surveyor, and his unworthy successor was William Benson, who built the rooms so badly that they soon had to be repaired, but since then they have survived.

The Cupola room was decorated by William Kent in the grand manner of the period. It had a massive marble chimney-piece. The walls were ornamented with Ionic pilasters, between which were niches in which gilded statues were placed, and above them were smaller recesses to take the collection of heads of the Roman poets which had been made by Charles I. The ceiling was painted to represent a mighty dome and in the middle was a panel with the star of the Order of the Garter.

Kent also decorated the grand staircase of the palace, with its beautiful, wrought-iron balustrade, as well as enlarging the upper landing. The walls he covered with paintings of groups of people connected with the palace, depicting them as peering over balconies. This was said to have been the King's idea and the paintings provide a fascinating picture of some of the palace personalities, including the Yeomen of the Guard, the two Turkish servants and Peter, the Wild Boy, who had been discovered in the woods of Hanover and presented to the King as a curiosity. There were more paintings on the ceiling, where Kent included himself as well as two of his pupils and his beautiful actress friend, with whom 'he lived on terms of intimacy'.

A year or two later alterations were made on the north side of Clock Court. The Prince of Wales Court to the west and the Princesses' Court to the east were added, both of them being surrounded by arcaded cloisters, and in the northern part of the western court a three-storeyed apartment, also decorated by Kent, was built for the Duchess of Kendal.

Many people disliked Kent's work. 'At Kensington the new Apartments built and adorned with paintings by Mr Kent are five rooms following each other at the head of the staircase,' wrote George Vertue. Of the Cupola room, he said: 'Niches of Marble and pedestals with statues gilt with burnished gold' ... make 'a terrible glaring show and truly Gothic, according to the weakness of the conception of the Surveyors and Controllers of the King's Works, or their private piques. In the next Room being the largest in the middle of the Ceiling one large long Oval wherein is represented Jupiter coming to Danae, not in a Cloud of gold (but of Snow) the other parts of this Ceiling are Ornaments; the next and fifth room the Ceiling in Imitation of the Ancient Roman Subterranean Ornaments – poor stuff. All these paintings are so far short of the like works done here in England before by Verrio, Cook, Streeter, Laguerre, Thornhill, Ricci, Pellegrini etc., in Nobelmen's Houses in Town and Country'.

Whether or not one admires this kind of mural decoration, there seems to have been some fairly acrimonious professional jealousy in regard to Kent and his work, which may have been generated by the growing dislike for the King and more particularly the Duchess of Kendal, so tall, thin and unprepossessing that the lampoonists soon dubbed her the Lamp-post. The chief grievance against the Duchess was her habit of persuading the King to make State appointments which proved extremely profitable to herself. However, the business of selling appointments and monopolies was current practice and the King was probably not as bad as he was often painted.

A contemporary describes him as 'short of stature and very corpulent, his cheeks are protuberant and his eyes too big, he looks kind and amiable, but those who do not like him say that he is not generous in money matters'.

His position was not easy. He was well aware of the strength of the Jacobite party in England and seems to have thought their claims reasonable. The Duchess of Kendal had been decidedly nervous of coming to England at all, remembering that it was little more than sixty years since the English had put to death a King with whom they had been displeased.

On meeting the Recorder of London for the first time, the King, regretting his lack of knowledge of the English language, had asked him to inform his people of his principles: 'I never forsake a friend; I will endeavour to do justice to every body: and I fear nobody.' And when he met his ministers he said that, as he knew little of English customs or the Constitution, he was prepared to put himself entirely in their hands and be guided by them. 'Then you become completely answerable for everything that I do,' he explained diplomatically, thereby instituting the Cabinet system of government which has remained ever since.

Perhaps because of his bitterness against Sophia Dorothea, he developed an aversion to his son, who was created Prince of Wales after his arrival in England. By 1717 they had quarrelled violently and the Prince and his wife, the future Queen Caroline, were turned out of all the Royal palaces and established themselves at Leicester House, on the north side of Leicester Square, where they were soon surrounded by a court which was a good deal livelier and more cultured than the King's. The children, however, were forced to remain with their grandfather and the Duchess of Portland was appointed governess to the three Princesses. The youngest child, a boy, died in infancy, and the eldest, the future Frederick, Prince of Wales was, by the order of his grandfather, still in Hanover, completing his education.

Living at Sandford Manor, at Sandy End, on the Fulham and Chelsea border, at the time of George I's accession was Joseph Addison. 'We dined at a country house near Chelsea where Mr Addison often retired,' wrote Swift to Stella in September 1710. The house is said to have been built for Nell Gwynn when she gave up her land in Chelsea in order that the Royal Hospital could be built, but this story is probably apocryphal. Addison, born in 1672, was already an important figure in the Whig party as well as having achieved literary fame.

During Queen Anne's reign, until the fall of the Whigs in 1710, he had been Under-Secretary of State and Secretary to the Lord Lieutenant of Ireland. Then, out of office and with time on his hands, he began writing regularly for Steele's *The Tatler*.

Richard Steele, born in Dublin in 1672, had lost his father when he was still a child and had been educated and sent to Oxford by his uncle, secretary of the Lord Lieutenant, the great Duke of Ormonde, who so many years earlier had secretly wooed his bride Elizabeth at Holland House. The Duke, who had lived on until 1685, also befriended Steele when he was a boy.

He had founded *The Tatler* in 1709, the year before Addison joined him. It was issued three times a week and by the time it was closed in 1711 Addison had contributed sixty papers. Swift, who disliked its Whig politics, although he had once been an adherent of the party, described *The Tatler* as 'cruel, dull and dry', but it was highly successful and brought enduring fame to Addison and Steele.

Addison's essay on *Quack Doctors* is an amusing reflection on the gullibility of people of the early eighteenth century, when confronted by the mysteries of the medical profession, which, like the interest in Don Saltero's Knackatory, seems so difficult to reconcile with their achievements in art and architecture and their intellectual attainments in other fields. 'I remember when our island was shaken with an earthquake some years ago, there was an impudent mountebank who sold pills which (as he told the country people) were very good against an earthquake,' wrote Addison. His cure for most human ills, either of the body or the spirit was abstinence. 'I am persuaded that if . . . a whole people were to enter into a course of abstinence, and eat nothing but water and gruel for a fortnight, it would abate the rage and animosity of parties, and not a little contribute to the cure of a distracted nation,' he said, a panacea which the Government might try today, if all else fails.

Steele brought *The Tatler* to an end to make way for *The Spectator*, which first appeared two months later. This was a daily and it continued until the end of 1712, running to 555 numbers which Addison and Steele wrote between them. Then Steele replaced it with *The Guardian*, another daily, costing one penny, and their collaboration continued, their chief meeting-place being Button's Coffee House in Russell Street, Covent Garden. Button had been a servant of the Countess of Warwick's family and he opened the coffee house after Will's, on the other side of the street, had declined in popularity after the death of Dryden, who had held court there for many years.

Contributors to *The Guardian* were invited to send their manuscripts to Button's and the famous lion's head with its wide-open mouth was placed at the door, so that they could be dropped into it and received in the box held in the lion's paws. 'Whatever the Lion swallows I shall digest for the use of the public,' promised Addison.

One of his own most amusing contributions to *The Guardian* was his essay *On Naked Bosoms*, another reflection on the social life of the English in Queen Anne's day. '. . . the clergy during the time of Cromwell's usurpation, were very much taken up in reforming the female world, and showing the vanity of those outward ornaments in which the sex so much delights,' he wrote. 'I have heard a whole sermon against whitewash, and have known a coloured ribbon made the mark of the unconverted. The clergy of the present age are not transported with these indiscreet favours, as knowing that it is hard for a reformer to avoid ridicule, when he is severe on subjects which are rather apt to produce mirth than seriousness. For this reason, I look upon myself to be of great use to these good men . . .

'Thus much I thought fit to premise before I resume the subject which I have already handled. I mean the naked bosoms of our

British ladies. I hope they will not take it ill of me, if I still beg that they will be covered . . .'

By 1713, with Steele becoming an increasingly militant Whig and Addison preoccupied in combating the libels of the jealous Pope, *The Guardian* closed. Early in 1714 Steele was elected to Parliament but a few weeks later was expelled for sedition.

Addison at Sandford Manor had long been in love with the widowed Countess of Warwick, still living at Holland House, only a short walk away, across the fields, and as early as 1708 was writing charming letters to her nine-year-old son – letters which show how completely rural Kensington still was.

'My dear Lord, I have employed the whole neighbourhood in looking after birds' nests, and not altogether without success. My man found one last night; but it proved a hen's, with fifteen eggs in it, covered with an old brooding duck. . . . This morning I have news brought to me of a nest that has abundance of little eggs, streaked with red and blue veins . . . some say they are sky-larks; others will have them to be a canary-bird's; but I am much mistaken in the turn and colour of the eggs, if they are not full of tom-tits . . .

'Since I am so near your Lordship, methinks that after having passed the day among the more severe studies, you may often take a trip hither, and relax yourself with these curiosities of nature . . .'

A week later he was inviting the little Earl to 'a concert of music which I have found out in a neighbouring wood. It begins precisely at six in the evening, and consists of a blackbird, a thrush, a robin-red-breast and a bull-finch. There is a lark, that, by way of overture, sings and mounts till she is almost out of hearing; and afterwards falls down leisurely . . . drops to the ground, or as soon as she has ended her song; the whole is concluded by a nightingale, that has a much better voice than Mrs Tofts, and something of Italian manners in her divisions.

'If your Lordship will honour me with your company, I will promise to entertain you with much better music, and more agreeable scenes, than you ever met with at the Opera . . .'

With the accession of George I and the return of the Whigs to power, Addison was once more made Chief Secretary for Ireland, an appointment which left him time to continue his writing. The gay and feckless Steele was elected to Parliament again and in 1715 he was knighted. He and his wife Prue had been living at a small house in Chelsea, where Cheyne Walk was later to be built, and round about this time they moved to a house in Kensington Square.

In August 1716 Addison at last married the Countess of Warwick and moved to Holland House. His long courtship, as Dr Johnson observed, was not unlike Sir Roger de Coverley's pursuit of his haughty widow. The marriage was said to have been unhappy, but this story may have arisen through jealous gossip and Pope's spiteful comment that he had 'married discord', and have had little foundation in fact. Another legend of Addison at Holland House is that he used to pace up and down the long library 'between two bottles of wine . . . taking a glass of each as he arrived at each end of the room'. And those who maintained that he was unhappy alleged that he used to escape from the Countess' sharp tongue by retiring to the White Horse Inn at the bottom of Holland Lane.

Addison left no direct evidence of his state of mind at this time, but he did write: 'everyone ought to reflect how much more unhappy he might be than he really is'.

He was already a sick man, suffering from both dropsy and asthma, but he continued to write. In April 1717 he was appointed a Secretary of State, but in less than a year he was forced to resign through increasing ill-health. For the next year he lived mainly at Holland House, seldom visiting his town house in Albemarle Street. In January 1719 the Countess gave birth to their only child, Charlotte, who lived on until the end of the century, unmarried, at Addison's Warwickshire home at Bilton.

Steele's turn of good fortune did not last. In 1718 he lost a great deal of money in an unsound business speculation, but far worse than this disaster was the death of his 'dear Prue' shortly afterwards. Swift had complained to Stella, a year or two earlier, that Steele 'was governed by his wife, most abominably' and was the worst company in the world 'till he has a bottle of wine in his head', but Steele loved his wife dearly and never recovered from her death. Early in the following year he quarrelled with Addison over the politics of the Peerage Bill. It proved the end of the friendship which had meant so much to them both and before it could be mended Addison died at Holland House, in June 1719.

Before his death he sent for his stepson, the young Earl of Warwick and taking his hand murmured: 'See in what peace a Christian can die.'

Steele was to live for another ten years but after launching another short-lived periodical, *The Theatre*, and writing one or two pamphlets and plays, he was so heavily in debt that he left Kensington and went to stay with his friend Bishop Hoadly at Hereford for a time and then moved on to a property of Prue's in Carmarthen. Here in 1729 he died of a stroke, but 'he retained his cheerful sweetness of temper to the last, and would often be carried out on a summer's evening, where the country lads and lasses were assembled in their rural sports, and with his pencil wrote an order for a new gown to the best dancer'.

The young Lord Warwick was barely twenty when his stepfather died and seems to have been a difficult and dissolute young man, despite Addison's affectionate concern for him. In 1721, only two years later, he succumbed to a fever and died.

Holland House passed to William Edwardes, grandson of the second Earl of Holland. Edwardes, whose name survives in Edwardes Square, was many years later to be created Baron Kensington, but he spent little, if any, time at Holland House. It was leased from time to time to a succession of tenants and fell into a sad state of disrepair, but during the reign of George II the Fox family took it on a long lease and in 1768 Henry Fox, the youngest son of Sir Stephen Fox, born when his father was seventy-six, bought it outright and became the first Lord Holland of a new line.

Campden House was still in the possession of the Noël family at the beginning of George I's reign, but they had leased it to the Dowager Countess of Burlington and her son Richard, and in 1719 they sold it to Lord Lechmere, who lived there until 1735.

George I died on 11 June 1727 at Osnaburgh, on his way to pay a visit to Hanover. He had had a strong premonition of his death, for he never forgot that an old wise-woman had once foretold that he would not long survive Sophia Dorothea, and she had died at Ahlden only a few weeks earlier.

The Prince of Wales was in residence at Richmond when Sir Robert Walpole brought him the news of his father's death. He returned at once to Leicester House for a few days, but 'on the 19th the Court removed to Kensington' recorded Lord Hervey.

VII

George II and Kensington

LIKE his father, George II preferred Kensington Palace to the other Royal residences – St James' Palace, Richmond Lodge, Hampton Court and Windsor, and spent much of his time there: and after a short period of doubt, Sir Robert Walpole continued in office as his Prime Minister.

The King formed the habit of visiting his Hanoverian possessions every three years, for several months each time, and during these absences Queen Caroline acted as Regent. The King loved her in his own strange way. She was more intelligent and cultured and, though he would have been the last to admit it during her lifetime, she exercised great power over him. She in turn was greatly influenced by Sir Robert Walpole and frequently acted as intermediary between him and the King.

When he was Prince of Wales the King had taken one of the Queen's ladies-in-waiting, Mrs Howard, who later became the Countess of Suffolk, for his mistress. According to Lord Hervey, 'he passed every evening of his life, three or four hours, in Mrs Howard's lodging, who, as dresser to the Princess, always in waiting, was lodged all the year round in the Court'.

At the time of his accession, George II was forty-three, Queen Caroline forty-two and Mrs Howard, already very deaf, forty-six. She knew that the King had little real feeling left for her and that his true affections lay with Queen Caroline, and so did the Queen, who bore the situation with remarkable tact and diplomacy. As Lord Hervey put it: 'The Queen, knowing the vanity of her husband's temper, and that he must have some woman for the world to believe he lay with, wisely suffered to remain in that situation whom she despised and had got the better of, for fear of making room for a successor whom he might really love, and that might get the better of her.'

Lord Hervey, six years younger than Queen Caroline, was appointed Vice-Chamberlain to the Royal Household in 1730 and became a great favourite of the Queen and the Princesses. He was also a good friend of the Prince of Wales, whom the King was persuaded to summon from Hanover shortly after his accession, until the Prince became the lover of Hervey's mistress, Anne Vane, after which the friendship cooled.

Frederick, Prince of Wales, was a difficult young man and before ong was quarrelling bitterly with his parents over his allowance, his mistresses and the problem of whom he should marry.

Queen Caroline, for all the difficulties of her marriage, had compensations, one of which was her love of gardens. Although Henry Wise had made tentative plans for the redesigning of the gardens at Kensington during Queen Anne's time, it was not until the last year of George I's reign that Wise and his partner Charles Bridgeman submitted a final plan. Wise retired in 1728 and Bridgeman became the royal gardener, with the task of carrying out the scheme.

The Broad Walk, 80 feet wide and more than half a mile long, had already been planted and the excavations for the Round Pond begun before the new reign and Queen Caroline happily superintended the completion of these projects, spending large sums of money which the King thought were coming from her own funds until he later received the bills. The Round Pond was finished and filled with water in 1728. Then, at the Queen's suggestion, the pools which Wise had planned along the course of the West Bourne river were joined to form the new Serpentine river. This work, which was very costly, involving a vast amount of excavation, took place during 1730 and the spring of 1731, and at one stage the Queen, raising the old complaint that Kensington Palace was damp, had decided to have a new Royal Palace built in Hyde Park, but the idea did not go beyond a plan and a model and was finally abandoned on the grounds of cost.

The planting of the avenues leading to the Round Pond was completed and on Saturdays, the day that the King and his Court went to

Richmond, the gardens were open to the public, though no one would have thought of entering them except in formal clothes. The Broad Walk became a promenade of high fashion, and it was here that the farthingale was first seen in England, said to have been first worn by Queen Caroline when Princess of Wales and her ladies-in-waiting. 'People would throng to see them; the ladies would take the opportunity of showing themselves, like pea-hens, in the walks; persons of fashion, privileged to enter the gardens, would avail themselves of the privilege; and at last the public would obtain admission, and the raree-show would be complete. The full-dress promenade, it seems, was at first confined to Saturdays; it was afterwards changed to Sundays and continued on that day till the custom went out with the closing days of George III:'* and by that time the gardens were open to the public every day of the week.

Moreover, the roads approaching the palace had improved and there was a turnpike at Knightsbridge and another in Kensington, opposite the gates of Holland House, the tolls from the turnpikes being used to maintain and improve the highway. But in 1736 Lord Hervey, in a letter to his mother, wrote: 'The road beyond this place (Kensington) and London is grown so infamously bad, that we live here in the same solitude as we should do if cast on a rock in the middle of the ocean, and all the Londoners tell us there is between them and us a great impassable gulf of mud. There are two roads through the park, but the new one is so convex and the old one so concave, that by this extreme of faults they agree in the common one of being, like the high road, impassable.'

At the palace Queen Caroline occupied Queen Mary's apartments and gallery and had Wren's panelling painted in gold and white, while the King settled into King William's rooms.

Domestic life was stormy. The King actively disliked the Prince of Wales and did not speak to him. His temper was uncertain but usually bad and when his family or his ministers annoyed him he was given to venting his spleen 'even on his innocent wig, while his clever spouse, Queen Caroline, stood by, maintaining her dignity and self-possession, and, consequently her ascendancy over him'.

So admirably did she play her part that by 1734 Sir Robert Walpole was saying to her: 'Your Majesty knows that this country is entirely in your hands, that the fondness the King has for you, the opinion he has of your affection, and the regard he has for your judgement, are the only reins by which it is possible to restrain the

* Walford, *Old and New London*.

natural violence of his temper, or to guide him through any part where he is wanted to go.'

'Her predominant passion was pride, and the darling pleasure of her soul was power,' wrote Lord Hervey, 'but she was forced to gratify one to gain the other, as some people do health, by a strict and painful régime, which few besides herself could have her patience to support and resolution to adhere to.'

The valetudinarian Lord Hervey certainly knew all about 'strict and painful régimes' for he was said to have existed on tea, asses' milk and a biscuit, with an apple once a week, but he was an entertaining writer, and in his *Memoirs of the Reign of George II* he recalled Sir Robert having said of the King that 'to talk to him of compassion, consideration of past services, charity and bounty was making use of words that with him had no meaning'.

Finding himself alone on one occasion with the Princess Royal, who had been married to the deformed and ill-favoured Prince of Orange and was on a visit to Kensington, Lord Hervey asked her why the King had been in such a particularly bad mood that day. 'My God!' she replied, 'I am ashamed for you, who have been so long about Papa, to know so little of him as when he is the most peevish and snappish to think it is the most material things that have made him so. When great points go as he would not have them, he frets and is bad to himself; but when he is in his worst humours, and the devil to everybody that comes near him, it is always because one of his pages has powdered his periwig ill, or a housemaid set a chair where it does not use to stand, or something of that kind.'

Late in the summer of 1734 Lady Suffolk, 'who had long borne His Majesty's contempt, neglect, snubs, and ill-humour with a resignation that few people who felt so sensibly could have suffered so patiently, at last resolved to withdraw herself from these severe trials, from which no advantage accrued but the conscious pride of her own fortitude in supporting them with prudence.'

She asked permission to take the cure at Bath for six weeks and when she returned to St James' for the King's birthday she found that the affair was finished and no objections were raised to her marriage, the following year, to Mr George Berkeley, who was 'neither young, handsome, healthy, nor rich'.

In 1735 the King was making preparations for his usual visit to Hanover. Walpole and the Cabinet were apprehensive of the King leaving England at this time, because of strained relations with Prussia, but Walpole could not persuade the Queen to prevent his going.

She saw the potential danger 'of blowing up his warlike disposition'
but, observed Hervey, it was offset by 'the pleasure that resulted to
her pride from the éclat of the regency, and the convenience and ease
of her being mistress of all those hours that were not employed in
writing, to do what she pleased, which was never her case for two
hours together when the King was in England.' Moreover, 'she had
the certainty of being, for six months at least, not only free from the
conjugal fatigue of being obliged to entertain him twenty hours in
the twenty-four, but also from the more irksome office of being set
up to receive the quotidian sallies of a temper that, let it be charged by
what hand it would, used always to discharge the hottest fire, on
some pretence or other, upon her.'

So the King departed, and in Hanover he met Madame Walmoden, who became his new mistress. He was besotted with her and
stayed away for nearly eight months, but each week he sent the
Queen voluminous letters of forty, fifty and sometimes sixty pages,
describing his new love in the most extraordinarily intimate detail,
so that 'had the Queen been a painter she might have drawn her
rival's picture at six hundred miles distance.' He also, said Hervey,
gave the Queen 'the account of his buying her, and what he gave for
her, which, considering the rank of the purchaser, and the merits of
the purchase as he set them forth, I think he had no great reason to
brag of, when the first price, according to his report, was only one
thousand ducats – a much greater proof of his economy than his
passion.'

All these letters the Queen showed to Sir Robert Walpole, who as
usual advised her to be patient and acquiescent, assuring her that this
was the only way for her to maintain her strong position.

When he could spare time from Madame Walmoden, King
George arranged for the marriage of the Prince of Wales, who by
this time was twenty-eight, with the seventeen-year-old Princess
Augusta of Saxe Gotha. He then departed for England, arriving at
Kensington Palace on Sunday, 26 October, just as the Queen was returning from chapel. As he alighted from his coach, she greeted him
with her usual affection at the gates, but he was in no sweet mood,
apart from being overtired, through travelling without pause for
more than three days, for no particular reason, 'only for the pleasure
of bragging how quick he moved'.

'Everybody shared the warm and frequent sallies of his abominable
temper,' said Hervey, 'and everybody imputed them to what was the
joint though not the sole cause of these eruptions, which was the

affliction he felt for the change of a German life to an English one, with the society of a stale wife instead of a new mistress; and, what grated more than all the rest, the transition to limited from unlimited power.'

He stayed at Kensington for only two days, after which he moved to London for his birthday celebrations, but during that brief visit he managed to raise a rumpus about the palace pictures. The Queen had a genuine appreciation of drawing and painting and it was she who discovered a large collection of long-forgotten Holbein sketches in an old bureau at the palace. During the King's stay in Hanover, she had 'taken several very bad pictures out of the great drawing-room at Kensington, and put very good ones in their places. The King, affecting, for the sake of contradiction to dislike this change, or, from his extreme ignorance in painting, really disapproving it, told Lord Hervey, as Vice-Chamberlain, that he would have every new picture taken away, and every old one replaced. Lord Hervey, who had a mind to make his court to the Queen by opposing this order, asked if His Majesty would not give leave for the two Van Dycks at least, on each side of the chimney, to remain, instead of those two sign-posts, done by nobody knew who, that had been removed to make way for them.' To which the King answered, 'My Lord, I have a great respect for your taste in that you understand, but in pictures I beg leave to follow my own. I suppose you assisted the Queen with your fine advice when she was pulling my house to pieces and spoil-ing all my furniture. Thank God, at least she has left the walls stand-ing! As for the Vandykes, I do not care whether they are changed or no; but for the picture with the dirty frame over the door, and the three nasty little children,* I will have them taken away, and the old ones restored; I will have it done too tomorrow morning before I go to London, or else I know it will not be done at all.'

Lord Hervey assured the King that the pictures should be restored without fail, although he knew that they had already been sent either to Windsor or Hampton Court and that some of the frames had been altered to fit the fresh pictures. However, the next morning, the King appeared to have forgotten all about it. He joined his family after breakfast for a few minutes, 'snubbed the Queen, who was drinking chocolate, for being always stuffing, the Princess Emily for not hear-ing him, the Princess Caroline for being grown fat, the Duke for standing awkwardly, Lord Hervey for not knowing what relation the Prince of Sultzbach was to the Elector Palatine, and then carried

* Probably Van Dyck's painting of Charles I's children, now at Windsor.

the Queen to walk, and be resnubbed, in the garden.' He then departed for St James', giving them all time to recover the pictures and replace them.

The King obviously needed a new mistress to amuse him while he was in England and parted from Madame Walmoden. Sir Robert assured the Queen that she must rely on her head rather than her person to hold her power over the King and suggested that Lady Tankerville be brought to Kensington to catch his eye and his fancy. To Sir Robert Walpole's dismay, the bait failed and the King took instead to Lady Deloraine, the Princesses' governess, whom Walpole disliked intensely, believing her to be dangerous, with a 'weak head, a pretty face, a lying tongue and a false heart'.

However, the King now spent nearly every evening in the Princesses' apartments with Lady Deloraine and, although 'he never used to be civil to the Queen, even when he was kind', he was now 'abominably and perpetually so harsh and rough, that she could never speak one word uncontradicted, nor do any one act unreproved.' Yet despite the liaison with Deloraine, he spent two or three hours of every morning writing page after page of love letters to Madame Walmoden, whom he had promised to visit the following spring.

Towards the end of April 1736, the little Princess Augusta arrived at Greenwich for her marriage to the Prince of Wales. She was a good-natured but plain little soul. Nevertheless, Frederick seemed disposed to be amiable to her and the marriage took place late on the evening of her arrival, at St James' Palace.

About a fortnight later the King left for Hanover and Madame Walmoden, with the Queen once more as Regent and the Court at Kensington. His romance had a slight setback this time for while he was staying at Herrenhausen a gardener noticed a ladder outside Madame Walmoden's lodgings, leaning against her bedroom window. He thought it was a thief and gave the alarm, but to everyone's embarrassment a search of the grounds produced only a Monsieur Schulenberg, a relative of the Duchess of Kendal. The Officer of the Guard ordered his release but tongues wagged and Madame Walmoden, in a panic, took the story quickly to the King, so that he should hear it first from her own lips. She said it was all a plot of the Schulenberg family to destroy their happiness and had been instigated by Madame d'Elite, another member of the family, whom the King had favoured before he had met the Walmoden.

The King was puzzled and wrote to the long-suffering Queen

Caroline for her opinion and advice, at the same time asking her to consult Sir Robert. The result of that letter was that the Queen, from long habit of self-abasement where the King's women were concerned, suggested that the King should bring Madame Walmoden to England, even describing the arrangements she would make for her accommodation at the palace. In the meantime, Madame Walmoden had talked herself out of a very awkward situation and was as high as ever in the King's favour, but deemed it wiser not to accept the Queen's invitation.

The King had ordered the Prince of Wales to make Kensington his principal place of residence during his absence, but the Prince, being jealous of his mother's Regency, was as difficult as he dare be without promoting open conflict. The Princess kept her drawing-room there every Monday morning and the Prince his levée, and they were sometimes there on a Thursday, but the rest of the week they spent either at Kew or St James's. The King complained in his letters to the Queen 'for letting them ramble about in that manner', but the Queen replied, reasonably enough, that 'they neither asked her leave to go out, nor were of an age to be locked up'.

The King returned to England at the end of the year, being nearly shipwrecked in the North Sea on the way. He arrived in a surprisingly amiable mood, but he had caught cold on the journey and was ill in bed for several days, and then he took up with Lady Deloraine again, who was still at Court. 'The King as usual talked to the Queen of his lying with Lady Deloraine, and the Queen to Lord Hervey, and Sir Robert Walpole talked of it with little ceremony. Sir Robert Walpole said to Lord Hervey he was not sorry the King had got a new plaything but wished His Majesty had taken somebody that was less mischievous than that lying bitch.'

By this time the Princess of Wales was pregnant. The King insisted that the child should be born at Hampton Court and as the time drew near the Court moved there. However, the Prince of Wales wished the birth to be at St James'. He said later that he had not received the King's command, but the general opinion at the time was that he had no intention of submitting to the King's dictation.

When the Princess' labour began, somewhat prematurely, though she begged him 'for God's sake . . . to let her stay quiet', he insisted on her being half-carried, half-dragged, in the greatest secrecy, through the long dark corridors of Windsor and down the back staircases to a waiting carriage. She was bundled into it with two of her dressers and her lady-in-waiting, Lady Archibald, who was also

Holland House – the great staircase (from *The History of Royal Residences*, W. H. Pyne, 1819)

Cremorne Gardens
From an engraving by Walter Greaves

Gough House in 1828 (it is now part of the Victoria Hospital for
Children, Tite Street)

Cromwell House, Old Brompton

The Gilt Room, Holland House, 1846 (lithograph by F. W. Halme from
the drawing by C. J. Richardson)

The Crystal Palace in Hyde Park
The Great Exhibition, 1851

Inside the Crystal Palace

Chelsea Bridge in 1852

The Rotunda, Ranelagh Gardens in the eighteenth century

Shrewsbury House, Cheyne Walk

Aubrey House (formerly Notting Hill House)

The Old Church, Chelsea

Paradise Row, Chelsea

Winchester House, Chelsea

King's Road, Chelsea, *c.* 1866

the Prince's mistress, and he ordered the coachman to drive full gallop to London.

More than once on the way they thought they would have to stop, so that the Princess could have her baby at some wayside dwelling, but they eventually reached St James' Palace at ten o'clock at night. No preparation had been made and she was put to bed between two table-cloths, where in less than an hour she was delivered of a premature daughter – 'a little rat of a girl, about the bigness of a good large toothpick case', said Lord Hervey.

When the King heard the news he was furiously angry with the Prince, both for flouting his wishes in regard to the birthplace of an heir to the throne and his callous folly in endangering the life of his young wife. The Queen went to see them and was kind to the Princess though appalled at the Prince's conduct, and there was nothing she could do, even if she had wanted to, to prevent the final breach with the King, who ordered him to leave the palace as soon as the Princess was well enough to be moved, though he allowed her to keep her baby.

They left St James' Palace on 12 September 1737 and shortly afterwards moved into the Duke of Norfolk's house in St James' Square, then to Leicester House and later to Carlton House.

'My dear first-born,' said the Queen to Lord Hervey, 'is the greatest ass, and the greatest liar, and the greatest *canaille*, and the greatest beast, in the whole world, and . . . I most heartily wish he was out of it . . . I hope, in God, I shall never see him again.'

Her wish was granted in an unexpected way, for only a few weeks later she was taken mortally ill at St James'. The doctors advised all the current remedies, Daffy's Elixir, mint water, snake-root, Sir Walter Raleigh's Cordial, whisky and brandy. Nothing did any good. More doctors were called, including Sir Hans Sloane. She was blooded and purged to no avail.

It was discovered that she had a rupture which she had concealed from everyone but the King for fourteen years. Surgeons attempted to operate but it was too late, and when the King knew that she was past all hope of recovery he was desolate. She had frequently said that she would like him to marry again after her death and she repeated the wish now, whereupon 'his sobs began to rise and his tears to fall with double vehemence'. Whilst in the midst of this passion, wiping his eyes, and sobbing between every word, with much ado he got out this answer: 'Non – j'aurau – des – maîtresses.' To which the Queen made no other reply than: 'Ah! mon Dieu! cela n'empêche pas.'

'I know this episode will hardly be credited, but it is literally true,' adds Hervey in his Memoirs, and he was in close attendance on the Queen all through her illness.

The King refused to allow the Prince of Wales to visit his mother and she felt so bitterly about him that even on her deathbed she said to the King: 'I am so far from desiring to see him, that nothing but your absolute command should ever make me consent to it.'

After two or three weeks of intense suffering, the Queen died, and the King grieved for her sincerely, extolling her virtues in a manner which would have given her deep happiness if she had been alive to hear him.

When the first shock was over, however, Sir Robert Walpole suggested tentatively that he take steps to bring Madame Walmoden over from Hanover and, while awaiting her arrival, renew his liaison with Lady Deloraine. At the mention of Lady Deloraine, the King grumbled that 'she stank of Spanish wine so abominably that he could not bear her', but Lady Deloraine prevailed and until Madame Walmoden arrived a few months later he resumed his affair with her, as 'he neither cared to be at the trouble nor expense of a new mistress in the interim'.

Lord Hervey did not stay at the palace after the Queen's death. He was given the appointment of Lord Privy Seal in 1739 but he was a chronically sick man and in 1743 he died. The tale of George II's private life was taken up by Horace Walpole, Sir Robert's supposedly second son, though there are reasons to think that he may, in fact, have been the son of Lord Hervey's elder brother.

When Madame Walmoden arrived in England she was established as the King's mistress and created the Countess of Yarmouth, but she was kept very much in the background and given no special privileges. Lady Deloraine remained at Court for a time, as governess and companion to the Princesses still, but there was bitter rivalry between the two women, and on 8 October 1742 Horace Walpole, in a letter to Sir Horace Mann, said:

'There has been a great fracas at Kensington; one of the Princesses pulled the chair from under Countess Deloraine at cards, who, being provoked that her Monarch was diverted with her disgrace, with the malice of a hobby-horse, gave him just such another fall. But alas! the Monarch, like Louis XIV, is mortal in the part that touched the ground, and was so hurt and angry, that the Countess is disgraced, and her German rival remains in the sole and quiet possession of her royal master's favour.'

That is the last we ever hear of Lady Deloraine and the King seems to have settled down in comparatively peaceful domesticity with the Countess of Yarmouth, but the Court now became very quiet and dull. At Kensington many of the rooms were locked and shuttered. Sir Robert Walpole did not continue in office for very long after the death of the Queen, being dismissed in 1739 for his unwillingness to take part in the long-threatened War of the Austrian Succession, in which the King was mainly concerned for the safety of his Hanoverian possessions.

He formed an army of Hanoverian and English troops, financed with English money, and led them personally to victory at the Battle of Dettingen in 1743. He was a brave soldier, the last English monarch to command his troops on the battlefield, and his conduct made him more popular than at any time during his reign. The tables were turned two years later, with the French victory at Fontenoy, in 1745, which gave them the confidence to support the Jacobite rebellion of Charles Edward Stuart later in the year, but the King was unperturbed by the Jacobites and after their suppression and the end of the war, which came with the Peace of Aix-la-Chapelle in 1748, the Countess of Yarmouth persuaded him to attend a celebration masqued ball at Ranelagh.★

For the most part, however, he lived quietly at Kensington with the Countess. She occupied Lady Suffolk's old rooms and in 1749 Horace Walpole in a letter to Sir Horace Mann, wrote: 'my Lady Yarmouth has an ague, and is forced to keep a constant fire in her room against the damps. When my Lady Suffolk lived in that apartment, the floor produced a constant crop of mushrooms. Though there are so many vacant chambers, the King hoards all he can, and has locked up half the palace since the Queen's death: so he does at St James', and I believe would put the rooms out to interest, if he could get a closet a year for them! Somebody told my Lady Yarmouth they wondered she would live in that unwholesome apartment, when there are so many other rooms: she replied, "Mais pas pour moi".'

In 1751 Frederick, the Prince of Wales, died suddenly and unexpectedly, at Carlton House, leaving his eldest son, the thirteen-year-old Prince George, as the heir to the throne.

Five years later began the Seven Years War with France. For the first two years matters went disastrously for the English, both in North America and Europe, where both Frederick of Prussia and the

★ See Chapter 9, p. 104.

Duke of Cumberland were in retreat. When England's fortunes were at their lowest ebb and her government at its most inept, there appeared on the political scene William Pitt. 'I know that I can save the country,' he declared, 'and I know that no other man can.'

He produced a plan for the campaign in North America which, under the leadership of Amherst, Lawrence and Wolfe, and culminating in Wolfe's capture of Quebec, systematically reduced the French to total capitulation.

In 1760, the year after the capture of Quebec, George II, at the age of seventy-six, died of a stroke, in the closet leading from his bedroom at Kensington Palace: and the young Prince George, only twenty-two, became George III of England.

He 'desired to be excused living at Kensington' and Lady Yarmouth retired discreetly to Hanover again, where she died five years later. No English monarch was to live at Kensington Palace for the next sixty years, although many members of the Royal Family were to be given apartments there from time to time.

South of Holland House, between the main road and the little village of Earls Court, there was still nothing but fields and market gardens, but by the 1760s there were two or three houses on the eastern corner, where the present Earls Court Road joins the High Street, and here the first turnpike toll-gate was built.

At Holland House, Henry Fox was making many improvements, but he had by no means so good a reputation as his father. He had begun his Parliamentary career as a Tory, but soon became attached to the Whigs, the party which was in power throughout most of the eighteenth century. The methods he used to amass his wealth were little different from those of his father and were in common practice, even though they were corrupt. But when he became Paymaster-General and increased his private fortune to half a million pounds, by speculation with public money, he nearly ran into serious trouble by not paying the accounts promptly. By 1768 he was accused of being 'a public defaulter of unaccounted millions' and John Wilkes called him 'that person whom every man of honour despises, and every lover of his country is bound to curse'. However, Henry was never directly challenged and though in public life there were some who detested him, in private he was a generous and devoted husband and father.

It was not until 1744, when he was thirty-nine, that Henry married, after falling in love with the beautiful Lady Caroline Lennox, whose father was the Duke of Richmond, a grandson of Charles II by the

Duchess of Portsmouth. The Richmonds would not countenance the match. They were of the blood royal and had very different plans for their daughter. However, Caroline was twenty-one and had a will of her own: and she was quite determined to marry Henry. The story goes that her parents had already planned for her to meet a suitor of their choice, and on the appointed evening told her to dress herself as becomingly as possible. In desperation, she cut off her eyebrows, and presented such an odd appearance that her enraged parents had to postpone the meeting and ordered her to stay in her room. The following morning she had vanished, and the next they heard of her was that she had eloped with Henry Fox and been married at the chapel in the Fleet Prison, which among its other amenities offered facilities for the quick and secret marriage of runaway couples. The Duke and Duchess of Richmond were furiously angry and it was five years before they were to forgive Caroline, but she and Henry were blissfully happy. They lived at Holland House in princely style and prospered. Their three sons to survive infancy were Stephen, the second Lord Holland, who died in his late twenties, Charles James, who was destined for lasting fame, and Henry Edward, who became a general in the army.

Henry Fox was a lavish and generous host and the parties and receptions he gave at Holland House, beginning with the grand house-warming ball in 1747, were important social occasions.

He and Lady Caroline made many improvements to the gardens as well as the house. In 1750 he was writing to Peter Collinson: 'If you will permit me, Lady Caroline has a thousand questions to ask you about flowers and I not much fewer about plants.' And the following year he was enquiring about trees. 'I want to raise a quantity of male spreading Cypress and other Cypresses from seed. Can you procure me any cones? I want likewise some acorns of Scarlet Oak, and a bushel or more of Chestnuts for sowing!'

Lady Caroline had a younger sister, Sarah. As a little girl she had run up to George II in Kensington Gardens and enchanted him with her charm and beauty. Both her parents died a few years after Caroline's marriage and Sarah was sent to her sister, Lady Kildare, in Ireland for a time, returning in 1759, when she was fourteen, to live at Holland House, with Henry Fox and Caroline, who were her guardians.

With Lady Susan Fox-Strangways, a daughter of Henry's eldest brother, Lord Ilchester, she attended the Court at Kensington Palace. Old George II, nearing the end of his life, was interested to see his small friend now grown into a beautiful girl, and the young Prince of Wales, meeting her for the first time, fell hopelessly in love.

Horace Walpole described her as 'a very young lady of the most blooming beauty, and shining with all the grace of unaffected but animated nature', and after seeing her in a performance of *Jane Shore*, which was acted at Holland House, he was even more lyrical. 'She was more beautiful than you can conceive. When Lady Sarah was in white, with her hair about her ears, and on the ground, no Magdalen by Corregio was half as lovely and expressive.'

When the Prince came to the throne, his passion for Lady Sarah was greater than ever, though as yet he had confided in no one except Lady Susan. However, Henry Fox and many others were well aware of what was happening, and the prospect of becoming the brother-in-law of the Queen of England was obviously delightful to him. Walpole wrote that, in the summer of 1761, though Henry Fox 'went himself to bathe in the sea (possibly to disguise his intrigue), he left Lady Sarah at Holland House, where she appeared every morning in a field close to the great road (where the King passed on horseback) in a fancied habit, making hay.'

And while Lady Sarah dallied in the hayfields, waiting to become Queen of England, her nephew Charles James, only five years younger, was already showing the brilliance he was to display in later life. He was not actually born at Holland House, as the mansion was in the hands of the builders at the time, but he spent all his childhood there and always recalled those early years and the devotion of his parents with deep happiness. In 1756 he was sent to the fashionable Huguenot School at Wandsworth and two years later to Eton.

Kensington House, the Duchess of Portsmouth's old home, which later in the century was to become a Jesuit seminary, had become a school by now, run by Dr Johnson's friend Elphinstone, who was caricatured by Smollett in *Roderick Random*. Campden House was also to become a school towards the end of the century – a very select boarding-school for young ladies. Among its distinguished pupils was Maria Fagniani, who afterwards became Lady Hertford. Her unpropitious start in life brought her ample recompense, for both George Selwyn and the Duke of Queensberry believed themselves to be her father and both left her large fortunes. However, the school was far from luxurious and one of its bitterest critics was Arthur Young, for his daughter died there in 1797 and he ascribed her death to the bad school food and the general ill-treatment of the girls, who were cooped up for hours at a time with no opportunity for proper exercise.

During the middle years of the eighteenth century, Kensington was changing only very slowly. Kensington Square was at the height of its fashion during the reign of George II and accommodation was sought so eagerly that at one time there was 'an ambassador, a bishop and a physician occupying apartments in one house'.

Yet Brompton, where the Victorian South Kensington was to be built, was still essentially rural, with its nurseries and cottages, its woods and small Georgian mansions standing in their own large gardens. Along the Gore, between Kensington village and Knights-bridge, Gore House, where the Albert Hall now stands, was little more than a cottage in a large garden, and Kingston House had not yet been built.

The road to Knightsbridge was still lonely and dangerous. In 1740 the *Gentleman's Magazine* reported that 'The Bristol Mail was robbed, a little beyond Knightsbridge by a man on foot, who took the Bath and Bristol bags, and, mounting the post boy's horse, rode off towards London'. Four years later three men were executed for highway robberies in Knightsbridge and a few weeks later a footpad was shot dead. As late as 1780, Knightsbridge was described as 'still a village a little to the east of Kensington, with many public-houses and several new buildings lately erected, but none of them sufficiently remarkable to admit of particular description'. It was 'quite out of London. The stream ran open, the streets were unpaved and un-lighted, and a Maypole was still on the village green'.

VIII

George III and Kensington

PRINCESS AUGUSTA and her friend and adviser, Lord Bute, had no intention of allowing the young George III to marry Lady Sarah Lennox, and as soon as they saw how the wind was blowing the Princess sent her private ambassador to Hanover, to choose a bride for the new King from among the several available Princesses. He selected the seventeen-year-old Charlotte of Mecklenburg-Strelitz, and, wrote Walpole, 'so complete was the King's deference to the will of his mother, that he blindly accepted the bride she had chosen for him; though to the very day of the council, he carried on his courtship of Lady Sarah; so she did not doubt of receiving the crown for him, till she heard the public declaration of it being designed for another.'

Yet she must have had some advance information, for the day before the announcement, which was made on 8 July 1761, she wrote to Lady Susan from Holland House:

'My dearest Susan,

'. . . To begin to astonish you as much as I was I must tell you that the . . . is going to be married to a Princess of Mecklenburg and that I am sure of it.

'. . . I shall take care to shew that I am not mortified to anybody, but if it is true that one can vex anybody with a reserved cold manner, he shall have it I promise him. Now as to what I think about it myself excepting this little revenge I have almost forgiven him, luckily for me I did not love him, and only liked, nor did the title weigh anything with me. So little at least my disappointment did not *affect* my spirits above one hour or two, I believe; I did not cry I assure you which I believe you will, as I know you were more set upon it than I was, the thing I am most angry at is looking so like a fool as I shall for having gone so often for nothing, but I don't much care, if he was to change his mind again (which can't be tho') and not give a *very very* good reason for his conduct I would not have him ...'

So instead of being a Royal bride, Lady Sarah was one of Queen Charlotte's ten bridesmaids, when she was married at St James' Palace on the evening of her arrival in England, but onlookers afterwards declared that throughout the ceremony the King had his eyes on Lady Sarah instead of on his bride.

Within a few months she had married Sir Charles Bunbury, but before long had deserted him for Lord William Gordon and finally married the Honourable George Napier and became the mother of three famous generals.

Henry Fox and Lady Caroline lived on at Holland House, organising the amateur theatricals for which the house was renowned, tending the gardens and adding to their valuable collection of pictures, inherited from Sir Stephen Fox and the Richmond family, by commissioning new family portraits from Sir Joshua Reynolds and buying Hogarths and the work of other contemporary artists.

Henry was given his peerage in 1763 and became Lord Holland of Foxley in Wiltshire and, when he finally bought Holland House five years later, he made it over to his wife. He had bought his elder son, Stephen a seat in Parliament, but both Stephen, who became Lord Ilchester, and Charles were wildly extravagant and ran into appalling debts, which time and again their indulgent father settled for them.

As a boy, Charles was devoted to Lady Susan Fox-Strangways. He was still at Eton when, in 1764, she desolated him and disgraced the family by eloping with William O'Brien, a Drury Lane actor who had been helping with some of the Holland House theatrical productions. She married him at the actors' church, St Paul's, Covent Garden. As a profession, acting was still regarded as barely respectable and London society was aghast. Walpole, in a letter to the Earl of Hertford, said that Lord Ilchester 'was almost distracted – even a footman were preferable. The publicity of the Lord's profession perpetuates the mortification. I could not have believed Lady Susan would have stooped so low.'

Lord Holland sent the couple to America, but Lady Susan never recovered her social status. Charles left Eton, went to Oxford for two years and then on the Grand Tour, and when he returned to England, still only nineteen, he found that, like Stephen, his father had bought him a seat in Parliament.

Charles quickly made his mark and before he was twenty had become a junior Lord of the Admiralty under Lord North. He was brilliant and very popular among his own circle, but he was too rich. Not only did he drink heavily, but, like Stephen, gambled disastrously at Brooks and Almacks. He was a clear, honest thinker and a brilliant speaker, though his youthful arrogance was often to make him the centre of stormy debate. By 1772 he had become a junior Lord of the Treasury, but his gambling debts rose as quickly as the success of his parliamentary career, until they reached the enormous sum of £100,000, and in 1774 he was dismissed office 'for great flippancy in the House towards Lord North', as Walpole put it, the dismissal having been demanded by George III, who disliked him and his radical views intensely. That year Stephen had a son, which meant that Charles was removed one degree further from the inheritance of his father's wealth. His credit immediately dropped but his worried and long-suffering father yet again settled his debts, though later that year he died, a sad and broken man, and Lady Caroline survived him by only three weeks. To add to the family tragedies, Stephen, Lord Ilchester, died a month or two later, at the age of twenty-nine, leaving his infant son, Henry Richard, not yet twelve months old, as the third Lord Holland.

Charles' fortunes had sunk very low but he was by no means penniless, for his father had left him an adequate income, and perhaps from the shock of such a multitude of bereavements, he now matured. As Walpole said, 'the vices of his youth were affected, and his solidity natural'.

His good qualities – his humanity, kindliness and incorruptible integrity – now prevailed over the profligate tendencies which had broken his father's heart and Charles James Fox became a champion of the people. 'The true freedom of the people is to be found only in a free and independent Parliament,' he declared. He never became Prime Minister but was twice Foreign Secretary, devoting himself to trying to achieve an extension of the franchise, which culminated in the Reform Bill, the emancipation of the slaves and the removal of the social and political restrictions on Roman Catholics. These reforms did not come about during his lifetime, for he died in 1806, the same year as his great opponent William Pitt the Younger, but he has always been remembered as a vital force in creating the movements which made them ultimately inevitable.

All through these years he had been devoted to his nephew and instilled in him the Whig principles which were to make the influence of the Holland House circle so important during the early years of the nineteenth century.

After the death of Stephen, Lady Holland did not live at Holland House but took the infant Henry and his older sister Caroline to live with her brother at Ampthill Park in Bedfordshire. Two years later she died and the children were brought up by their mother's relations, Henry being sent to Eton and Oxford.

Holland House was let, first to Lord Rosebery and then to a Mr Bearcroft: and in 1794 Charles James was writing to Henry, by then a young man of twenty: 'Poor Holland House is said to be in a bad way; I have not seen it, but I find there is a terrible outcry against its weakness, so that I fear it cannot stand.'

George III did not use Kensington Palace after his accession, choosing first St James' Palace and then Buckingham House for his London residence. The State apartments at Kensington Palace were closed and most of the pictures moved to St James'.

The Dowager Duchess of Newcastle was given apartments there and so was Lord Hertford, the Lord Chamberlain, and until 1764 Horace Walpole's sister lived there as housekeeper. Then she was promoted to Windsor and her successor was Miss Rachel Lloyd, who amused herself by giving card parties, her guests including Lady Holland and Lady Mary Coke, a lady-in-waiting of Princess Amelia, one of the King's aunts. When the Princess and Lady Mary visited the palace in 1768, Lady Mary remarked: 'There is not much left; the bed Queen Anne died in is taken away and likewise Queen Mary's. One could scarcely imagine it would have been worth his Majesty's while to have removed beds that have been there so long. . . . It is all so changed that there is hardly any knowing it again.'

However, under the care of Sir John Hill, the gardens were maintained and the Broad Walk was as fashionable as it had ever been. In 1773 members of the Macaroni club ran races there every Sunday evening 'to the high amusement and contempt of the mob, and yet the mob will be ambitious of being fashionable and will run races too'.

The Macaronis were extremely rich and fashionable young men, affecting their own distinctive manner of dress, with skin-tight trousers and very small tricorns, which they perched low on their

foreheads. They founded their club, which was mainly given over
to gambling, after doing the Grand Tour and discovering the delights of Italian macaroni, which was always included in the club
menu.

Towards the end of the century, Kensington Gardens was becoming too popular for some tastes, for in 1793 Sir Gilbert Eliot wrote to
his wife: 'All I know of the country is Kensington Gardens, where I
walked on Sunday with La Porte, one of my French schoolfellows.
It is really extremely pretty; but its rusticity was in some degree
diminished by the resemblance of the entrance and the battle to get
in to the pit door when Garrick acted. It is literally hardly safe for a
woman.'

A few years later a snob was writing of:

> 'The vulgar folks, who run
> To thy fair gardens, Kensington;
> . . .
> To be immortal – if they could.'

And by that time the fashionable promenade had moved east again,
to Hyde Park Corner.

However, throughout the eighteenth century Kensington became
increasingly fashionable as a place of residence for the aristocracy and
the wealthy, even after the Court had left the palace, supplanting the
seventeenth-century popularity of Covent Garden, Bloomsbury,
Lincoln's Inn Fields and the Strand.

Elizabeth Chudleigh was one of Kensington's most notorious
residents during the 1770s. She was well-born, the daughter of
Colonel Chudleigh, the Governor of Chelsea Hospital, but in 1726,
when she was only six years old, he died. She and her mother were
left with very little money and retired to the country, but Elizabeth
grew into a beauty and by the time she was twenty she was befriended by the future Earl of Bath, who secured her appointment as
a maid-of-honour to Augusta, Princess of Wales. The young Duke
of Hamilton fell in love with her just before departing for the Grand
Tour, but his correspondence either went astray or was intercepted,
and when he returned to England he married someone else. A few
weeks later Elizabeth went to stay with an aunt in Hampshire, and at
the Winchester races met the Honourable Augustus Hervey, the
younger son of John, Lord Hervey, and a grandson of the Earl of
Bristol, who was serving in the navy. Still smarting from the Duke
of Hamilton's behaviour, Elizabeth agreed to marry Augustus, but

as he had little money and she did not wish to give up her position at the Princess of Wales' Court, she insisted that it must be a secret wedding. On 4 April 1744, the marriage took place late at night, in the greatest secrecy, at the Lainston Chapel, near Winchester, but was not entered in the Chapel register. A few days later Augustus set sail for the West Indies and Elizabeth, still calling herself Miss Chudleigh, returned to the Court at Leicester House, spending her off-duty time with her mother in Conduit Street.

Her husband returned to England in 1746 and the following year Elizabeth had a baby, still in the greatest secrecy, in lodgings at Chelsea. The baby died and Elizabeth and Augustus began to quarrel. When he returned to sea they parted for good and Elizabeth, still keeping her marriage a secret, went back to Court, where she enjoyed herself enormously, drank deeply and was generally regarded as being 'free in her ways'.

George II took a fancy to her for a time, gave her a gold watch and made her mother a housekeeper at Windsor. By 1759 Elizabeth heard that the Earl of Bristol was dying. This meant that her brother-in-law would be the new Earl and a potentially valuable connection, so she took steps to ensure that her marriage could be in no doubt. She went down to Winchester, visited the vicar who had performed the ceremony, though by this time he was on his deathbed, and insisted that the details of the wedding be inserted properly in the Chapel register.

She soon found that she had acted too hastily for on her return to London she met the Duke of Kingston who fell in love with her and wanted to marry. She prevaricated but became his mistress and continued to enjoy life, giving riotous and notorious parties and travelling a good deal on the Continent. She bought herself a plot of land in the fields of Kensington Gore, fronting the Kensington Road, and proceeded to build for herself a handsome villa set in a large garden.

One of her visitors was Count Frederick Kielmansegge who in his *Diary of a Journey to England* (1761–2) had this to say: 'On the morning of the 15th March (1762) we were invited by Miss Chudleigh to a concert; she does not live really in town, but opposite Hyde Park in a row of houses called Knightsbridge. Her house can justly be called a gem; it contains a quantity of handsome and costly furniture and other curiosities and objects of value, chosen and arranged with the greatest taste, so that you cannot fail to admire it greatly. There is hardly a place in the whole house left bare or without decoration, like a doll's house. Everything is in perfect harmony. The view in front over Hyde Park, and at the back over Chelsea, is considered with truth one of the finest that could be pictured.

'At noon, a rather good concert began. Miss Brandt, who generally sings, and an Italian called Tenducci, were the performers. The Prince of Mecklenburg and a large and select company were present. About half-past two, when the concert was over, we were invited to lunch in the dining-room downstairs, where music was going on with two good French horns; a so-called "ambigue" was served at a very long table, on which was everything which could be brought together – cakes, sandwiches, cold and smoked meat, ham, jelly, fruit, etc. Small side-tables were arranged for coffee, tea, chocolate, etc., so that I must say it was the most perfect feast of its kind.'

The Count went on to say that everyone knew that Miss Chudleigh had a husband from whom she was separated and that she had never announced the marriage as she wanted to keep her position as Maid of Honour to the Princess of Wales. 'That she has been kept during all this time by the Duke of Kingston, from whom she received all her riches, house, and garden, is just as well known.'

In 1765 Frederick II, writing to the Electress Dowager of Saxony, commented: 'Nothing particular happened save the appearance of an English lady, Madam Chudleigh, who emptied two bottles of wine and staggered as she danced and nearly fell to the floor.'

Soon Augustus arrived on the scene. He wanted to marry again and said he was suing her for divorce. Elizabeth, not fancying the scandal of a divorce, now refused to admit she was ever married. She took legal action and Augustus and his advisers put up such a poor defence that in 1769 she was declared a spinster, married the Duke and they established themselves respectably in her new mansion which they called Kingston House. Here they lived in ducal splendour, giving the most magnificent parties, but four years later the frustrated Augustus petitioned the King for a new trial. The law moved slowly and before Elizabeth was indicted the Duke of Kingston had died and she was abroad, visiting Italy. When she heard what was afoot she decided to return at once to Kingston House. Being short of ready cash for the journey, she arrived at the office of the English banker in Rome with a loaded pistol, so he did not hesitate to supply her with the necessary funds.

By the time the trial began, in April 1776, Augustus had succeeded to the family title of the Earl of Bristol and had arrayed a formidable army of witnesses, including the widow of the vicar who had married them, the surgeon who had delivered the baby and the inevitable maidservant.

Elizabeth, tried by her peers, was found guilty of bigamy and perjury. She could have suffered the corporal punishment of being burnt on the hand, but claimed the privilege of her peerage and, although the Attorney-General expressed his unwillingness, the peers allowed it. In an open boat, she managed to escape from England before worse befell her, deprived of her title but still owning a vast amount of money. Augustus was now free to divorce her but died before proceedings could be brought. Elizabeth never saw Kingston House again, but still calling herself the 'Duchess of Kingston' she landed in Russia, where she was received by the Empress Catharine and bought herself an estate near St Petersburg, which she called Chudleigh. Here she set up an establishment for the making of brandy, but she was a restless soul and even this assurance of a regular supply of hard liquor could not keep her long in Russia. She departed for Paris and then went to Rome for a spell, where she is said to have 'lived scandalously'. She moved again to Paris and here she died, in 1788, at the age of sixty-eight, making a last salute to the Establishment by leaving a legacy to the Pope in her will.

Kingston House remained empty for many years until it was bought, early in the nineteenth century, by Viscount Ennismore, afterwards the Earl of Listowel, and later it became the home of the Marquis of Wellesley, the elder brother of the Duke of Wellington.

IX

The Chelsea Bun House, Ranelagh and the Physic Garden

DURING the early years of the seventeenth century there were three theatres in Southwark, and a warm friendship was established between the theatre folk and the watermen who rowed their customers over to the south bank. During the Commonwealth, these theatres were closed and the watermen lost valuable business. With the Restoration and the establishment of the Theatre Royal, Drury Lane, the old warmth of feeling between the theatre and the watermen revived. In the early years of the eighteenth century the resident comedian at Drury Lane was the Irishman, Thomas Doggett. 'As an actor he was a great observer of Nature; and as a singer he had no competitor,' wrote Colley Cibber. Doggett ultimately formed a joint actor-managership with Cibber and Robert Wilks. He was a staunch Whig and, with the accession of the Hanoverians, he inaugurated the Thames watermen's race from London Bridge to Chelsea, leaving in his will enough money for the race to be run annually.

'In 1715, the year after George I came to the throne, Doggett, to quicken the industry and raise a laudable emulation in our young men of the Thames, whereby they not only may acquire a knowledge of the river but a skill in managing the oar with dexterity, gave an orange-coloured coat and silver badge, on which was sculptured the Hanoverian Horse, to the successful candidate of six young watermen just out of their apprentice, to be rowed for on the 1st

August, when the current was strongest against them, starting from the Old Swan at London Bridge to the Swan at Chelsea.'*

The race was first run in 1722, the year after Doggett's death, 1st August being the anniversary of George I's accession. The coat for the prizewinner contained a golden guinea in each pocket and the Fishmongers' Company, of which Doggett was a member, contributed prizes for the runners up, their barge-master being the umpire. In 1780 the Swan at Chelsea was turned into a brewery and the goal became the new Swan, on the other side of the Physic Garden. The race was a great excitement and amusement for Chelsea and the winner was always carried into the tavern for a celebration. It was run until well into the nineteenth century, when bridges, roads and railways made the watermens' trade obsolete, but has recently been revived.

Another Chelsea diversion was the old Bun House, which was established late in the seventeenth century and possessed a museum designed to rival that of Don Saltero's. The Bun House was at the western end of Jew's Row – which is now the Pimlico Road – and close to the gardens of Ranelagh House. It was a long, one-storey building, with a colonnade over the pavement, in the shelter of which customers could buy their buns at the windows, and inside was a large room in which the curiosities were exhibited.

Chelsea buns – rare Chelsea buns; smoking hot, piping hot Chelsea buns – were famous all through the eighteenth century, and the genuine article was made with eggs, butter, sugar, lemon and spice. Swift tried one, but thought nothing of it. 'I bought one today in my walk; it cost me a penny; it was stale,' he complained to Stella, 'and I did not like it.' Nevertheless, the Chelsea Bun House was extremely fashionable for many years, the most successful proprietor being Mrs Hands, whose family was connected with poor Mary Gwynn, Nell's mother, who fell into the river. Miss Manning described the arrival there one day of one of the ladies of high fashion, Lady Betty Spadille, 'in the yellow autumn of life, with no resources but "Green Tea and Brag". How well I remember her arriving at our bun-house in her peach-coloured sacque, Mechlin head, and red-heeled shoes, the foreparts richly embroidered with silver; loudly talking and laughing, and turning her head right and left, now to this beau now to t'other, who fluttered round her with their clouded canes and perfumed wigs . . .'

George II and Queen Caroline often paid visits to the Bun House with the princesses, and George III and Queen Charlotte were also

* J. T. Smith, *A Book For a Rainy Day.*

customers. When Queen Charlotte presented Mrs Hands with a half-gallon silver mug containing five guineas, the poor lady was quite overwhelmed and Queen Charlotte's gift became one of the most treasured exhibits of the museum.

On Good Friday mornings the Bun House also made hot-cross buns, but they were so popular that they almost caused a riot. Hundreds of people would arrive, clamouring for buns, and at last, in 1793, Mrs Hands had to put up a notice, stating that 'in consequence of the great concourse of people which assembled before her house at a very early hour, on the morning of Good Friday last, by which her neighbours (with whom she had always lived in friendship and repute) have been much alarmed and annoyed; it having been also intimated, that to encourage or countenance a tumultuous assembly at this particular period might be attended with consequences more serious than have hitherto been apprehended; desirous, therefore, of testifying her regard and obedience to those laws by which she is happily protected, she is determined, though much to her loss, not to sell CROSS BUNS on that day to any person whatever, but Chelsea buns as usual.'

It is odd that the English dread of Jacobinism should have stopped the sale of so innocent a commodity as a hot-cross bun.

When the bankrupt Lord Ranelagh died in 1712, his daughter, Lady Jones, friend of Mary Astell, was allowed to live on in Ranelagh House and was even granted a small pension. Here on one memorable occasion in 1715, she was visited by George I, during a great water pageant, and as the royal flotillas came up the river people heard for the first time, drifting across the water, Handel's beautiful *Water Music*, which he had composed especially for the occasion and which he conducted from one of the barges, as it was performed by an orchestra of fifty players.

It was not until 1733 that Ranelagh House and its gardens were put up for auction. Pleasure gardens and tea gardens had long been popular and in Stuart times Vauxhall Gardens had been fashionable. Now Lacy, a joint patentee of Drury Lane with David Garrick, bought Ranelagh House and part of the gardens, with a view to creating an even more elegant pleasure garden. The first venture failed, but a few years later a new company was formed, and the Royal Hospital authorities who, all along, had opposed the scheme, were aghast as they saw the great rotunda or 'Musick Theater' being built close to Ranelagh House, with which it was later connected by a corridor. The rotunda was nearly as big as the Albert Hall was to be in the next century, and an affront to Wren's beautiful hospital. However, plans proceeded and the rotunda and pleasure gardens were opened in 1742, with a public breakfast and a blaze of publicity.

Most of the first visitors were enthusiastic, marvelling at the great building with its tiers of boxes, its large floor for dancing and concerts, its magnificent chandeliers, as well as the temple of Pan and the Venetian temple, built across the canal, all of which had been added to the gardens. Others, however, were doubtful, particularly in the first weeks. 'The pomp and splendour of a Roman amphitheatre are devoted to no better use than a twelvepenny entertainment of cold ham and chicken,' snarled one visitor.

A Frenchman, writing in the *Gentleman's Magazine* in 1742, said that, dumb with surprise and astonishment, he found himself 'in the middle of a vast amphitheatre, for structure Roman, for decorations of paint and gilding as gay as the Asiatic; four grand portals in the manner of the ancient triumphal arches, and four times twelve boxes in a double row, with suitable pilasters between, for the whole interior of this wonderful fabric – save that in the middle a magnificent orchestra rises to the roof, from which depend several large branches, which contain a great number of candles enclosed in crystal glasses, at once to light and adorn this spacious rotunda. Groups of well-dressed persons were disposed in the boxes, numbers covered the area, all manner of refreshments were within call, and music of all kinds echoed, though not intelligibly, from every one of these elegant retreats.'

But he quickly became satiated with so much glitter and noise. 'In five minutes I was familiar with the whole and every part; in the five next indifference took place; in five more my eyes grew dazzled, my head became giddy, and all night I dreamed of Vanity Fair.'

Horace Walpole was by no means impressed at his first visit. 'I was there last night,' he said, 'but did not find the joy of it. Vauxhall a little better for the garden is pleasanter and one goes by water.' But two years later he had changed his opinion. 'Every night constantly I go to Ranelagh, which has totally beat Vauxhall,' he wrote. 'Nobody goes anywhere else – everyone goes there. My Lord Chesterfield is so fond of it that he says he has ordered all his letters to be directed there.' And by 1748, he was writing: 'Ranelagh is so crowded that in going there t'other night in a string of coaches, we had a stop of six and thirty minutes.'

At first morning concerts were given in the rotunda, but when employers complained that young men and apprentices were being lured from their businesses, the hour of opening was changed to the early evening, the management providing a succession of programmes of dancing, masqued balls, firework displays, puppet shows and concerts, at some of which Handel's oratorios were performed, while food and drink were served in the privacy of the boxes.

One of the most memorable occasions was the Grand Masqued Ball in 1749, held to celebrate the Peace of Aix-la-Chapelle, when George II attended and there were said to be two thousand visitors. 'It was by far the best understood and prettiest spectacle I ever saw – nothing in a fairy tale ever surpassed it,' wrote Horace Walpole, and went on to describe the marquees in the garden, the maypole, round which masqued peasants danced to the music of a pipe and tabor, the huntsmen with their horns, the harlequins and scaramouches in the little temple on the mount, the gondola on the canal, the orchestras hidden away in secluded corners of the garden, the little shops outside the rotunda, selling Dresden and Japanese china, the booths for tea and wine, the gaming tables and the dancing, the orange trees, 'with small lamps in each orange'.

The ball was so successful that another masquerade was held a few weeks later. The King again attended and also the Duke of Cumberland, dressed in an 'Old English habit, but so enormously corpulent that he looked like Cacofoco, the drunken captain in *Rule a Wife and Have a Wife.*' All the ladies of the Court were there 'in vast beauty, Miss Pitt with a red veil which made her look gloriously handsome. . . . Miss Chudleigh was "Iphigenia" and so lightly clad that you would have taken her for Andromeda. The maids of honour were so offended that they would not speak to her.'

Even Dr Johnson enjoyed Ranelagh, believing it, somewhat mistakenly, to be a place of 'innocent recreation', and poor Oliver Goldsmith, even when his fortunes were at their lowest ebb, liked to go there with Dr Johnson and Sir Joshua Reynolds, and when he could afford it would treat his Irish cousin to a visit.

Handel's *Messiah* and Dibdin's *Ephesian Matron* were heard there and Mozart, at the age of eight, performed on the harpsichord and organ.

Throughout the middle years of the eighteenth century, Ranelagh remained fashionable and saw many glittering occasions, none more so than Lord North's regatta in the summer of 1776, when the whole river, 'from London Bridge to the Ship Tavern, Millbank, was covered with pleasure vessels' and on both sides of the river 'bad liquor with short measure was plentifully retailed'. A procession of barges bearing the Dukes of Gloucester and Cumberland, Richmond and Montagu, the Lord Mayor and a hundred or more elegant ladies, to the accompaniment of cannon, drums, fifes, horns and trumpets moved 'in picturesque irregularity' to Ranelagh.

'In a word, from the mixed multitude of lords and liverymen, pinks and pickpockets, dukes and dustmen, drabs and duchesses, the whole scene afforded an admirable picture of High Life below Stairs and Low Life Above.'

When they landed at Ranelagh, there were great junketings, although the supper, which cost seven hundred guineas, was contracted and said to have been bad and poorly supplied with wine.

By the 1780s, although the gardens were opened on Mondays, Wednesdays and Fridays, and there were special celebrations for anniversaries such as Royal births and marriages, as well as grand subscription parties, Ranelagh's glory was fading. There were several famous parties held there after this time, including a ball given by the Knights of the Bath and an entertainment by the Spanish ambassador, when the King and Queen ate from gold plate and the boxes of the rotunda became a 'Spanish camp', each tent guarded by a boy in Spanish uniform. The gallery was a temple of Flora and 'a hundred valets in scarlet and gold, and as many footmen, in sky-blue and silver, waited on the company'.

Nevertheless the general attendance on ordinary occasions began to fall. The 'top ten thousand' were no longer amused. The proprietors had to make economies. The standard of entertainment and catering fell, and with it the moral tone, which had never been particularly high.

Respectable ladies might walk in the gardens during the day time, when admission was only a shilling, but few were seen there in the evenings, unless it were a special gala, graced by some celebrity such as the beautiful Duchess of Devonshire, when the tickets would cost anything from one to two guineas.

Ordinary evening tickets were only half a crown or five shillings, including a supper of 'beef, ham, savoy cake, orange, veal, pastry, jelly and blancmange' with wine extra, and the company often stayed all night, until long after dawn. But Ranelagh had become tedious, and of the endless promenade round the rotunda, Bloomfield wrote:

> 'Fair maids, who at home, in their haste,
> Had left all their clothes but a train,

> Swept the floor clean, as slowly they passed,
> Then – walked round and swept it again.'

And for the ladies of the town who came to Ranelagh with a prospective eye, a popular song reminded them that 'bright eyes were intended to languish, not stare'.

> 'But if Amazon-like you attack your gallants
> And put us in fear of our lives,
> You may do very well for sisters and aunts,
> But believe me, you'll ne'er becomes wives.'

The journey to Ranelagh from London was no mean hazard after dark and visitors were in real danger from attack by footpads. The Ranelagh advertisements invariably included a note that 'there will be a proper patrol, well-armed, continually passing between the Rooms and Hyde Park Corner, and good guard at the back of Chelsea College'. Pensioners at the hospital, which was called the college still, long after it had ceased to be one, were often recruited for this duty, being paid by the Ranelagh proprietors.

In 1793 a costumier in Wilderness Row, close to Ranelagh, advertising fancy dress for hire, assured his customers that they would be conducted safely to the gardens.

By the end of the century, Ranelagh was too run down ever to recover. One of its last entertainments was a balloon ascent, the balloon landing an hour later at Colchester, but even this spectacle was not enough to save the gardens. Ballooning was no longer new, in any case, for as early as 1786 Blanchard and Jeffries had made the Channel crossing in three hours. In 1805 Ranelagh was closed. The rotunda and Lord Ranelagh's beautiful house were pulled down and the gardens dismantled.

The Bun House had flourished all through the prosperous days of Ranelagh, being maintained by four generations of the Hands family. Then it was sold and was never the same. The closing of Ranelagh hastened its end. A rival establishment opened near by, but Chelsea buns became as outmoded as Ranelagh. Early in the 1850s the old Bun House was closed and demolished and the contents of the museum were sold.

After studying botany at Chelsea and anatomy and medicine in London, Paris and Montpelier, where he began to make his plant collection, Hans Sloane had been elected a Fellow of the Royal Society in

1685, at the age of twenty-five, and two years later became a Fellow
of the Royal College of Physicians. He then went to Jamaica, as
physician to the governor, the Duke of Albemarle, where he began
a study of tropical plants, but very soon after his arrival the Duke
died, and Sloane felt obliged to accompany the bereaved Duchess
back to England. Fifteen months later, therefore, they were making
the return journey, Sloane bringing with him many specimens of
tropical plants which he presented to the Physic Garden. He also
tried to bring back some fauna, but the alligator died, the iguana,
frightened by a sailor, jumped overboard, and the yellow snake,
seven feet long, caused so much havoc and alarm when it escaped
from its water-jar that the Duchess' footman shot it.

In London, Sloane set up a very successful practice as a physician.
In 1693 he was made Secretary of the Royal Society and edited their
Philosophical Transactions, as well as publishing his *Natural History
of Jamaica*, which brought him much acclaim from his fellow scientists. He was appointed physician to Christ's Hospital and in 1708
was made a member of the Royal Academy in Paris.

In London his skill as a physician became famous and Queen Anne,
who had long forgiven old Dr Radcliffe for reporting in her younger
days that 'she had only the vapours and is as well as any woman
breathing, if she could only be persuaded to believe it', often consulted Dr Sloane during her last illness.

Sloane was a great advocate of 'peruvian bark' – the bark of the
cinchona tree, from which quinine and other drugs are obtained –
and he spent large sums of money importing it to England, for the
benefit of his patients.

In 1716 George I created him a baronet, the first English physician
to receive an hereditary title, and he was appointed Physician-
General to the army. By 1719 he was elected President of the College
of Physicians, and in 1727, on the death of Sir Isaac Newton, he was
made President of the Royal Society, and George II appointed him
Physician in Ordinary.

This steady success, as well as a very rich wife, brought Sir Hans
great wealth, much of which he spent on research and in adding to
his wonderful natural history and antiquities collection.

He had bought Chelsea manor from the Cheyne family in 1712,
but he continued to live on at his house in Bloomsbury for many
more years. Yet he never lost his love for the little Physic Garden,
where he had studied in his youth, and when the Cheyne lease expired in 1722 he granted the freehold of the garden to the Society of

Apothecaries, on condition that it 'should at all times be continued as a Physic Garden, for the manifestation of the power and wonder and goodness of God's creation; and that the apprentices might learn to distinguish good and useful plants from hurtful ones'.

The Society was to pay a ground rent of £5 a year and deliver each year to the Royal Society specimens of fifty new plants, till their number should amount to two thousand.

The Society of Apothecaries had found great difficulty in maintaining the gardens up till this time, through lack of money. In 1674 the garden had been walled, the north wall facing on to Paradise Row, and the four magnificent cedars which had been planted about this time still flourished, but the gardens had fallen into neglect.

With Sir Hans Sloane's gift they were now revived. At his suggestion, Philip Miller, one of the most gifted of gardeners, was appointed as a salaried director, and he worked at Chelsea from 1722 until his death in 1771. He devoted himself to the introduction and acclimatization of exotic and rare plants, arranging for them to be sent to the garden from all parts of the world, and here he wrote his magnificent *Dictionary of Gardening*.

In 1732 Sir Hans laid the foundation stone of a new greenhouse along the north wall of the garden, with a library and gardener's quarters. The garden was laid out in broad divisions and the plants, trees and shrubs grown in orderly rows, according to their botanical classifications, so that they could be easily identified and studied. The river-front was wharfed, and from the little boathouse, the four-man boat rowed specimens down river for study and inspection at the Apothecaries' hall.

In 1734 Mrs Elizabeth Blackwell arrived at the garden. She was the wife of Dr Alexander Blackwell, a physician turned printer, who had become hopelessly in debt and been sent to prison. Elizabeth obtained permission from the Apothecaries to compile her *Curious Herbal*. She took a house in Swan Walk and settled down to draw five hundred of the most medicinally valuable plants growing in the garden. Many of her drawings were engraved on copperplate and she then coloured them by hand. She worked so hard that by 1739, with Philip Miller's help, the herbal was finished and published. It made a lot of money and she was able to pay Alexander's debts and obtain his release from prison. For a few years he lived with her contentedly in Swan Walk, but then he went to Sweden. The end of his story is a mystery. He was appointed physician to the King and became involved in conspiracy in high places.

In 1747 the *Gentleman's Magazine* reported: 'Sweden, July 29, was beheaded at Stockholm Dr Blackwell the Physician. He confessed some secrets to Dr Folstadius, a Protestant clergyman, which the torture could not extort. It is said he prayed with great devotion; but that having laid his head wrong, he remarked jocosely that, being his first experiment, no wonder that he should want a little instruction.'

Poor Elizabeth stayed on in Chelsea and died eleven years later, being buried in the old churchyard in 1758.

In 1736 the great Linnaeus visited the garden and recorded that 'Miller of Chelsea permitted me to collect many plants in the Garden, and gave me several dried specimens collected in South America.'

The following year the Apothecaries erected a marble statue of Sir Hans by Rysbrack. It first stood in the new building but a few years later he was moved into the centre of the garden, where he stands to this day, in his doctor's robes.

In 1741 Hans Sloane began removing his museum from Bloomsbury to the palace at Chelsea. He was an old man now, a widower and an invalid, but he took great joy in his collections. Many of the ground-floor rooms of the old palace were filled with antiquities from Egypt, Greece, Etruria and Rome, others with geological specimens and coins. The long gallery upstairs was filled with cases of natural history specimens and from it opened his magnificent library.

He died in 1753 and was buried in the old churchyard. The heiresses to his fortune were his two daughters, Mrs Stanley and Lady Cadogan, with a reversion to the Cadogan family. He bequeathed the manor-house and his collection to a body of trustees, asking them to offer them to the country for £20,000, a sum which was considerably less than a quarter of their real value. He obviously hoped that the manor-house would be a permanent home for his museum, but after much discussion, Parliament, having agreed to the purchase, decided that it would be better to house it, along with the Harleian Collection and the Cottonian Library, both of which they had recently acquired, in the Duke of Montagu's mansion in Bloomsbury which was available and which they bought for the purpose, thereby establishing the British Museum.

Sloane did not make any further gifts to the Physic Garden in his will, but the Apothecaries were now able to maintain it. On Miller's death, William Forsyth (after whom forsythia was named) was appointed gardener and in 1733 William Curtis, who founded the

Botanical Magazine, became demonstrator of plants, giving lectures to students in the garden. This was the year that two of the famous cedars of Lebanon had to be felled, though the other two were to survive for another century or more.

Curtis also built the rock garden, incorporating into it some porous lava brought from Iceland by Sir Joseph Banks. Sir Joseph did a great deal of work for the garden, presenting seeds and dozens of plants he had collected on his travels, and while he was studying there he lived with his mother in Swan Walk, perhaps in the same house where Elizabeth Blackwell had laboured at her *Curious Herbal*.

X

Men of Letters in Eighteenth-Century Chelsea

DEFOE called Chelsea a 'town of palaces', but one by one throughout the eighteenth century the palaces and mansions disappeared, although other great houses were built, as well as many smaller ones, and Chelsea remained, for many years to come, fashionable, gay and elegant.

In 1717 there were about 350 houses in Chelsea and sixty years later there were twice that number, as well as many more cottages.

On the site of Danvers House a small silk factory was established and a mulberry garden planted. It never attained the success of Spitalfields, but in 1723 Thoresby recorded that he had seen 'at Mr Gates' a sample of the satin made at Chelsea of English silk for the Princess of Wales, very rich and beautiful'. Two years later a small tapestry works was set up by Le Blom, but it did not last for long.

John Gay had been the Duchess of Monmouth's secretary, until they quarrelled, and it was in 1726 that Gay offered *The Beggar's Opera* to John Rich, who made a fortune from it at his theatre in Lincoln's Inn.

In 1723 the beautiful Argyll House, which still stands in the King's Road, was built by the Venetian architect, Giacomo Leoni. It was originally intended for John Perris, but from 1769 to 1770 John, the fourth Duke of Argyll, spent his last years here. It is now number 211 King's Road, and the three houses next to it, up to the corner of Glebe Place, were built about the same time, delightful examples of early eighteenth-century domestic architecture, standing to this day, full of memories and a little mysterious behind their iron railings. In number 215 lived Dr Arne, who at one time was the tutor of Dr Burney, and a 150 years later it was to be the home of Ellen Terry.

Gough House, just west of the Royal Hospital, was built about 1707 by the third Earl of Carberry, who had made his fortune from the slave trade, while Governor of Jamaica. Anthony Ashley Cooper, the third Earl of Shaftesbury, fell in love with Carberry's daughter, but Carberry would not countenance the match, considering both the fortune and manner of living of the suitor too modest. So the Earl of Shaftesbury married a girl from a less pretentious family and became 'as happy a man as ever', while the Earl's poor daughter was married to the Marquis of Winchester, who forsook her at the church door and later married Polly Peachum. The Earl of Carberry died that same year – 1713 – and Gough House was bought by the Gough family, who lived there throughout the eighteenth century, after which time the house became for a time a boarding-school for girls and was later incorporated into the Victoria Hospital for Children.

Not much is known of the fate of Boyle's house in Little Chelsea. At Shaftesbury House near by, Lord Shaftesbury's friend Locke is said to have written some of his essays in a summer-house built in the garden under the shade of a giant yew tree. The Earl died in 1719 and later eighteenth-century residents of Shaftesbury House included Narcissus Luttrell, the annalist, diarist and bibliographer, who claimed to have cultivated twenty-five different kinds of pear trees in the beautiful garden, and Serjeant Wynne, the author of *Eunomus*. Long after the house had been converted into a Victorian workhouse the yew tree survived.

It was in 1711 that Dean Swift wrote to Stella: 'I design in two days if possible to go to lodge at Chelsea for the air, and put myself under the necessity of walking to and from London every day.' He took lodgings in Church Lane – now Church Street – and a few days later was reporting: 'I got here in the stage coach with Patrick and my portmanteau for sixpence and pay six shillings a week for one silly room with confounded coarse sheets.' The lodging was next to Dr Atterbury's house, and yet 'I shall not like the place better for that,' he added sourly. Nevertheless, they became close friends. The Doctor and Mrs Atterbury showed Swift many kindnesses and he often dined with them during the next two or three years.

But by the 1730s Addison and Steele, Dr Atterbury and Gay were all dead, and by 1740 the caustic, brilliant, disappointed Swift had become senile, seen at the last gazing into a mirror and murmuring piteously to himself 'Poor old man! Poor old man!'

At Lindsey House, adjoining Beaufort House, where the Earl of Lindsey had lived until the beginning of the century, there arrived in 1751 Count Zinzendorf, the head of the Moravians, who planned to found a Moravian community in Chelsea. He bought Lindsey House and a plot of land from the Beaufort House grounds for a burial-ground. He also rented a piece of land on which he intended to house a community of some three hundred families, who were to earn their living in some unspecified factory work and exist in a state of idyllic beatitude. The beautiful Lindsey House was intended mainly as a 'pilgrim house' for visiting Moravian missionaries from Europe and America. The Utopian community, which he called Sharon, did not succeed, but the Count lived on in Lindsey House until 1770. Five years later Lindsey House was converted into five large dwellings which still remain as numbers 96 to 100 Cheyne Walk.

In 1753 Tobias Smollett came to live in part of the divided Monmouth House, hoping that the clean, country air of Chelsea would improve the health of his little daughter, who was an only child. This was the year that old Hans Sloane died. He had already been responsible for the demolition of Sir Thomas More's house. Now his own home, the old Royal Tudor palace, was pulled down and the houses which are now numbers 19 to 26 Cheyne Walk were built.

Smollett was thirty-two when he came to Chelsea. He had been practising in London as a doctor, the profession for which he was trained. He had barely made a living as a doctor, but had already published, with considerable success, his first two novels *Roderick Random* and *Peregrine Pickles*. At Chelsea, he devoted himself to writing, becoming by turns, as Thackeray said: 'reviewer and historian, critic, medical writer, poet and pamphleteer'. His earlier literary success was by no means maintained, and he had a hard struggle to survive, enduring the drudgery of hours of hack work in order to make ends meet.

He was often accused of being quarrelsome and cantankerous, but he was beset by disappointments and financial worries, as well as grief for his dying daughter, and underneath the irritability was a kind and generous heart. He was often to be seen at the Swan and Don Saltero's, and was entranced by Ranelagh, which he said, looked 'like the enchanted palace of genii adorned with the most exquisite performances of painting, carving and gilding'.

During the ten years he lived at Monmouth House he was visited by most of the literary lions of the day, Dr Johnson, Goldsmith and Sterne, as well as Garrick, Wilkes and John Hunter, and every Sunday he kept open house to 'unfortunate brothers of the quill', whom he treated to 'beef, pudding and potatoes, port, punch, and Calvert's entire butt-beer'.

In 1756 he became editor of the *Critical Review*, which involved him in much controversy, and a few years later Admiral Knowles charged him with libel. He was fined £100 and imprisoned for three months, and it was shortly after this that his cherished daughter, at the age of fifteen, died of tuberculosis. Grief-stricken, he left Chelsea and did not return. For the next two years he travelled in France and Italy, but he did not forget Chelsea and some of the happy times he had spent there. 'I cannot help respecting Chelsea as a second native place, notwithstanding the irreparable misfortunes which happened to me while I resided in it,' he wrote to a friend in 1763. Back in England, he published in 1769 *The Adventures of an Atom*, a political satire which roused another storm of indignation, and the following year, in failing health and no longer able to contend with the 'sea of trouble' in which he was floundering, he went abroad again, eventually settling in a cottage near Leghorn. Here he wrote his last novel *Humphrey Clinker*, part of which is set in Chelsea, but he died in September 1771, before he had time to learn of its great success.

For Smollett, the struggle to earn a living never ceased and, as Faulkner said of him: 'He should seem to have deserved a better lot than he met with.' His temper was 'like a gusty wind – frosty but kindly' and all his life, wrote Sir Walter Scott, 'he practised the virtues of generosity and benevolence, though often, like his own Matthew Bramble, under the disguise of peevishness and irritability'.

Throughout the eighteenth century Chelsea's fame for its beautiful gardens was as strong as ever. Early in the century the Society of Gardeners was formed by twenty working nurserymen, who used to meet regularly at Newhall's coffee house in Chelsea, to discuss specimens and new varieties of plants they had grown, which they brought for exhibition. One of these members was Thomas Fairchild, who in 1722 published his gardening book, *The City Gardener*.

Early in the century the Earl of Huntingdon built a house on the river-front at the western end of Chelsea, called Chelsea Farm, and in 1778 the house was acquired by Lord Cremorne, who employed James Wyatt to enlarge and improve it. Lady Cremorne, who was a great-granddaughter of William Penn, was renowned for her skill as a housewife. The servant troubles which were to beset poor Jane Carlyle a century later were unknown to Lady Cremorne, for the story goes that her housekeeper stayed with her for forty-eight years, and in all that time not one woman servant left, except to be married. Both Lord and Lady Cremorne lived on into the nineteenth century, Lord Cremorne dying in 1813 and Lady Cremorne in 1825.

Adjoining Chelsea Farm, which became known as Cremorne House, Dr Benjamin Hoadley, the good friend of Richard Steele, had built another elegant mansion, and on his death in 1760 it came into the possession of the Earl of Ashburnham, and was known as Ashburnham House.

Politically and socially, the most important house in Chelsea during the first half of the eighteenth century was, of course, Sir Robert Walpole's villa, Walpole House. This had been built on land adjoining Gough House, which had originally been acquired for the Royal Hospital. In 1690 the ground was leased to William Jephson, who built the original house and, after it had changed hands several times, Sir Robert Walpole bought it. Here, from 1723, he spent part of every summer for the next twenty years, improving and enlarging the house and transferring to it some of his Van Dycks and other pictures from Houghton, and tending the four acres of riverside garden in which he built his octagonal summer-house, a large glass-house, designed by Vanbrugh, and the famous shell grotto.

His son Horace lived here during his early years, before he departed to Twickenham, where he flouted the Palladian architectural tradition which had persisted since the days of Inigo Jones and Christopher Wren, and built himself his 'little Gothic castle'.

Sir Robert sometimes entertained Queen Caroline at Walpole House and on these occasions, despite the humiliations she suffered from the King, she asserted her Royal dignity in full measure. Lady Walpole was permitted to sit at table with the Queen and the Royal members of her entourage, but Sir Robert stood behind the Queen's chair, and after offering her the first dish, retired to another room, to dine with the rest of her suite.

In 1729 he gave a magnificent entertainment for the Queen and the Royal Family at Walpole House. The dinner was held in the green-house, a special kitchen with twenty fireplaces being built for the occasion in the Hospital stable-yard adjoining the grounds. 'After dinner Her Majesty and the Royal family retired to the Banqueting-House on the river to drink Tea; where were several Barges of fine musick, playing at the Time. After which they returned to the Green House, where the illustrious company were entertained with a Ball, and afterwards supp'd in the same place.'

After Queen Caroline's death in 1737 Walpole's power declined. In 1742 he resigned office and retired to his home at Houghton Hall, but by 1745 he was dead. Walpole House changed hands several times within the next few years, but the last tenant, Lord Yarborough, surrendered the unexpired part of the lease to the Crown in 1798, and eventually it became an Infirmary for the Hospital pensioners.

The year that Sir Robert Walpole left Chelsea there arrived as resident physician at the Hospital that extraordinary character Messenger Monsey, who held office for forty-six years, until his death in 1788 at the age of ninety-six. He was born in Norfolk in 1693, the son of a country parson, and after studying medicine at Cambridge, he settled in Bury for the next twenty-five years to the humdrum life of a country doctor.

Lord Godolphin, on his way to Newmarket one day, was seized with an apoplectic fit, and it was Dr Monsey who was called to attend him. Godolphin was so pleased with his cure and so attracted to the doctor, that he brought him to London, to live with him as his companion and physician. He introduced him to all the right people, including Lord Chesterfield, Sir Robert Walpole and David Garrick, and Doctor Monsey acquired, if not polish, a vast amount of amusement and a lot of money.

When Godolphin died, Dr Monsey lost his comfortable home, but was soon appointed physician to the Royal Hospital. He was a great character, and beneath all his bluster, a kindly soul. He was also a great letter writer, one of his many correspondents being the learned Mrs Carter. After his retirement to Chelsea, his friends must have feared he was missing the gay days of London, but to Mrs Montagu, that other erudite member of London society, he wrote: 'Wasn't I a miserable country doctor between twenty-five and thirty years, and is it possible to conceive such a one wouldn't be glad to rest after riding his horse to a jelly almost risquing his neck night and day after a parcel of sc-l l-rds, sorry rascals and fantastical misses who sometimes did and sometimes did not give me something for hearing all their nonsensical complaints, and now and then curing the real ones? Is it nothing to have got rid of the stupidity and slip-sloppery of drivling nurses and conceited chambermaids and waiting women, and what is worse, the perplexity of obscure cases, the difficulty of relieving plain ones, and the perpetual anxiety and distress of mind about all . . .?'

'Nerves' he described as 'modern cant . . . that absurd jargon which the Bold assert roundly and fools cover their ignorance with.'

Dr Monsey had an ingenious method for extracting teeth. He tied the end of a piece of catgut round the tooth and the other end to a perforated bullet, with which he loaded his revolver. Then, 'the revolver being held in the proper direction . . . by touching the trigger a troublesome companion and a disagreeable operation were evaded.' When one victim cried out, at the last minute, that he had changed his mind, Monsey shouted back: 'but I have not and you are a fool and a coward for your pains'. Whereupon the shot was fired and out came the tooth.

Boswell tells us that at a supper party at the Crown and Anchor in the Strand, Dr Johnson was 'vehement against old Dr Monsey, of Chelsea College, as a fellow who swore and talked bawdy' but he was a forthright, honest and amusing old man, notwithstanding. During his last years at the hospital, Fanny Burney's father Dr Burney was appointed organist, and he lived there until his death in 1814, finding his sojourn so perfectly to his taste, wrote Fanny, 'that he never wished to change his abode'.

XI

Chelsea Porcelain

DURING the eighteenth century, many aspects of living among the wealthy English reached a degree of elegance which had never been known before, and the craftsmanship of furniture, silver, glass and china has probably never been surpassed. In regard to furniture, the Dutch marquetry of William and Mary's reign was a short-lived fashion and the plain walnut furniture of Queen Anne's time gave place to mahogany, partly because supplies of walnut were becoming increasingly expensive and difficult to come by, but also because, during the reign of George I, supplies of mahogany became available from the West Indies. William Kent designed beautiful furniture to fit his Palladian houses, including marble-topped side-tables with elaborately carved and gilded legs, which were often surmounted by a small mirror in a gilded frame, flanked by candelabra. In 1753 Chippendale opened his workshops in St Martin's Lane and a few years later Hepplewhite began business in Cripplegate.

Georgian silver and glass were as beautiful in design and workmanship as the furniture, and now began an interest in china and porcelain. The middle classes and artisans were still using pewter plates and mugs, and in the remote country districts even the medieval wooden platters were not unusual. But in London and the big cities the fashion for china and porcelain tableware grew steadily.

Earthenware pottery is one of the earliest of the arts, but porcelain is relatively new, having been first made in China about twelve hundred years ago.

In England, earthenware pottery was made from medieval times, and during the sixteenth century it was imported from Europe. Among these imports was stoneware, which is earthenware baked at such an intensity of heat that it becomes hard and impervious.

In 1671, John Dwight of Fulham opened the first English factory for the manufacture of stoneware, claiming in his patent that he had discovered 'the mystery and invention of making . . . stoneware, vulgarly called Cologne ware . . . never before made in England.'

His factory turned out utilitarian stoneware bottles and jugs in great numbers, some of which were engraved with patterns of birds and flowers, work which was probably done by glass engravers. He also produced a few stoneware figures as, for example, the heads of Charles II and James II, both of which are now in the Victoria and Albert Museum. The most charming of them all is the sad little figure of Lydia Dwight, his small daughter, who 'dyed March 3, 1673'. She lies with her eyes closed, her hands meekly folded in prayer, and an expression of touching resignation on her beautifully modelled little face.

Dwight renewed his patent for the manufacture of stoneware in 1684, but five years later he was bringing a lawsuit against the Wedgwood brothers of Burslem, James Morley of Nottingham and John and David Elers of Fulham, all of whom had also begun manufacturing stoneware.

It was during these years that Chinese porcelain was being brought to Europe by the various East India companies, along with their cargoes of tea, and among the rich it became immensely popular. Collecting became the fashion. Queen Mary is thought to have begun the craze, and it was during her reign that the first walnut china cabinets were made for its display, with glass doors and the typical 'inverted cup' legs.

During the reign of Queen Anne, Addison described a porcelain piece he had seen at a friend's house – 'inclosed in a kind of Square, one of the prettiest grotesque works that I ever saw and made up of scaramouches, Lions, Monkeys, Mandarines, Trees, Shells and a thousand odd figures in China ware'.

Porcelain is a stoneware made from kaolin, or china clay, and fused with 'patuntse', a china stone: and it is glazed with a mixture of china-stone, lime and potash. This true porcelain is white and translucent and came to be known as 'hard paste'. 'Soft pastes' are imitations of true porcelain, in which ground glass and other substances are mixed with the clay, and a lead glaze is fused on to the surface.

As the highly-priced Chinese porcelain dinner and tea services, figure groups and vases were brought in ever-increasing numbers from the East, European potters and chemists experimented to try to find the secret of its manufacture. Dwight, in his original patent, claimed to have discovered the method of manufacture of 'transparent earthenware, commonly known by the name of porcelain and China and Persian ware', as well as his stoneware, but he never produced any. However, he did imitate the unglazed red stoneware from China, known as 'red porcelain', which was considered the best material for teapots, and when the Elers brothers left Fulham for Staffordshire, these red teapots were soon being made there too, from the red clay of Stafford.

It was at the Meissen factory near Dresden, opened in 1710, that European hard paste porcelain was first made, and Kändler of Meissen produced the first European porcelain figures. Much of the Meissen work was copied from the Chinese, and when it was imported to England, the collecting craze spread. By 1714 Addison had found it tedious, complaining that the habit of filling the best rooms of the houses of ladies of fashion with china had become absurd. He could remember, he said, when the largest article of china was a coffee cup, but it had now swelled to vases as large as 'half a hogshead', and Gay was moved to write:

> 'What rival's here? A China jar!
> China's the passion of her soul,
> A cup, a plate, a dish, a bowl,
> Can kindle wishes in her breast,
> Inflame with joy, or break her rest.'

In 1738 the French porcelain factory opened at Vincennes, and very soon afterwards Thomas Briand introduced the industry to England. In 1743 he showed specimens of his soft-paste porcelain to the Royal Society, the Journal Book recording: 'Mr Bryand, a Stranger, that was present, shew'd the Society several Specimens of a sort of Fine Ware made here (in London) by himself from native materials of our own Country which appear'd to be in all respects as good as any of the finest Porcelaine or China Ware; and he said that it was much preferable for its fineness to the ware of Dresden, and seem'd to answer the Character of the true Japan. For when broken, it appears like broken sugar, and not like Glass as the Dresden ware does: and that if it be heated red-hot, and immediately put into Cold water it will not fly or break. And that this ware, before it be glaz'd (a Specimen of which he shew'd) is firm enough to stand the heat of a Glasshouse furnace.'

During the early 1740s several porcelain factories were opened in England. The Bow factory was in business by 1744 but the Chelsea factory, at the corner of Justice Walk and Lawrence Street, seems to have opened even earlier, perhaps in 1742, the year that saw the opening of Ranelagh Gardens.

Very little is known about the early days of the factory, but by about 1745 Charles Gouyn was directing it in partnership with Nicholas Sprimont, a Flemish Huguenot, who had been a silver-smith in Soho. Gouyn soon disappears from the story and Sprimont remained in sole management, being financed by Sir Everard Fawkener, secretary to the Duke of Cumberland, and also, in all probability, by the Duke himself. The factory was not large. The land Sprimont leased for £24 a year measured 85 feet from east to west and 90 feet from north to south along Lawrence Street. It was an 'aggregate of old timber workshops, in an avenue of lime trees, added on to each other' as the business grew, and the workmen lived in cottages close by. Alongside the narrow roadway by the river, with its river wall and wooden railing, the factory had its own small wharf, for the unloading of the clay and other materials, and it seems possible, although there is no tangible proof, and Briand assured the Royal Society that his porcelain was made from English materials, that some of the clay may have come from China.

Betew, in *Nollekens and His Times*, writing of the closing of the factory, more than twenty years later, said: 'Ay, that was a curious failure; the cunning rogues produced very white and delicate ware, but then they had their clay from China; which, when the Chinese found out, they would not let the Captains have any more clay for ballast, and the consequence was, the concern failed.'

This was not the reason for the factory closing, but may be considered additional support for the theory that some of the original clay used at Chelsea came from China.

In the ramshackle little buildings in Lawrence Street were the slip house, where the wet clay was mixed, measured and prepared, the slip itself being clay mixed with water to the consistency of cream; the potters' shop, where plates and dishes were pressed and moulded; the modelling room where figures were modelled and then broken up for casting, the casts of the legs, arms, heads and bodies of the little figures being then reassembled and joined with clay slip; the moulders' shop where wax and lead moulds were made; and the kilns where the porcelain was arranged on shelves for firing, each piece being placed on three or four cone-shaped stilts.

After firing, the biscuit porcelain was taken to the glazing room and dipped in lead glaze, a process which in Victorian times was to prove deadly, for many workers in the pottery towns were to die through the poison in the lead glaze being absorbed through their wet hands and arms. After glazing, the porcelain was fired again and then the creamy white pieces were ready for painting. The paints were enamels made from pigments derived from oxides such as copper, manganese, iron and antimony, and the enamel painters were English, French and Flemish.

Chaffer, in his *Marks and Monograms*, quotes from an old man with a rather shaky memory, who had worked at the Chelsea factory. He said that Sprimont was first employed at a salary of a guinea a day, with certain allowances for apprentices, and other emoluments. 'I think Sir Everard died about 1755, much reduced in circumstances, when Mr Sprimont became sole proprietor, and having amassed a fortune, he travelled about England, and the manufactory was shut up for about two years, for he neither would let nor carry it on himself. I then went to work at Bow for a short time. I went to work again at Chelsea for Mr Sprimont, after being absent about two or three years, where I stopped till I engaged with Mr Duesbury to go to Derby, which was about the year 1763.'

The first Chelsea mark, from about 1745 until perhaps as late as 1749, was an incised triangle. The name Chelsea was inscribed and sometimes the date. This soft paste porcelain was like opaque glass. Mixed with the clay was a compound of silica which was ground with lime and chalk, and when held up to the light the porcelain showed bright flecks in the translucency. The mixture was not stable and pieces often collapsed during firing, which meant that the finished specimens were expensive.

The characteristic forms of this early Chelsea were derived from the shapes being used for silver, the best known being the little 'goat and bee' cream jugs, in the form of a pair of reclining goats supporting the jug, on to which a bee was moulded.

Cups and saucers and other tableware were made, sometimes unpainted but fluted and decorated with applied sprays of leaves and flowers, sometimes painted with Japanese patterns which were derived from Meissen. Often tiny flowers and insects were painted on the pieces, apparently haphazardly, but actually to conceal flaws in the porcelain.

Very few figures from this period now exist and probably not many were made, but a few teapots in the form of grotesque China-men's heads have survived.

From the time that Sprimont became sole manager of the factory, he gradually evolved a finer-grained porcelain, with a thinner glaze, which enabled him to produce his delicate masterpieces. The mark during this second period was a raised anchor embossed on an oval medallion. The anchor was unpainted until 1752 and from then until about 1754 it was sometimes painted red. Chelsea porcelain of this period can be recognised, when held to the light, by the presence of small, bright spots.

During these few years the Chelsea factory produced beautifully painted porcelain, two of the favourite themes being Aesop's *Fables* and the Lady and Pavilion. The Oriental and Meissen influences were strong and a letter written in 1751 by Sir Charles Hanbury Williams, English Ambassador at Dresden, confirms this borrowing. He wrote: 'I received a letter about ten days ago from Sir Everard Fawkener who is, I believe, concerned in the manufacture of china at Chelsea. He desired me to send over models for different pieces from hence in order to furnish the undertakers with good designs, and would have me send over fifty or three score pounds worth. But I thought it better and cheaper for the manufacturers to give them leave to take any of my china from Holland House and to copy what they like.'

The factory had not produced a great many original figures as yet, but the Italian comedy characters – the Doctor, the Harlequin, the Jester, the Columbine, the Pantaloon and Scaramouche the servant were very popular, and also the figure of the Nurse in Elizabethan costume, which had earlier been made in earthenware. They also made some white portrait busts of the Duke of Cumberland, George, Prince of Wales, and George II, which it seems possible were model-led by Roubiliac.

Small painted birds were favourite ornaments, often displayed on dining-tables. Many of these birds were modelled from engravings in George Edwards' book *The Natural History of Uncommon Birds*, which had been published in 1743, and one of Sprimont's artists, William Duesbury, who later became proprietor of the Derby fac-tory, recorded in his account book painting 'Flapwing birds, Bool-finch Birds, Topknot Birds, King Fishiers and Hostrigis' at two shillings a pair.

From about 1754 the Chelsea mark changed to a plain red anchor painted on the glaze, and this third phase lasted until about 1756. Sprimont had overcome some earlier difficulties in fixing the enamel, and this was perhaps the finest period for Chelsea porcelain, the factory producing work that ranks with the best in Europe. It included tableware and vases, as well as delightful figures and figure groups, many still showing Meissen, Chinese and Japanese influence, but others the individual creativeness of the painters and modellers at Chelsea, who drew their inspiration from the life around them in the rapidly growing waterside village.

They made beautifully modelled and painted figures, not more than five or six inches high, of the people they saw every day in Chelsea, fishermen, gardeners, vegetable sellers, flower sellers, beggars, itinerant musicians, watermen wearing the Doggett coat and badge, masqueraders from Ranelagh. And they adapted the flowers from Philip Miller's *The Gardener's Dictionary* for their painted decoration.

They also made porcelain 'toys' – charming conceits such as scent-bottles, patch-boxes, snuff-boxes and the like – and the scent-bottles were particularly enchanting as well as ingenious, as for example a bottle in the form of a vase of flowers, with a butterfly for a stopper, a girl kneeling in confession to a monk, with two billing doves for a stopper, a boy playing a bagpipe, with a rose for a stopper, a cupid encircling a heart with a wreath of roses, with a metal bird for a stopper.

Occasionally they used little Battersea enamel stoppers from the factory on the other side of the river, but the production of Battersea enamel was short-lived, the factory opening in 1753 and closing in 1756.

Animal and vegetable shapes were used for tureens and dishes and the factory also produced miniature models of fruit and vegetables, such as artichokes and cauliflowers.

The enamelled decorations on dinner services and other pieces of tableware were often copied from the paintings of Watteau, Tenier and Boucher. Aesop's *Fables* appear again in this period and O'Neale painted them on a dinner service which at one time belonged to Warren Hastings.

Many splendid figures were made, some taken from Kändler's models at Meissen, others from engravings. Red Anchor figures include gods and goddesses from Greek and Roman mythology, emblematic figures, figures from the London theatre, such as David

Garrick and Mrs Cibber, and figures from the Italian comedy and Aesop's *Fables*. The group of Chinese musicians is an outstanding piece of work, an arrangement of four musicians facing outwards round a raised centre designed to carry a table lustre, and the Woman Killing a Hen is a wonderfully vigorous example from the Aesop collection.

At the end of 1756 Sprimont closed the factory, probably because he was ill, and when he reopened it in 1758 he changed the mark to a gold anchor, which he continued to use until he sold the factory in 1769. At this time he introduced bone ash into the porcelain, which made it denser and harder, and used a somewhat thicker and richer glaze.

The Gold Anchor period was influenced more by Sèvres than Meissen and is characterised by elaborate gilding, which before this time had been used rather sparingly. Sprimont also used for the first time the new 'mazarin' blue and the deep claret ground so often seen in Sèvres ware. In the figure groups, the background of trees and foliage is very elaborate and the simple bases of the Red Anchor pieces has changed to rococo.

Vases were decorated with elaborate figure paintings, after Rubens and Tenier, as well as exotic birds, flowers, fruit and chinoiserie.

The factory was making a great deal of money for the corpulent Sprimont. He had a splendid house in Chelsea and a country seat in Dorset, and he used to ride to London in a gilded cabriolet and pair. Nevertheless, in 1759 he had to plead for government protection against the import of Dresden china, protesting that 'the undertakers (of Chelsea) last winter sold to the value of more than £3,500, which is a great deal, considering that the thing (porcelain strengthened with bone ash) is new. . . . The manufacture in England has been carried on by great labour and a large expense; it is in many respects to the full as good as Dresden. . . . It is now daily improving, and already employs at least one hundred hands, of which is a nursery of thirty lads, taken from the parishes and charity schools, and bred to design and painting – arts very much wanted here, and which are of the greatest use in our silk and printed linen manufactories.'

Reginald Blunt, in his book *The Wonderful Village*, quotes from a contemporary writer who affirms that Sprimont's establishment did indeed occupy a great number of both sexes, but adds that this propinquity proved very injurious to their morals.

One of the most important orders Sprimont received was for the famous Mecklenburg service, made in 1763 and valued at £1,200, as a present from George III and Queen Charlotte for the Queen's brother, the Duke of Mecklenburg.

Dr Johnson was interested in porcelain and had an idea he could mprove its manufacture. 'He even applied to the directors of the Chelsea China Works,' writes Walford, 'and was allowed to bake his compositions in their ovens in Lawrence Street. He was accordingly accustomed to go down with his housekeeper, above twice a week, and stay the whole day, she carrying a basket of provisions with her. The doctor, who was not allowed to enter the mixing room, had access to every other part of the premises, and formed his composition in a particular apartment without being overlooked by anyone. He had also free access to the ovens, and superintended the whole process; but he completely failed, both as to composition and baking, for his materials always yielded to the intensity of the heat, while those of the Company came out of the furnace perfect and complete.'

For the most part, Sprimont sold his wares by annual auction in London. The first was held in 1754 at Mr Ford's in the Haymarket, when he offered 'épergnes and services for Desserts, beautiful groups of figures, round and oval dishes, tureens and plates, etc.'. Sales were also held in the big provincial cities and in this same year, 1754, eighty lots were being offered for auction in York, conveyed there presumably by pack-horse train.

By 1769 Sprimont was a sick man and the production declined. The following year he sold the factory to William Duesbury and John Heath of the Derby works. A few days later, Christie held a four-day sale of 'Chelsea Porcelaine by Order of Mr Nicholas Sprimont', and shortly afterwards Sprimont died.

Duesbury operated the Chelsea factory until 1783, but only in a very small way, for there were few employees left. In 1771 there were only seven, and one horse was sufficient to operate the machinery. Many of the Chelsea models and moulds were sent up to Derby. From those remaining, the production during the last years of the Chelsea factory was known as Chelsea-Derby, but much of the Chelsea work now followed the tradition of Derby rather than Chelsea, and it is difficult to distinguish Chelsea from Derby. At first the mark was a gold anchor with a D. In 1773 appeared the crowned anchor and sometimes a Crown and a D, without the anchor.

By 1783 Duesbury became ill. He closed the factory at Chelsea and transferred the rest of the plant, moulds and models to his factory in Derby, where his son joined him in partnership.

By the end of the century, the Chelsea factory was pulled down and new little houses built on the site. Years later, under the garden at the back of number 32 Church Street, three kilns were discovered, with a few rejects on the shelves, which had lost shape in firing. They included an unglazed cup with a Chinese painted decoration, an oval dish-cover, a cos lettuce and a cock and hen group. And in the early 1920s Reginald Blunt discovered the remains of some dome-topped kilns in the cellar of a house at the south-east corner of Justice Walk.

In 1768, Josiah Wedgwood and his partner Thomas Bentley began moving their Burslem factory to their new factory, with its village for the workmen, which they called Etruria. Plain biscuitware from the Wedgwood factory was often sent away for enamelling, and in this same year they opened a decorating shop at Great Newport Street, adjoining their London salerooms. They soon found that they needed larger premises and decided to move to Chelsea, where they leased a plot of ground where Glebe Place now stands, the site stretching from Upper Cheyne Row to the King's Road.

Wedgwood had just taken out a patent for 'ornamenting earthen and porcelain ware with an encaustic gold bronze, together with a peculiar species of encaustic painting in various colours in imitation of the ancient Etruscan and Roman earthenware'.

In Chelsea they put up sheds, buildings and kilns, and for the next five years Wedgwood biscuitware was brought here from Etruria, by pack-horse trains and wagons, for enamelling, encaustic painting and glazing. Many of Wedgwood's decorators came to live and work in Chelsea, including James Bakewell, Ralph Unwin, Nathaniel Cooper, John Roberts, his son and two daughters, and Mr and Mrs Wilcox, Miss Gleeson and Miss Pars. Payment seems to have been graded according to skill and also to social status, which must have presented many a knotty problem. Miss Gleeson, for example, received twelve shillings a week, but Miss Pars, perhaps less skilful and certainly less gently born, never rose above ten shillings and six-pence.

David Rhodes, Wedgwood's master foreman, lived in Little Cheyne Row, and Thomas Bentley also took up residence for a while in Upper Cheyne Row.

Much of Wedgwood's best border decoration of tea and dinner-ware, as well as enamelling on creamware, was done at Chelsea during this time, but the most important undertaking was the famous Imperial Russian dinner service, made in 1773-4 for the Empress Catherine, for the La Grenouillière palace at St Petersburg.

This consisted of more than eight hundred pieces of creamware, each piece having a border decoration of oak leaves and berries and being painted with one or more views of the seats of the English nobility and gentry, set in English landscapes. In all, there were nearly two thousand different scenes, painted in a mulberry purple, and each piece bore the green frog mark of La Grenouillière.

The ware was packed in panniers, loaded on to the backs of ponies, and the 150-mile journey from Etruria to Chelsea took several days. This was just before the Trent–Mersey canal was opened, which made the transport of Wedgwood's pottery so much safer.

The selection of the houses to be painted on the Russian dinner service was no mean task and Sir Josiah realised he might cause offence to those whose homes he had omitted. 'It is a pity,' he wrote to Bentley, who was supervising the decoration, 'but we had more large dishes in the service. As it is, it will seem, and be in reality, too great a partiality for a County Esquire, though he does happen to be our neighbour and a good man, to occupy so capital a situation as a large dish when there is but two or four in the whole service.' Later he wrote again to Chelsea, when the question of putting the service on view to the public before its despatch was being discussed: 'For suppose a Gentn thinks himself neglected either by the omission of his seat when his neighbours is taken, or by putting it on a small piece, or not flattering it sufficiently. He then becomes our enemy, gains some of the Artists to his party, and Damns it with the Rusn Ambassador and with everyone he is able.' These subtle, social problems seem to have been satisfactorily resolved in the end, and after the safe despatch of the service to St Petersburg, the Wedgwood painting shops at Chelsea were abandoned and the buildings demolished.

XII

Turner, the Carlyles and Leigh Hunt
in Chelsea

BY 1800 Chelsea was no longer a village. It had become a small country town, with a population of twelve thousand. Yet, like so many country towns, it still retained its village atmosphere, particularly by the unchanging riverside, where fishermen still hauled up their boats on the sandy, pebbly shore, drank at the waterside taverns and exchanged news with the watermen, plying for hire.

By 1834, when Thomas and Jane Carlyle came to Chelsea, the population had more than trebled, yet this was still the slow-moving world of the horse and stage-coach, for the railway age was only just dawning. The days of Ranelagh were over, the house and the rotunda had been demolished and the gardens were a weedy waste. At the other end of Chelsea, Cremorne House, which Faulkner had described as 'one of the most delightful retreats in the vicinity of London', had been bought by the Baron de Beaufain, who had turned it into a sporting club for 'various skilful and manly exercises – swimming, rowing, shooting, fencing, archery, riding, skating, coursing, hunting and racing', which he called the Stadium.

The King's Road was still lined with nursery gardens, but by the 1830s there was new building along both sides, between the widely-scattered eighteenth-century mansions. At the eastern end was the Duke of York's school for the children of soldiers, built in 1810, and next to it Whitelands House, a girls' boarding-school, which had been established in 1772.

In the heyday of Ranelagh, the way from Westminster lay through the Five Fields, a lonely stretch of country notorious for its dangerous footpads. At Jenny Whim's tavern there was a bridge over the reservoirs of the Chelsea Water Works to what is now the Pimlico Road, and then the way led past the old Bun House to the Chelsea boundary. In the early years of the nineteenth century the builders were encroaching on the Five Fields and covering it with the bricks and mortar of Pimlico and Belgravia.

In 1777 Henry Holland took from Lord Cadogan a lease of 100 acres of the isolated 'black lands', lying between Knightsbridge and Chelsea, and here he built Hans Town, a building development where Sloane Street, Upper and Lower Cadogan Place and Hans Place were later to appear. In Hans Place he also built his own house, the Pavilion, which was a model for the classical villa he built for the Prince Regent at Brighton, shortly after the Prince's secret marriage to Maria Fitzherbert. The villa had originally been a farmhouse, and by 1815 it was rebuilt yet again, when John Nash transformed it into the Oriental pavilion which still stands.

The first Battersea bridge was built in 1771, a wooden structure, 28 feet wide, the tolls being a shilling for a carriage and four horses, eightpence for a carriage and pair, a penny for a horse and a halfpenny for a foot passenger.

The two most populated parts of Chelsea were Paradise Row and Church Lane, which was later to be known as Church Street, and here were the main shops, old Thomas Faulkner, the distinguished historian of Chelsea, having his bookshop at number 1, Paradise Row.

At the Royal Hospital, John Soane had supervised the conversion of Sir Robert Walpole's house into an infirmary for the pensioners, who at first were carried there from the main building in sedan chairs.

Lord Palmerston had made increased provision for the maintenance of the hospital during his term of office as Secretary for War and as early as 1823 the new amenity of gas was being supplied to the buildings by the recently formed Chelsea gas-works. During the 1830s, Lord John Russell made many reforms in the organisation of the hospital, which included increasing comforts for the veterans of the Napoleonic Wars.

The Physic Garden, with its water gates and steps leading down to the river, was still flourishing. Botany was no longer so essential a part of the medical students' training, but students still came regularly to the garden, to the lectures of John Lindley, who was appointed lecturer in botany in 1836.

Along the river-front, which was to be known as Cheyne Walk, was a low wooden railing, protecting the brick river embankment, built up from the sandy shores a few feet below, and the walk was shaded by a row of beautiful elm trees. The houses along the walk were widely spaced, but with the passing years the spaces soon disappeared.

The little parish church of St Luke had become too small for the growing population and in 1821 work was begun on the new St Luke's church in Sydney Street, to the north of the King's Road, but the old church, with its memorials and tombs and precious memories, remained as a Chapel of Ease.

When Jane and Thomas Carlyle arrived at number 5 Cheyne Row, in the summer of 1834, from Craigenputtock, plans were already under way for the building of the squares which were to become known as Chelsea Square, Carlyle Square and Paulton's Square. Some houses were already built and the squares were all completed by the middle of the century.

Thomas Carlyle was thirty-eight when he came to Chelsea and he was to live in the same house until he died in 1881, although Jane, six years younger, died suddenly in 1866.

Their letters have left a brilliantly vivid picture of their life together in Chelsea, though it was a strange marriage and it seems possible that it was never consummated. The clever, talented Jane had been deeply in love with Carlyle's friend, Edward Irving, and they would have married if Irving had not been already engaged before he met Jane. Carlyle fell in love with her, but for a long time she refused to consider marriage. Yet when at last she did agree, they seemed contented enough, for all Carlyle's chronic indigestion and neurotic hatred of noise and Jane's migraines, excess of nervous energy and extortionate demands on her servants.

They were poor in the early days, for Carlyle's capital was only £200 when he came to London to make a living by his writing, but they were delighted with their little house, already 120 years old, which they rented for £35 a year.

'Chelsea is unfashionable,' wrote Carlyle. 'It was once the resort of the Court and great however; hence numerous old houses in it, at once cheap and excellent.' It had now become 'a genteel neighbourhood, two old ladies on one side, unknown character on the other, but with "pianos"'.

Number 5, which in 1877, with the building of more houses in the Row, was renumbered 24, was an eight-roomed house, with two rooms on each floor and a large closet extending from each of the back rooms on the three floors above the basement.

'A right old strong, roomy brick house, likely to see *three* races of their modern fashionable fall before it comes down,' said Carlyle.

The house still stands, for it is now a property of the National Trust, and it seems much smaller than it appears in many drawings or even photographs, and certainly in Carlyle's description of the 'dark, panelled hallway leading through an archway into the garden, past a broadish stair, with massive balustrades (in the old style) corniced and as thick as one's thigh'. But it is a wonderful example of a Queen Anne dwelling house, and with the Carlyles' furniture still there, it breathes the atmosphere of their letters, their domestic trials, their sufferings and triumphs and simple contentment.

In the basement were a front and back kitchen. In the front kitchen was a kitchen range with trivets for kettles and saucepans, a sliding hook for a stewpot, a roasting jack and a baking oven at the side. The stone sink was supplied with water from a pump, which drew on a well under the stone floor, but later, in 1852, when main water was supplied to the house, Jane had a boiler installed, with a two-gallon cistern which was filled each day from a tap at the sink.

Here, amidst the black beetles and mice, a succession of maids, sometimes a child of fifteen, sometimes a middle-aged alcoholic, slept in the four-poster bed, to which they would retire each evening at about eight o'clock after the kitchen range had been allowed to die out.

In the back kitchen, which was used as a wash-house, were the larder and coal-house, and here Carlyle also fixed a primitive shower-bath for himself.

The two little ground-floor sitting-rooms, of which the front was used as a dining-room, had pink-and-white flowered wallpaper and Jane was delighted that the landlord had painted nearly all the pine panelling throughout the house 'almost white'. For many years, the first-floor front-room was a study–drawing room, with Jane's bedroom behind and Carlyle's bedroom at the top of the house, along with the spare room for visitors. Later, in a desperate effort to secure absolute silence for his work, Carlyle had an attic study built above the third floor, with no windows to let in the street noises and a large skylight for ventilation, but it was not the success he hoped for, for it was bitterly cold in winter and oppressively hot in summer and it let in a fresh set of noises which he had never heard before – church bells and hooters and sirens from the river – so that, according to Jane, it became the noisiest room in the house.

The garden, with its discreetly secluded earth closet, was a little patch 75 feet long and 20 feet wide, enclosed by a high brick wall, part of which was the surviving wall of Henry VIII's kitchen garden. Here the Carlyles lovingly tended their two vines, the cherry tree, the walnut tree and their 'two miserable rose bushes'.

Jane loved her little house and in 1835 was boasting: 'We have no bugs yet – and I do not know of any other house among all my acquaintance that so much can be said for'. Unfortunately she spoke too soon, for it was not long before she discovered the maid's bed in the kitchen crawling with them and ordered it to be burnt, much to the surprise and indignation of the maid, who protested that bugs were 'inevitable to London'.

'Our row, which for the last three doors or so is a street, and none of the noblest', wrote Carlyle, 'runs out upon a "Parade" . . . running along the shores of the river, a broad highway with huge, shady trees, boats lying moored and a smell of shipping and tar', and he went on to describe the 'white-trowsered, white-shirted Cockneys dashing by like arrows in their long canoes of boats; beyond the green, beautiful knolls of Surrey . . . a most artificial, green-painted yet lively, fresh and most operatic looking business'.

'Chelsea', he said, 'was a singularly heterogeneous kind of spot, very dirty and confused in some places, quite beautiful in others.'

Just round the corner, in Upper Cheyne Row, Leigh Hunt had recently moved, with his wife and seven children, and the Hunts and Carlyles were soon exchanging visits. Leigh Hunt was fifty, but still struggling to maintain his large family by his writing. He had been a friend of Charles Lamb. He had helped his brother in the production of various short-lived periodicals, none of which had made much money for them. He had suffered two years' imprisonment in the King's Bench prison at the Borough, for criticising the Prince Regent, whom he had called 'a fat Adonis of fifty'.

Soon after he was freed, he took his family to Italy on the advice of Shelley, to join forces with Byron in the establishing of a Liberal Quarterly Review. It was shortly after his arrival that Shelley was drowned and Leigh Hunt was one of those present at the cremation. The literary venture with Byron failed. Byron became perceptibly cooler in his attitude to Hunt and the brief partnership ended. By 1825 Hunt was back in England, still writing his essays and poetry and still promoting a succession of periodicals which did not pay.

In the early 1830s the Hunts moved from 'the noise and dust of the New Road' to 'a corner in Chelsea'. The house in Upper Cheyne Row – number 4 which has since been changed to number 22, was, he said, 'of the old-fashioned sort which I have always loved best, familiar to the eyes of my parents, and associated with childhood. It had seats in the windows, a small third room on the first floor, of which I made a sanctum, and there were a few lime trees in front, which in their due season diffused a fragrance.'

He loved the peace of Chelsea. 'A little back room in a street in London is farther removed from the noise than the front room in a country town,' he declared. He felt at 'the end of the world. The air of the neighbouring river so refreshing and the quiet of the "no thoroughfare" so full of repose that although our fortunes were at their worst, and my health almost of a piece with them, I felt for some weeks as if I could sit still for ever, embalmed in silence.'

While Carlyle was soon complaining about the noisy cries of the street vendors, Leigh Hunt enjoyed 'the quaintness and melodiousness' of their songs, 'which procured them the reputation of having been composed by Purcell and others. . . . 'There was,' he said, 'an old seller of fish, in particular, whose cry of "shrimps as large as prawns" was such a regular, long-drawn and truly pleasing melody, that in spite of his hoarse, and I am afraid, drunken voice, I used to wish for it of an evening, and hail it when it came.'

Carlyle could not fail to like the charming, sweet-natured Hunt, with his Georgian elegance and leisurely manner, but he could not understand his feckless way of life and disapproved of what he, quite unjustly, deemed his indolence.

'His house,' wrote Carlyle, 'excels all you have ever read of a political Tinkerdom, without parallel even in literature. In his family room where are a sickly large wife and a whole school of well-conditioned wild children, you will find half-a-dozen old ricketty chairs gathered from half-a-dozen different hucksters and all seeming engaged, and just pausing, in a violent hornpipe. On these and around them and over the dusty table and ragged carpet lie all kinds of litter – books, papers, egg-shells, scissors and last night when I was there, the torn heart of a quartern loaf.'

Here, in his dressing-gown, Hunt would engage on 'the liveliest dialogue on philosophy and the prospects of man (who is to be beyond measure happy yet)'.

The house-proud Jane, with her solid mahogany, horse-hair covered dining-room chairs, her piano, her four-posters, one with green curtains and the other with red, her insistence on incessant scrubbing and cleaning, was openly disapproving, particularly when Mrs Hunt began 'borrowing' and not returning. That Jane could not stand, for, as she confided in a letter to a friend, Mrs Hunt had 'eight guineas a week to keep house on' and should have been able to manage.

The acquaintanceship did not ripen into friendship. The Carlyles allowed it to fade and when the Hunts moved to Kensington in 1840 it ended. But the Hunts did not take offence. Leigh Hunt described Carlyle as 'one of the kindest and best, as well as most eloquent of men', though prone to be over-critical at times.

Carlyle had set to work on his *French Revolution* soon after their arrival at Cheyne Row, and the first volume was finished five months later, at the beginning of 1835. In February he gave the manuscript to John Stuart Mill to read. A few weeks later, Mill arrived at Cheyne Row 'pale as Hector's ghost'. He had a terrible confession to make. A housemaid had mistakenly used the manu-script to light a fire and all but two or three pages had vanished.

To a man of Carlyle's nervous, highly strung temperament, who expended so much of himself in his writing, it was an almost un-bearable blow. Five months' work wasted – and he was no nearer earning any sorely-needed money. Yet he took the news with great courage. Mill was able to make financial amends to the extent of a hundred pounds and Carlyle set grimly to work again. By September the whole of the first volume was rewritten, and the complete work was published in 1837.

Yet Carlyle had fits of terrible depression while he was writing. 'It is twenty-three months since I earned a penny by the craft of litera-ture, and yet I know no fault I have committed . . .' he said. 'I am tempted to go to America . . . I shall quit literature; it does not invite me. Providence warns me to have done with it. I have failed in the Divine, Infernal Universe.'

The *French Revolution* brought him fame if not wealth, and the lectures he was invited to give brought him an additional income, though he hated public speaking. 'Oh heaven, I cannot "speak"; I can only gasp and writhe and stutter, a spectacle to gods and fashion-ables – being forced to it by want of money,' he wrote to Emerson in 1839.

Success and security came to the Carlyles slowly but steadily through the years, and with it marched the changing pace of Chelsea. At first Carlyle was complaining of the early morning crowing of the cocks in the next door garden. Then he wrote of the everlasting sound of 'men, women and children, omnibuses, carriages ... steeple bells, door bells, gentleman raps, twopenny post-raps, footmen ...' And yet, after the solitude of Craigenputtock, he was fascinated by the life of London, 'the torrent of vehicles and faces ... the slow-rolling, all-defying waggon, like a mountain in action, to dejected Hackney-coach ... the *distracted* Cab, which always some *blackguard* drives, with the fury of Jehu; the huge Omnibus ... Butchers' and Brewers' and Bakers' Drays: all these, with Wheelbarrows, trucks, dog-carts, and a nameless flood of other *sma' trash*, hold on unweariedly, their ever-vexed, chaotic way. And then of foot passengers! From the King to the Beggar; all with a look of care and endeavour; and as if there *were* really "Deevil a thing but one man oppressing another".'

The King was William IV who, with Queen Adelaide, had been visiting Chelsea Hospital. The Queen was very unpopular at the time and was nervous, convinced that a revolution in England was imminent. 'Poor Queen, after all!' wrote Jane. 'She looked so frostbitten and anxious! Curtsied, with such cowering hurriedness, to the veriest rabble that was ever seen. I was wae to look at her...' William, being more democratic than his queen, was better liked. 'Poor old fellow,' said Carlyle. 'He looked fresh and decent; clear as from spring water.'

But when the fascination of the London scene faded, there remained the noises, which still plagued him endlessly and intolerably. New neighbours arrived with more crowing cocks, but Carlyle persuaded the landlord to have the birds removed. A young lady began practising the piano on the other side of his study wall, but he wrote her such a charming letter that she either had the piano moved elsewhere or stopped playing it altogether.

Cheyne Row was becoming busier, and to the sounds of the street vendors and the horses and carts were added the jangle of the organ-grinders and the shrill wrangles of a Punch and Judy show. 'Vile yellow Italians' complained Carlyle distractedly. In 1855 the Cremorne Gardens were opened and the noise of the fireworks and the excited, wondering cries of the spectators came floating in through the skylight of the newly-constructed 'silent' study, to add further to his distress.

Carlyle wrote frenziedly that London was 'the noisiest Babylon

that ever raged and *fumed* (with coal smoke) on the face of the Planet'
– a sad change from the days when he first arrived in Chelsea, and
Cheyne Row at night had been 'pure and silent as at Puttock; and the
gas light shimmer of the great Babylon hangs stretched from side to
side of our horizon'.

Gas was laid on at Cheyne Row in 1852, the same year that they
received main water, but it was expensive and the light was not as
good as candle or lamplight, so at first they had only two jets, one
over the front door and the other in the kitchen.

With his increasing fame, there were many distinguished visitors
to Cheyne Row, including the Brownings, Tennyson, Dickens,
Thackeray, Ruskin, Chopin, Mazzini, Emerson, on his occasional
visits to England, Harriet Martineau, the Macreadys, Fanny Kemble
and some of the Pre-Raphaelites and their associates, though Carlyle's views on their paintings were far from encouraging. When Holman Hunt showed him *The Light of the World*, Carlyle studied it
grimly for a few moments and then released an explosive, vehement
denunciation. It was a 'mere papistical fantasy', an 'empty make-
believe' and 'wilful blindness'. 'That may be your idea of Jesus
Christ, but I've another of my own which I very much prefer . . . no
puir, weak-faced nonentity', he said.

Despite Carlyle's success and fame, each new work he undertook
caused him intense mental suffering and hours of sleeplessness and
worry, which made him ill with dyspepsia and melancholia. His *Life
of Cromwell*, finished in 1845, took him two years to write, and
Frederick the Great, begun in 1852, was not completed until 1865, a
year before Jane's death.

For exercise, Carlyle bought himself a horse, on which he would
ride over the old wooden Battersea bridge to the country lanes of
Clapham and Wandsworth. From the hills of Sydenham, he looked
back over London, 'the monster quite buried, its smoke rising like
a great, dusky-coloured mountain, melting into the infinite clear
sky'.

The horse was an expensive luxury, costing him three to four
shillings a day, for feed and stabling. He sold it after a while and took
to a velocipede, but preferring the older method of transport was soon
buying a new mare. Occasionally he would set off on a week's riding
tour, and Froude, recalling Jane's description of Carlyle's preparations for one of these holidays, remarked that 'It struck me as rather
untender'. Many years later, Rossetti, talking over old times with the
young Hall Caine, said of Jane that she was 'a clever but rather bitter

little woman, with the one redeeming quality of unostentatious charity. The poor of Chelsea always spoke well of her.'

Perhaps poor Jane had more cause to be bitter than people realised at the time, for she had to contend with many frustrations and, for all his affection, an exceptionally difficult husband. Like him, she suffered from insomnia, and by the 1850s, after trying all manner of remedies such as henbane and chloroform, she was regularly taking morphine for her migraines and other nervous disorders. She was very sensitive to her husband's moods and suffered vicariously from the noises which caused him so much anguish. In 1853 she was writing to a friend: 'Cocks are springing up more and more till it seems as if the Universe were growing into one poultry yard. . . . All that has waked up Mr C. into the old phrenzy to be off "into silence".'

The letters of Jane and Thomas Carlyle provide an interesting commentary on the changing modes of travel and dress throughout the century. One of the Scottish servants of the 1830s made the journey from the west coast of Scotland to Liverpool by boat and then boarded the Umpire coach from Liverpool to London, which took her fifty hours. From the coach stop in Holborn she reached Chelsea by cab. In 1837 another servant was making the journey from Kirkaldy by sea, driving up to Chelsea from the St Katherine's dock.

In 1843, when Jane arrived from a visit to the south coast at Vauxhall station, a porter carried her trunk to the Chelsea steamer, for the last lap of the journey home. In 1859, when Jane and Thomas were both going to Scotland, Carlyle, with Charlotte the maid, his horse and the dog, went all the way by boat, while Jane travelled by train.

This was about the time when crinolines were at their most fashionable, following the first bustle craze, the second of which was to come in the 1880s. Jane refused to tight-lace or to wear either bustles or crinolines, but in one of her letters she described how a fashion-conscious Chelsea servant went out one Sunday with three dusters pinned under her skirt as a substitute for a bustle and, in 1864, soon after the decorators had been at work in number 5 Cheyne Row, she was writing to Carlyle: 'When the rooms are done, pray charge the maids not to rub on the clean paper with their abominably large crinolines.'

Jane loved long bus rides and from Chelsea she could ride on top of a horse-bus to Islington or Richmond for a shilling, and sometimes to

Hampstead Heath, where she would hire a donkey-chair: but towards the end of her life, Carlyle was able to buy her a brougham of her own.

In 1863 she was knocked down by a cab and was very ill for several months. She seemed to recover, but in 1866 she died, leaving an unfinished novel, and after that time Carlyle's niece Mary Aitken came to live at Cheyne Row with her husband, to look after the sad and silent old man for the last fifteen years of his life.

During the first half of the nineteenth century, living in strange anonymity, in a small cottage at the western end of Cheyne Walk, was William Turner. Turner was born in 1775, in humble circumstances, the son of a hairdresser in Maiden Lane, Covent Garden. His gifts developed very early and by the time he was fourteen he had become a pupil at the Royal Academy school. At twenty-three he was exhibiting his water-colours and his first oil-painting at the Royal Academy. His work sold well and, even in the early days, he never had any difficulty in earning a living.

With increasing confidence, he developed his style, until he achieved the wonderful effects of his greatest work, the dawns and sunsets which earned him the title of the 'Shakespeare of English painting'. During his twenties and thirties he travelled through France, Switzerland, Italy and Germany, painting in water-colour and oils, always successfully, but concentrating more and more on trying to capture the fugitive light of sun and clouds which always fascinated him. Many critics, including Thackeray, were inclined to ridicule these works of Turner's maturity at first, but Turner ignored them all. He was financially independent by now, having made a fortune from the sale of engravings of his etchings, as well as his paintings. He continued to paint as he wanted to, pursuing his private and individual purpose, and it was not long before the critics, influenced by Ruskin's deep admiration of his work, began to understand and appreciate what he was doing.

Turner had a studio in Queen Anne Street and also owned a house in Twickenham, where he lived with his widowed father until the old man's death in 1829. Turner never married, but after his father's death he began to lead a curious double life, spending part of his time at the house in Queen Anne Street, where a housekeeper looked after him, and the rest in the little cottage at 119 Cheyne Walk, where he adopted the name of the housekeeper there, Mrs Booth, a woman he had met at some seaside lodging. In Chelsea he was known as

Mr Booth, and for years no one suspected that Puggy Booth, the supposedly retired seafaring man, was the great William Turner.

He left a fortune of £140,000, but the amount of his wealth and the grandeur of his work were a sad contrast to his way of living. He was, said E. V. Lucas, 'grubby, miserly, jealous and squalid in his tastes', and it may well be that he had inherited something of his mother's insanity.

In 1846, Elizabeth Rigby, a friend of John Murray's, wrote of one of Turner's exhibitions: 'Turner living by the grace of Art. Turner proving how vulgar we are': but a week or two later, after she had called at Queen Anne Street, she wrote: 'The door was opened by a hag of a woman, for whom one hardly knew what to feel most, terror or pity . . . she showed us into a dining-room, which had penury and meanness written on every wall and article of furniture. . . . Then up into the gallery; a fine room – indeed, one of the best in London, but in a dilapidated state; his pictures the same. The great *Rise of Carthage* all mildewed and flaking off . . .'

The cottage in Cheyne Walk was no better, yet Turner loved it: and he did not keep its existence entirely a secret, although the housekeeper at Queen Anne Street seems to have known nothing about it. In the late 1830s he took John Martin and his son, Leopold, to see it. They crossed Hyde Park at Brompton and then made their way by footpaths through the market gardens to Chelsea. The Martins enjoyed the walk but the cottage they found to be a 'squalid place . . . the house had but three windows in front and was miserable in every respect'. Yet Turner saw nothing amiss and was in a jovial mood as Mrs Booth brought them porter and bread and cheese. He invited the Martins to admire the glorious view from his bedroom window. 'Here you see my study; sky and water; Are they not glorious?' he exclaimed. 'Here I have my lesson, night and day.'

On the roof of the narrow, three-storeyed cottage, with its three windows, one above the other, he had built a balustrade, with a stairway leading to it from inside the cottage, and here, wrapped in a dressing-gown, he spent hour after hour of entrancement, watching the changing pattern of the sky at dawn and sunset and the 'ever-moving clouds and river'.

Turner's last years were sad. He was a sick man and, among other disabilities, he had lost his teeth. When his friend the Reverend William Kingsley asked him to come and stay with him at Cambridge, Turner declined, saying that 'he was so nasty in his eating, the only way in which he could live being by sucking his meat'. 'The simple truth is,' wrote Kingsley later to Ruskin, 'his digestion failed thro' loss of teeth and he had to have recourse to stimulants and finally took too much.'

During his last illness, Turner was staying in the Cheyne Walk cottage. On 19 December 1851, Mrs Booth, seeing that the end was near, summoned his doctor. It was a grey and cloudy day, but in his last hour 'the sun burst forth and shone directly on him with that brilliancy which he loved to gaze on'.

From the bleak little room in the Chelsea cottage his body was taken for a few days lying-in-state at the equally dismal house in Queen Anne Street. Hundreds of people came to pay homage to the strange and lonely genius, and on 30 December his coffin was taken, in a long funeral cortège, to the solemn grandeur of a burial at St Paul's, where he was laid to rest in the crypt by the side of the tombs of Sir Joshua Reynolds and Sir Thomas Lawrence.

A year or two before Turner died, John Martin, who deeply admired Turner's work if not his cottage, also came to live in Cheyne Walk, occupying the middle part of the Moravians' old home, Lindsey House, which is now number 98 Cheyne Walk.

It was in this stretch of the Walk, known as Lindsey Row, that Mrs Gaskell had been born at number 93, in 1810, but her mother died less than four weeks later, and the baby was taken away, almost at once, to be cared for by an aunt in Cheshire.

From the balcony of one of the upper storeys of his house, Martin studied the sky which Turner knew so well and he introduced many of the Chelsea skies into his paintings. He made friends with Charles Greaves, the boat-builder whom Turner had employed to row him about the river, and Charles' son, Walter Greaves, was able to recall that 'whenever there was a storm and my father had to stay up all night to look after the boats, Martin used to say to him: "If there are good clouds and a good moon, ring my bell." When the bell rang, Martin would appear on the balcony to make his sketches.'

John Martin died in 1854, and from 1861 until his death in 1870 another Victorian artist, Daniel Maclise, lived in the house, but after his early years of popularity, Maclise became a saddened recluse, never recovering from his disappointment when the murals he had painted for the Houses of Parliament were unfavourably received.

XIII

Kensington Palace in the Early Nineteenth Century

T was in 1788 that George III had his first bout of madness, and although he recovered the following year, by 1811 he had become incurably insane. The Prince of Wales became Prince Regent until the old King's death in 1820, when he succeeded as George IV. As Prince of Wales he held his court at Carlton House, the mad old King being kept at Windsor, while Queen Charlotte and the unmarried Princesses spent most of their time at Kew and the other six Princes had their separate establishments.

The Prince of Wales was already married morganatically to Mrs Fitzherbert when in 1794 Caroline of Brunswick was chosen for his legal bride. From the moment she arrived in England the following year the Prince took a deep dislike to her, alleging that she was dirty, brash, unmannerly and unbalanced. They spent the wedding night together, but that first night was also the last. The following year the Princess Charlotte was born, but there is even a doubt as to whether she was, in fact, the Prince's child. Princess Caroline remained at Carlton House until after the birth of the Princess and was then ordered to leave. At first she refused, but the Prince and his current mistress, Lady Jersey, made life so impossible for her that she soon retired to Blackheath, while the Prince, wearying of his stormy passage with Lady Jersey, and encouraged by his doting sisters, turned again to Mrs Fitzherbert for a few years.

The Duke of Kent had been granted apartments at Kensington

Palace in 1799 but he had found them 'so comfortless as to be almost uninhabitable' and he did not live there until many years later, by which time he had made many improvements. The first Royal resident at the palace in the nineteenth century was Prince Augustus, second youngest of the Royal princes and in many ways the most likeable.

He was born in 1773 and as a young man of twenty, while travelling in Italy, had fallen deeply in love with Lady Augusta Murray, who was several years older than himself. He knew that the King would never consent to the marriage, as Lady Augusta was not of Royal birth, but insisted on being married to her in Rome, and on their return to England they were married again at St George's, Hanover Square. Neither marriage was recognised at Court and the couple lived abroad for many years with their two children. By 1801 they had agreed to part and Prince Augustus returned to England with the children. He was then given a parliamentary grant, created the Duke of Sussex and given apartments in Kensington Palace, where he moved in 1806, occupying the southern part of Clock Court, while his vast library of fifty thousand books was housed in the Long Gallery, where he liked to receive his visitors.

He was a friendly, genial man with many interests as well as his library. He had a fascinating collection of five thousand Bibles, which were arranged in a special Divinity room at the palace, and a valuable collection of clocks and watches. He was a great bird-lover and a keen gardener and took a great delight in the palace gardens, which since 1784 had been under the care of the excellent William Forsyth.

At Blackheath, Princess Caroline soon ran into serious trouble. She gave wild parties. She had men friends. And there was soon a small boy living in her household, called William Austin, for whose parentage there was no satisfactory story. A 'Discreet Enquiry' was held, the result of which was that she was acquitted of infidelity to the King, which would have been regarded as treason, but was reprimanded for 'indiscreet' conduct.

However, she was again admitted to Court and in 1808 was allotted apartments at Kensington Palace, so that she now became a neighbour of her brother-in-law, the Duke of Sussex.

The Dowager Duchess of Manchester moved out and preparations were made for the reception of the Princess of Wales. Her rooms were largely refurnished and redecorated and in her bedroom was installed 'a double headed Couch bedstead, carv'd heads and Paws, finished in Burnished Gold', which according to the Lord Chamberlain's accounts cost £106. 10.0 A new chaplain was appointed and the chapel refurnished, with 'scarlet cushions, curtains, etc.'

Here the Princess arrived, with William Austin, in June 1808, and proceeded to hold her Court, the Princess Charlotte being allowed to visit her twice a week.

For the first few years, Caroline put up a brave show at Kensington Palace and entertained a good deal, her circle including, during the early years, Lord and Lady Henry Fitzgerald, Lord Brougham, Lord and Lady Abercorn, Humphrey Davy, Lady Anne Hamilton, Lord Byron and Sir Walter Scott, but she was well aware of the fact that most of these people came to Kensington Palace more because they were opponents of the Prince of Wales than genuine friends of hers, and when the Prince became Regent she was not surprised to see them slowly disappear from her visitors' book.

'It was the besom of expediency which swept them all away,' commented one of her ladies-in-waiting.

The Princess was eccentric and may even have been a little mad, but whether this was inherent or brought about by the boredom, loneliness and unhappiness induced by the treatment she received in England it is difficult to tell. In 1810 one of her ladies-in-waiting wrote: 'The Princess does the most extraordinary things, apparently for no other purpose than to make her attendants stare. Very frequently she will take one of her ladies with her to walk in Kensington Gardens, who are accordingly dressed . . . in a costume very unsuited to the public highway; and, all of a sudden, she will bolt out of one of the smaller gates, and walk all over Bayswater, and along the Paddington Canal, at the risk of being insulted, or, if known, mobbed, enjoying the terror of the unfortunate attendant who may be destined to walk after her. One day, her royal highness inquired at all the doors of Bayswater and its neighbourhood if there were any houses to be let, and entered into many of them, till at last she came to one where some children of a friend of hers (Lord H.F.) were placed for change of air, and she was quite enchanted to be known by them, and to boast of her extraordinary mode of walking over the country.'

This escapade sounds like nothing more than the most tragic boredom, however disconcerting it may have been at the time to the ladies-in-waiting.

The following year Lady Brownlow described the Princess: 'Her figure was fat and somewhat shapeless; her face had probably been pretty in youth, for her nose was well formed, her complexion was good, and she had bright blue eyes; but their expression was bold – this, however, might be partly caused by the quantity of rouge she wore. Her fair hair hung in masses of curls on each side of her throat, like a lion's mane. Everybody, before the peace with France, dressed much according to their individual tastes; and her royal highness was of a showy turn; her gowns were generally ornamented with gold or silver spangles, and her satin boots were also embroidered with them. Sometimes she wore a scarlet mantle, with a gold trimming round it, hanging from her shoulders; and as she swam, so attired, down an English dance, with no regard to the figure, the effect was rather strange . . .'

She was clearly no match for the elegant, well-bred and always circumspect Mrs Fitzherbert.

'The Princess' parties themselves were marvellously heterogeneous in their composition,' continued Lady Brownlow. 'There were good people and very bad ones, fine ladies and fine gentlemen, humdrums and clever people . . .'

And in the end it was the humdrums who remained, hanging on for so long as the Princess could afford to entertain them.

She became acquainted with a family of Italian musicians called Sapio and rented two adjacent cottages in Bayswater, installing the Sapios in one and using the other for herself, where she 'could feel herself unshackled by the restraints of royalty and etiquette'. 'All the follies though not the elegance and splendour of Le Petit Trianon, were aped in the rural retreat of Bayswater,' declared Lady Brownlow, for here the Princess received 'a set of persons wholly unfit to be admitted to her society'. This was an oblique way of saying that she had become far too friendly with the Sapios, with whom she frequently took supper, the attraction being their young and very handsome son. Rumour soon had it that he was her lover, but before the scandal had become too widespread the Princess' Whig supporters had persuaded her to find another home for the Sapios.

By this time there were troubles with Princess Charlotte, who had always been difficult. Caroline was now said to be having an evil influence over her daughter and conniving at her love affair with a Captain Hesse, to the point of locking them in one of the palace bedrooms together, and by highly unsuitable and bawdy insinuations called through the keyhole, leaving them in no doubt as to what she expected of them.

Princess Charlotte told all this to her father, for she was highly skilled in the game of playing her parents off against each other. The result was that the Prince forbade Princess Charlotte to visit Kensington Palace except by his special permission. He also felt that it was high time his eighteen-year-old daughter was married and arranged for her engagement to the Prince of Orange. In this year, 1814, Caroline left Kensington Palace for good and went to live in Connaught Square.

When Charlotte realised not only that the Prince of Orange was a drunkard but that she would have to spend part of her life in Holland, she infuriated her father by breaking off the engagement and taking refuge with her mother in Connaught Square. Her uncle, the Duke of Cambridge, found her and brought her back to Carlton House, where a marriage with Prince Leopold of Saxe-Coburg was hastily arranged. She married him in 1816, but a year later she died in childbirth, the baby, a direct heir to the throne, also dying.

Princess Charlotte's death raised the problem of the succession. It was obviously unlikely that George and Caroline would ever come together again, and in any case George was now fifty-five and Caroline nearly fifty.

The next three princes were the Duke of York, who had been married for years and had no children, Prince William, who was to become the Duke of Clarence and was living at Richmond, in 'blameless irregularity' with Mrs Jordan and had a houseful of ten little Fitzclarences, not to mention Mrs Jordan's five children by a previous association, who were cosily housed in lodgings close by, and Prince Edward, the Duke of Kent, who was living in great contentment with Madame St Laurent.

In December 1817, the Duke of Kent talked over the problem with Thomas Creevey. 'As for the Duke of York, at his time of life and that of the Duchess, all issue, of course, is out of the question,' he said. 'The Duke of Clarence, I have no doubt, will marry if he can; but … besides a settlement such as it is proper for a Prince who marries expressly for a succession to the Throne, the Duke of Clarence demands the payment of all his debts, which are very great, and a handsome provision for each of his ten natural children … Should the Duke of Clarence not marry, the next prince in succession is myself; and altho' I trust I shall be at all times ready to obey any call my country may make upon me, God only knows the sacrifice it will be to make, whenever I shall think it my duty to become a married man. It is now seven-and-twenty years that Madame St Laurent and I have lived together.'

However, the dukes managed to extricate themselves from their amorous entanglements. The Duke of Clarence broke with the long-suffering Dorothy Jordan, who, in between her almost annual child-bearing, had managed to continue her acting career and so contribute materially to the always shaky household exchequer. The Government paid his £60,000 debts and provided for his ten children, whom he settled in a house in South Audley Street, with a gentlewoman to supervise the upbringing of the girls. He then set about looking for a suitable bride, but this took him longer than he expected and for the next year or two he lived in close company with the Prince Regent, providing nearly as much material for gossip and scandal.

The Duke of Kent, thinking that his brother Billy might in the end never marry at all, decided to ensure his own position in the succession. He left Madame St Laurent and married the widowed Princess Victoria of Leningen, sister of Leopold, who had been married to Princess Charlotte.

But at the same time, to the mortification of poor Madame St Laurent, who had made a dignified exit to Paris, the Queen Mother at last found a bride for Billy Clarence – Amelie Adelaide, daughter of the late Duke of Saxe Meiningen.

The two dukes were married on the same day, to the great satisfaction of the dying Queen Mother. The Duke of Clarence took his bride to live at Bushey and the Duke of Kent who, between 1806 and 1814, had spent £13,000 on making his Kensington Palace apartments more comfortable, now made them his permanent residence, with his new duchess and her daughter by her previous marriage, Princess Feodora. In 1819 a daughter was born to the Duchess of Kent at Kensington Palace, the witnesses being the Archbishop of Canterbury, the Duke of Wellington and Canning. They called her Victoria. Only nine months later, the Duke died, leaving the Duchess alone at Kensington with her baby daughter and the Princess Feodora, who married eight years later.

The Duke of Sussex lived on in his own quarters, a much loved man who helped many philanthropic causes and was President of the Society of Arts for many years. He was a staunch Whig and was often in conflict with his eldest brother, after he had quarrelled with the Whigs, both for his political views and because he had always been friendly with Caroline. The American ambassador describing a visit to Kensington Palace in the 1820s, when he dined with the Duke, wrote: 'The Duke sat at the head of the table in true old English style, and was full of cordiality and conversation. General principles of government coming to be spoken of, he expatiated on the blessings of free government, declaring that as all men, kings as well as others, were prone to abuse power when they got to possess it, the only safe course was to limit its exercise by the strictest constitutional rules.'

Another Royal resident at the palace was the Princess Sophia, the fifth of George III's daughters. She was born in 1777 and from a child had developed a passion for Thomas Garth, a Royal equerry who was thirty-three years older than herself. In 1799 she retired from Court for a time, suffering from some undiagnosed indisposition, and it was later revealed that she had had a son by Garth, though presumably without the King's knowledge, for Garth remained at Court and the King was particularly fond of him.

Princess Sophia returned to Court and attended the King and Queen, occasionally seeing her son in secret, but the romance with Garth seems to have petered out. With the death of Queen Charlotte and George III within a few months of each other in 1820, Princess Sophia was given apartments at Kensington Palace, on the first floor of the north-east corner of Clock Court, and here her son occasionally visited her. He joined the army but never rose above the rank of captain and, according to Greville, was 'an idiot as well as a rogue'. Old General Garth died in 1829, after which Captain Garth tried to blackmail the Royal Family into giving him an annuity of £3,000 a year in exchange for documents which proved that he was the son of Princess Sophia. The old scandal was revived, but as his parentage had never been in much doubt he found that he was wasting his time. He did not get his annuity and he disappeared, never to be heard of again, while Princess Sophia lived on at Kensington Palace, with her brother, sister-in-law and niece for neighbours.

After his accession, George IV had brought an action for divorce against Queen Caroline in the House of Lords. It was rejected but she was not allowed to attend the Coronation the following year and she left England for the Continent, where, only a few months later, she died.

George IV had deserted Mrs Fitzherbert again, this time for Lady Hertford, and had become extremely unpopular. The Duchess of Kent was hard-pressed for money and it was only because of an allowance from her brother Leopold that she was able to remain at Kensington Palace, for the King gave her nothing, but Leopold's allowance came from the annuity of £50,000 that had been settled on him by the British Parliament when he married Princess Charlotte. George IV died in 1830 and, as the Duke of York had died three

Brompton Square, Kensington

Kensington House, Kensington Road

Kensington Old Parish Church, 1809

Gloucester Lodge, Kensington

Thomas Carlyle's house in Cheyne Row, Chelsea (now No. 24, formerly
No. 5)

Don Salteros' Tavern and Coffee House
Cheyne Walk, Chelsea

Earl of Shaftesbury's house, Little Chelsea

Argyll House, King's Road, Chelsea

William Turner's cottage in Cheyne Walk, Chelsea, *c.* 1870

Cheyne Walk, Chelsea, *c.* 1870

Campden House, Kensington, from the south-east

Cheyne Walk and the Cadogan Pier, 1871

Lawrence Street, Chelsea in 1886 (Nos. 23, 24 and 25)

Exeter Street, Sloane Street, 1888 (Hans Crescent now occupies this site)

Natural History Museum, South Kensington

years earlier, Billy Clarence now came to the throne, as William IV.

He was a great deal more popular as a king than his brother, though he had a difficult temper and was a trial to his ministers.

At Kensington, Princess Sophia's apartments were now enlarged to include 'Queen Caroline's bedchamber, dressing-room, water-closet and little closet'. Princess Victoria had become next in succession to the throne and her mother was appointed Regent if the King died before Victoria was of age. The following year the Duchess' brother Leopold became the King of the Belgians and the Duchess, a rather silly woman, became insufferably full of her own importance. King William disliked her intensely and accused her of preventing him from seeing the little Princess Victoria, of whom he was very fond. This was true enough. The Duchess kept Victoria almost in isolation at Kensington Palace, with only her governess, the Baroness Lehzen, whom the Princess loved dearly, for company. She was never allowed to be alone. Every hour of the day was accounted for and she slept in her mother's room at night. She saw the Duke of Sussex, of whom she was always very fond, and also Princess Sophia but, except when her German cousins came to stay, she had few children to play with and the Duchess was determined to keep her, come what may, from all contact with the bastard Fitzclarences.

As a little girl, Victoria was often to be seen in Kensington Gardens, riding in her small pony carriage or on her donkey, which was a present from the Duke of York. When she was seven, Lord Albemarle records seeing her, in a large straw hat and white cotton dress, watering her plants in the Palace Gardens and, when she was about ten or eleven years old, Leigh Hunt met her in the Gardens, holding the hand of another little girl. 'A magnificent footman in scarlet came behind her, with the splendidest pair of calves in white stockings which we ever beheld.'

Very early in life, the Princess was made aware of her high destiny and despite her simple and secluded upbringing at the palace, her plump little mother, bustling around importantly, with a swirl of velvet skirts and a flurry of ostrich plumes, did all she could to enhance the Princess' prestige in public, as well as her own, the simplest journey to the seaside being turned into a Royal progress, designed to make the Princess of more consequence than the King himself. At the same time she took over an increasing number of the State apartments until in the end she and her household were occupying seventeen rooms.

By the time the Princess was fourteen she had grown resentful of her mother's attitude to her Uncle William, whom she liked, and was uncomfortably aware that her Uncle Leopold of the Belgians was plying her with advice which was not always in accordance with her mother's plans.

The real bone of contention, however, was Sir John Conroy, the Duchess of Kent's confidential secretary. King William was sixty-five when he succeeded to the throne but showed no signs of dying. With Conroy's connivance the Duchess therefore tried to advance the date of the Princess' coming of age, so that there would still be a reasonable chance of the Duchess becoming Regent, with Conroy as the power behind the throne.

Whether the Princess ever learned of this plan is not clear, but she certainly loathed Conroy and he was the cause of many bitter quarrels with her mother. The scandalmongers said that he was the Duchess' lover and that the Princess had once come upon them in each other's arms, though this has never been proved.

Conroy was also controller to Princess Sophia, who was similarly dominated by him, for he cheered her loneliness by flirting with her outrageously. In fact Conroy seems to have been a thoroughly unpleasant character, with few redeeming virtues. Princess Sophia became his willing spy and helped to poison the atmosphere of the palace by trying to procure the dismissal of the Baroness Lehzen and also the Baroness Spath, one of the Duchess' ladies-in-waiting who had dared to reprove her for her 'familiarities' with Conroy and had objected to his trying to gain precedence over her for his own mild and uncomprehending wife.

It was Conroy who, during the reign of George IV, had put about the story that the Duke of Cumberland was plotting to 'do away' with the Princess, but years later Victoria dismissed the story as 'all Sir John's invention and Princess Sophia's fearful falseness'.

By 1835 he was trying to persuade the Princess to promise that, on her accession, he should be her private secretary, but with only the devoted Lehzen to support her, she refused. Her mother was furious but Victoria was adamant. The following year her cousins Prince Ernst and Prince Albert came on a visit to England and from their first meeting Victoria loved Albert, seeing in him not only her future happiness but an escape from her domineering mother.

On her eighteenth birthday, King William sent her by a personal messenger an offer of £10,000 a year, entirely under her own control, an independent Privy Purse and the right to appoint her own ladies-in-waiting. Conroy and the Duchess tried to intercept this letter but failed. However, Conroy insisted on her replying with a letter dictated by himself, in which she accepted the money but declined the privileges, which meant that Conroy still had control of it. She was forced to sign the letter but at the same time dictated to Lehzen an exact account of what had happened.

As the King's final illness advanced the Princess had a last bitter quarrel with her mother about Conroy, but she was still only her mother's daughter and the affronted Duchess made the grave mistake of locking her up in her room in disgrace.

On 20 June 1837, shortly after two o'clock in the morning, King William died at Windsor. The Archbishop of Canterbury, Lord Conyngham, the Lord Chamberlain, and the King's physician set out at once for Kensington Palace. At six o'clock the Princess was awakened and led down to a sitting-room, which she entered alone, in her dressing-gown, to learn that she was now Queen of England: and at half past eleven that morning, dressed in black, she held her first Privy Council in the Red Saloon of the palace, impressing them all, and particularly Lord Melbourne, with her regal dignity and grace.

Behind the scenes, she dismissed Conroy from her household forthwith and had her bed moved from her mother's room. When the Duchess asked if there were anything she could do for her, the Queen replied: 'I should like to be left alone', and that night, for the first time in her life, she had dinner by herself, after a private talk with her Prime Minister, Lord Melbourne, who was to be such a dear and valued friend and adviser during the first difficult years of her reign.

Less than four weeks later she had left Kensington for Buckingham Palace. 'It was the *last time* that I slept at the poor old Palace,' she wrote in her diary for Thursday 13 July. 'I have gone through painful and disagreeable scenes here, 'tis true, but still I am fond of the poor old Palace . . . the poor rooms look so sad and deserted, everything being taken away.'

The Duchess of Kent also left Kensington and was given apartments in Buckingham Palace, though at a distance from the Queen's, and in 1839 Conroy was forced to resign from her household. After this, although the Duchess was for long bitterly jealous of both Lehzen and Lord Melbourne, her relationship with the Queen steadily improved.

Princess Sophia stayed on at Kensington Palace. Living alone with her personal frustrations, she becomes a tragic and sinister figure, as, with failing eyesight, she passed her lonely days at her spinning-wheel or her embroidery frame. In 1838 the cataract which had been threatening for some years made her totally blind and was found to be inoperable. She moved to York House near by, where her quarters were more convenient, but her spirit still haunts Kensington, for there is a story that the humming of her spinning-wheel can sometimes still be heard in the courts and corridors of the dark old palace.

When she died at York House in 1848 she left only £1,600, the assumption being that Conroy had filched most of her fortune from her during her lifetime.

The kind old Duke of Sussex had a far happier end. The wife from whom he had been so long separated died at last and he married the widowed Lady Cecilia Buggin. She was not of royal blood so technically this marriage was also illegal, but Queen Victoria, who had happy childhood memories of her uncle, created her Duchess of Inverness. As the Duke already held the title of Duke of Inverness this made them of equal rank and they lived together in great happiness, partly at Kensington Palace and partly at their small house overlooking Hyde Park; and when the Duke died, in 1843, the Duchess was allowed to stay on at Kensington Palace until her death thirty years later.

When the Hanoverian Court had been at Kensington, Kensington Square had been the most fashionable part of the village, for it was here that many of the ambassadors and courtiers resided, and those who could not find lodging in the Square stayed in the High Street, which by this time was lined with demure little seventeenth- and eighteenth-century houses, or found accommodation in scattered houses to the north, in the area of the old gravel-pits.

York House, where Princess Sophia spent her last years, was on the east side of Church Street, and above it stood Maitland House, the home of James Mill, father of John Stuart Mill. On the death of Lord Lechmere, in 1727, the Campden House estate had been bought by Stephen Pitt, who lived with his family in Little Campden House and let the big house for the young ladies' boarding-school. Orbell's Buildings, where Sir Isaac Newton died, had been thrown into one mansion again, known as Bullingham House. On Campden Hill stood Sheffield House and between Campden Hill and Holland Park was the mansion of Sir Robert Phillimore, who died in 1779. On the gravel-pits, Campden Hill Place and Campden Hill Square had been built, late in the seventeenth century.

From 1767 till 1788 Lady Mary Coke was living at Aubrey House, earlier known as Notting Hill House, her neighbours being Sir Robert Phillimore to the south and the Hollands to the south-west.

Lady Mary thought little of the sermons preached at St Mary Abbots. 'The clergyman did not preach a sermon to please me,' she wrote. 'I like practical discourses from the pulpit, and not historical digressions. He began by saying that the Virgin Mary was of Royal extraction but not having sufficient to support her pedigree, was in a low state. Whether any of his congregation will lead a better life for his informing them of these two circumstances I really can't tell, but I thought he might have said something more to the purpose.'

But she loved her garden, in which stood one of the famous medicinal wells, though she seems to have made no use of its waters for their alleged healing properties. 'I worked hard all day,' she recorded, 'tying up honeysuckles, sowing annuals and weeding. I wish my gardener took half as much pleasure as I do, for my garden would then be better.' And again: ''Tis a delightful day. I have planted a hundred perannual flowers that I had this morning from Mr Lee, but my work was twice interrupted by visitors.'

North of the Uxbridge road stretched open country. Lord Craven's house stood on Craven Hill and not far away was Notting Hill farm. As late as 1820 Faulkner described the Portobello Road as 'one of the most rural and pleasant walks in the summer in the vicinity of London' and in Bayswater Sir John Hill, the Royal gardener, had his physic garden, where he concocted strange herbal remedies of extremely doubtful medicinal value, despite their high prices, such as 'essence of waterdock' and 'Pectoral balsam of honey'.

The old Kensington Gore was a triangle of land with its apex at Knightsbridge and the base running southwards from Queen's Gate, its north side the Gore and its south side about where Gloucester Road and the Brompton Road now run: and until the end of the eighteenth century most of this land was given over to market gardens. On its eastern boundary stood Kent House, where the Duke of Kent lived before he moved to Kensington Palace. Close by was Park House, standing to the north of the Brompton Park nurseries of London and Wise. Rutland House, the home of the Duke of Rutland, was on the borders of Knightsbridge and the Gore, where Rutland Gate now stands, and to the west was Elizabeth Chudleigh's Kingston House.

Gore House had been rebuilt and was now a spacious Georgian villa behind a high brick wall, not unlike Kingston House, except that the first-floor drawing-room had a deep bay window, surmounted by a balustrade, built over the porch. Here lived a rich but parsimonious financier called Morgan, but in 1808 the house was taken by William Wilberforce. 'We are just one mile from the turn-pike gate at Hyde Park, yet having three acres of pleasure-ground around my house, or rather behind it, and several old trees, walnut and mulberry, of thick foliage,' he wrote, soon after he had moved there. 'I can sit and read under their shade, which I delight in doing, with as much admiration of the beauties of nature . . . as if I was 200 miles from the great city.'

The four other important houses in the Gore were Noël House, built in 1804, Grove House, close to Gore House, Colby House and Kensington House, where a few years after James Elphinstone left it, in 1778, the French Jesuits moved in to found their school.

North of the High Street, Lower Phillimore Place and Hornton Street were put up by speculative builders towards the end of the century and in the High Street itself, on the south side, where Ponting's store was later to be built, stood Scarsdale House, a late Tudor building which had been the home of the Scarsdale family until it was turned into yet another eighteenth-century boarding-school for young ladies. To the east, Young Street, leading into Kensington Square, had been begun by Young about the same time that he was building the houses in the Square. After the departure of the Court and its attendants, men of letters and retired army officers moved into Kensington Square and in 1792 Talleyrand arrived there, having escaped from Paris five days after the September massacres. He lodged at a house which has since been converted into numbers 36 and 37. Farther west, off the south side of the High Street, Wright's Lane was a row of neat villas built in 1774. Allen Street was not yet built but in the fields to the west Edwardes Square was laid out, to-wards the end of the century, by another speculative builder – a Frenchman this time, called Changier.

Edwardes Square is much larger than Kensington Square, though the houses, particularly on the east and west sides, are smaller, built in attractive terraces. They have three storeys and basements, tall sash-windows on the first floor and small paved courtyards in front. The spacious garden was planted with lawns, trees and shrubs and the gardener's lodge, which still stands, was built in the form of a small Greek temple.

Changier did not finish the Square. He failed and owing £100,000 he retired hastily to France, leaving the houses in the hands of his creditors.

South of Kensington High Street, the hamlet of Earls Court was approached by an avenue of elms, from which ran country lanes with a few isolated cottages and country houses, the most important of which was the manor-house, tenanted by the Hutchinson family, who cultivated a near-by farm.

In 1764 John Hunter, the great surgeon and physiologist, bought two acres of land in Earls Court, where he built a neat villa known as Earls Court House, which he gradually enlarged as his fortunes improved and where he lived until his death in 1793.

Hunter, realising that physiology was as essential to the surgeon as a knowledge of anatomy, made experiments and lengthy observations on animals, birds, fishes and insects, all of which he kept in the garden at Earls Court. The menagerie also included two leopards, a number of buffaloes, which he kept in order to observe the results of cross-breeding, and a small bull, which was presented to him by Queen Charlotte. In his pond he laid an oyster bed where he experimented on the artificial formation of pearls and in his kitchen he boiled the skeleton of the Irish giant O'Byrne, who attained the height of eight feet four inches. The copper in which this operation took place was long preserved as a showpiece for visitors and the skeleton ended up in the museum of the Royal College of Surgeons.

One of Hunter's most distinguished pupils was Edward Jenner, whose statue now stands in Kensington Gardens.

Next to Hunter's attractive villa Gunter the confectioner built a far more ostentatious house, set in sixty acres of land, with famous hothouses, orchards and kitchen gardens.

Near by, where Colehearne Mansions now stand, was Colehearne House, rebuilt by Wren on the site of an earlier house, but all the land to the east, which is now covered by the maze of Victorian museums and houses and is known broadly as South Kensington, was fields and gardens and shady country lanes. Walnut Tree Walk, now Redcliffe Gardens, joined Earls Court to Little Chelsea, and Selwood Terrace was then Sallad Lane. Gloucester Road was Hogmire Lane, shaded with trees and with a stone causeway in the middle. It ran from Brompton past Gloucester Lodge, a small classical villa set in six acres of garden, built by the Duchess of Gloucester, after her secret marriage to the Duke, a younger brother of George III. Her daughter, Princess Sophia of Gloucester, inherited it on her mother's death, in 1807, and sold it two years later to George Canning, who lived there for the rest of his life. Little Chelsea was a tiny hamlet in the midst of the fields and gardens of Old Brompton, which stretched from the Fulham Road to Knightsbridge.

Eight nurserymen had their gardens here, covering in all 124 acres. The largest firm, with thirty acres, were Gray and Company, the successors to London and Wise.

In their midst Hale House, which later was to be given its original name of Cromwell House, still stood. In 1754 Sir John Fleming bought it from the Methwold family and on his death it passed to his daughter, the Countess of Harrington, whose family held it until the Commissioners of the 1851 Exhibition bought it and built the Victoria and Albert Museum on the site.

To the south, where Onslow Square now stands, the Earls of Onslow lived in Onslow House.

By the end of the eighteenth century the population of Kensington had reached about 8,600. St Mary Abbots was still the only church and the seventeenth-century building, which had seemed so spacious when it replaced the medieval church, was becoming far too small. The old tower, which had been retained when the church was rebuilt, had become dangerous, and in 1772 it had to be pulled down and a new red-brick one built to take its place, but it was not until the middle of the nineteenth century that a new and larger church was built.

XIV

Holland House in the Early Nineteenth Century

WHILE the intrigues and quarrels of Conroy and the Duchess of Kent were taking place at Kensington Palace, Holland House, which had taken on an air of decay and melancholy during the childhood of the third Lord Holland, now revived and entered the most illustrious period of its history.

After leaving Oxford, Henry, Lord Holland, spent several years travelling on the Continent and in 1794, when he was twenty-one, he met the twenty-three-year-old Lady Webster. Elizabeth Webster had been born Elizabeth Vassall and when she and Henry met in Naples she had already had five children, of whom three had survived, and she was travelling with her husband, Sir Godfrey Webster, to whom she had been married when she was fifteen.

Elizabeth was beautiful, very intelligent and an heiress to her father's Jamaican fortune. Sir Godfrey, more than twice her age, was a drunkard and a gambler, ill-tempered and always short of money. Elizabeth was desperately unhappy and their home at Battle Abbey she described as 'a detested spot where I have languished in solitude and discontent the best years of my life'.

Henry and Elizabeth were soon deeply in love. 'Ld. H. is not handsome,' Elizabeth confided to her diary. 'He has on the contrary many personal defects, but his pleasingness of manner and liveliness of conversation get over them speedily.'

Already he was suffering from the gout which was to undermine his health all his life, but nevertheless she found him 'quite delightful. His gaiety beyond anything I ever knew.'

The Websters separated. Sir Godfrey returned to Battle Abbey and Elizabeth and Henry spent the next year or two travelling through Europe. Early in 1796 Elizabeth was pregnant and they returned to Kensington, but not yet to Holland House, their son Charles Richard being born at Brompton Park. The same year Elizabeth's father died, leaving her an income of £10,000 a year.

They were anxious to marry but Sir Godfrey made things as difficult as possible, insisting on an outright payment of £6,000 and, in addition, £8,000 a year of Elizabeth's income, as well as custody of the children, before he would consent to bring an action for divorce.

Henry and Elizabeth were so much in love that they accepted these monstrous terms and two days after the divorce they were married: and now that their position was regularised, they moved into Holland House and Henry took his place in the Lords, as a Whig.

They were both as enchanted with the old house as with each other. 'I have determined to make it both a town and country house and my regular and permanent residence,' wrote Henry to his sister Caroline, and only a few years later, in 1804, Caroline, who never married, though she could count Jeremy Bentham among her suitors, moved with her step-aunt into Little Holland House, a farm just to the south-west of the big house, which their grandfather had bought shortly after he had acquired the estate in 1768.

Elizabeth was shunned by the Court of George III and the more rigid leaders of society, because of her divorce, but she was too vital to be unduly concerned by their attempted ostracism and set about creating her own salon. Henry was only twenty-five when he delivered his maiden speech in the Lords, in 1798, but at once established himself as a worthy disciple of his uncle, Charles James Fox, following the best traditions of the eighteenth century Whig aristocrats. Ill-health had made him old for his years and he had already become a man of deep humanity and peace, a champion of freedom and, like many of his Whig friends at this time, and also Elizabeth, a sympathiser with Napoleon, seeing him as a child of the Revolution, born to lead the people of France to freedom from the oppression of the Bourbons.

In 1800, Webster, still incapable of managing his financial affairs and overcome with gambling debts, committed suicide. This meant that Elizabeth regained her fortune, though not her children, for Sir Godfrey had committed them to the care of a brother-in-law.

The money was to be extremely useful for the lavish entertainment on which she now embarked. A greater part of it, however, came from West Indian estates which were maintained by slave labour, and as the opposition to the slave trade increased and the slaves were eventually emancipated, her income dwindled. The emancipation of the slaves was brought about partly by her husband's work, but Elizabeth was too honest a thinker to protest and William Wilberforce, who by 1808 was living close by, at Gore House, was a frequent and always welcome visitor at Holland House.

Few women were among their guests but an increasing number of distinguished Whigs and men of letters, for the hospitality was generous and the conversation brilliant, Lord Holland's easy charm a foil to Lady Holland's sometimes overbearing and dictatorial manners.

In 1798 they entertained the Prince of Wales, with the Duke of Norfolk, Lord Suffolk, Lord Bessborough and the three young Whigs who were quickly rising to fame, Charles Gray, George Tierney and Samuel Whitbread. The Prince of Wales was strongly attached to the Whigs at this time, though when he became Regent he was to quarrel with them and change sides, mainly because of their opposition to the Regency Bill and their criticism of his treatment of Caroline, as Princess and Queen. Moreover he disliked Lord Holland's attitude to the Bourbons.

Many French visitors came to Holland House and Sheridan, Sydney Smith, Henry Luttrell and Samuel Rogers were among the regular guests, as well as Canning in the early days, before the national danger in the face of Napoleon's growing strength in Europe induced him to change his loyalty to Pitt.

The Duke of York, the Duke of Clarence and the Duke of Sussex were all to be met at Holland House from time to time and the Duke of Clarence was particularly fond of Lord Holland. Many years later, the Holland's illegitimate son, Charles Richard Fox, was to marry Mary Fitzclarence, so that the friendship continued after the Duke became William IV.

A permanent resident in the Holland household was Dr John Allen, who had first come to them, on the recommendation of Sydney Smith, in 1801, as a physician to their eldest son, Charles Richard, who was delicate. A second son, born in 1800, had died in infancy. The third, Henry Edward, born two years later, was also delicate, with a malformed leg. Mary, born in 1806, was a charming girl who ultimately married Lord Lilford, but the second daughter died in childhood and the third in infancy.

Dr Allen therefore stayed on at Holland House as physician to the family and also as the librarian, for he was a distinguished man of letters as well as a doctor, and as Lord Holland became increasingly crippled with gout, the cultured and good-natured Dr Allen became indispensable, acting as joint-host and making the entries in the Dinner Book, which Lady Holland had begun in 1799, as a record of her guests.

One of the earliest entries was the name of young William Lamb, whose first visit was in 1799, when he was twenty.

'William Lamb, a rising young genius, dines here for the first time today,' noted Lady Holland. 'Pleasant though superior' was her next verdict. 'Clever and agreeable and will improve when he gets over his love of singularity.'

During the early years of his career, William Lamb's life revolved round the four great Whig houses of London, Carlton House, Devonshire House, Holland House and his own home, Melbourne House, in Whitehall, where the family moved in 1789, after the Duke of York had expressed a fancy for their old home in Piccadilly and they had exchanged residences. It was at Devonshire House that William had met and fallen in love with Caroline, the daughter of the Duchess of Devonshire's sister, Lady Bessborough.

They were married in 1804 and although they were happy for a few years the unstable Caroline soon became impossible. One of her first love affairs was with Lady Holland's son by her first marriage, another Sir Godfrey Webster, a young rake who had inherited all his father's faults and none of his mother's graces.

Caroline soon met the full force of the indignation of Lady Bessborough, Lady Melbourne and Lady Holland, a formidable trio, and when Lady Holland said she was ready to admit that the affair was nothing more than an attempt on Caroline's part to attract attention to herself, the infuriated Caroline wrote back: 'As to the gnats and mites that dare to peck at me, let them look to themselves. If I choose, you shall see them lick the dust I tread on. Lady Holland, if this is the case, I shall be courted by you. . . . I remain more sincerely than you deserve, Caroline Lamb.'

By the summer of 1812 it was all over. Caroline declared that she was tired of Sir Godfrey and he was certainly bored with her, for he quietly vanished from the scene.

From early in that year the Hollands had welcomed the twenty-four-year-old Lord Byron to Holland House, not only for his radical views but for his literary gifts and his friendship with two of their established circle, Samuel Rogers and Thomas Moore. Byron was at his most charming in those days and was particularly fond of little Henry Fox, then ten years old, who, like himself, was lame.

When in March 1812, Byron published the first part of *Childe Harold*, he became a literary lion overnight. Everyone wanted to meet him, including Caroline Lamb. 'I must meet him. I am dying to meet him,' she declared to Samuel Rogers.

Her opportunity came when they both attended the same ball in London. Caroline asked for him to be presented to her. She waited dramatically as he was led forward to her, stared at him for a moment and then suddenly turned away, without speaking a word. That night she wrote in her diary: 'Bad, mad and dangerous to know.'

Two days later they met again at dinner at Holland House. Byron was far from cordial at first but before the evening was over they had agreed to meet again and their strange love affair was launched, though the truth of what really passed between them is difficult to trace, for as David Cecil says in his life of Lord Melbourne, 'they were both such confirmed liars, both so bent at all costs on making out a good cause for themselves, that it was impossible to trust a word that either says'.

This capricious affair did not impair Lord Holland's friendship with Byron. They collaborated in several literary works and, after Byron's marriage in 1815, he brought his wife to dine at Holland House on at least two occasions. When the marriage broke up the following year, Lord Holland acted as intermediary. Shortly afterwards, Byron went abroad and he died, in Greece, in 1824.

Lord Holland became a Privy Councillor and after the death of his uncle, in 1806, was made Lord Privy Seal, with a seat in the Cabinet, but as the Tories gained power and his prospects of being a Whig Prime Minister faded, he widened his interests to include literature as well as politics, though still stoutly maintaining his liberal views and his opposition to the war with France.

He wrote the Life of Lope de Vega and also a biography of Guillende Castro and both he and Lady Holland wrote verse. The *Edinburgh Review* was founded by members of the Holland House circle – Francis Jeffrey, Sydney Smith, Francis Horner and Henry Brougham, and Lady Holland sometimes corrected the proofs.

After the death of Charles James Fox, the Whigs, sorely lacking a leader, were divided, falling into three main groups, the Grenvillites, who formed the right wing, the Foxites of the Holland House Circle and 'The Mountain', which represented the most practical and vigorous reformers. The Foxites were more academic and intransigent and thus it came about that long after Napoleon had revealed himself as a dictator and had proclaimed himself emperor, the Hollands were still supporting him as the liberator of France.

In 1802 they had met him in Paris and Lady Holland, like most women, had been captivated by his voice, 'so melodious that no heart can resist'.

Talleyrand, another visitor at Holland House, had supported Napoleon for years, and when he turned against him Lady Holland accused him of treachery, but Lord Holland began to have second thoughts. Nevertheless, he was successful in pleading with the Government that Napoleon be treated with less harshness during his captivity, and in this he was warmly supported by the Duke of Sussex.

When Napoleon was living on Elba, the Hollands, staying at the time in Italy, sent him English newspapers, and on his return to Paris they were against the renewal of the war with France, saying that he should be given another chance to prove himself.

Even after Waterloo and his confinement on St Helena, they obtained permission to send him books and many other gifts, including some of Lady Holland's plum jam. He never wrote to them but they received a grateful letter from his mother and, when he died in 1823, it was found that he had left Lady Holland a gold snuff box, in which he had placed a brief note of thanks.

For a few years, Holland House was the centre of the English Napoleonists and in 1816 Louis Napoleon even consulted Lord Holland about his chances of being allowed to live in England, but gradually the Hollands began to take a more rational and realistic view of Napoleon and the position which they held for so long as the centre of fashionable Whig society was maintained.

People sometimes left the circle, as, for example, Henry Brougham, who did not visit Holland House from 1810 until 1816, but then, with Napoleon a lost cause and the war with France over, he asked to return and was received with all the old warmth.

There was no rancour. The ideas discussed so freely at Holland House were, in a sense, above politics, and many Tories were invited there as well as Whigs, if they had something to contribute to intellectual and literary life.

There was nothing quite like this place in all Europe, a lovely old Jacobean country mansion, so close to London yet set in beautiful grounds and run in eighteenth-century splendour, with a steward to supervise the butler and footmen, the pages and gentlewomen-in-waiting, and the army of household servants.

Nearly every evening of the week, when the Hollands were in residence, distinguished Whigs could be seen driving through the fields of Kensington to dine or stay at Holland House. After dark the way was dangerous, for footpads still lurked in the country lanes and around the turnpike, and because of this the Hollands often took a house in London for brief periods, during the winter, for Lady Holland was far too nervous to undertake the drive to Kensington after a theatre or evening party. In 1821, when Lord Holland was at Ampthill for a day or two, she was writing to her son Henry: 'Dear Papa will return, I trust, before footpad hour . . .'

Dinner was usually served in the Gilt Room, the guests assembling in the large drawing-room behind it. It was often extremely cold, for the old house was draughty, and the tables, more often than not, were overcrowded, but no one minded, even though Lady Holland could at times be tiresomely overbearing, insisting on her guests changing places at the last minute and indulging in similar irritating fads. She even seemed to dominate her husband and sometimes ordered him about with a harsh brusqueness, but he took it in good part, knowing that fundamentally she adored him, as he did her. For all her eccentricities, Lady Holland never forgot that Lord Holland was the presiding genius of the house and the magnet which drew the visitors.

The food and wine at Holland House were impeccable and she was an excellent hostess, generous and kind-hearted beneath an austere manner, interested in all new thought and always willing to give help if it were needed. Most people enjoyed themselves thoroughly during their visits, though she had been known to cause a young guest agonies of embarrassment by summoning him to her room to talk, while her page Edgar knelt at her feet and, plunging his hands beneath her skirts, proceeded to rub her legs to ease her rheumatism.

During these years the gardens at Holland House were carefully tended and early in their residence the Dutch garden was established. The house itself needed constant attention and was a never-ending source of expense, the worst calamity being in 1832, when the rain suddenly poured through the roof of Lady Holland's dressing-room. It was about this time that a new heating system was installed, which at least made the house more comfortable for Lord Holland, with his increasingly severe gout.

By this time Lord Holland had been obliged to sell some of his land for building developments and by the 1830s new houses had been built to the west of the estate, on the east side of the new Addison Road. Kensington was growing, for Edwardes Square was completed and also Earl's Terrace, the row of twenty-five large houses facing on to the High Street, on which building had begun about 1811.

In 1820 the Tory Sir Walter Scott was invited to Holland House and he paid another visit in 1828, after which Lady Holland wrote to her son:

'... W. Scott dined & slept here Saturday. He was remarkably entertaining, full of legendary lore; some of his anecdotes he told admirably & briefly. . . . I never saw any person admire more this lovely place. The day was bright and fine; the nightingales in full song, & the rich blossoms and foliage quite magnificent.'

In 1830, with the fall of Wellington and Peel's Tory Government, the Whigs at last came to power, but by this time Lord Holland's gout was so severe that, for weeks at a time, he was confined to a wheeled chair, while Lady Holland had become very stout. Lord Holland was not well enough to accept the post of Foreign Secretary, which otherwise he could have filled so admirably, but was given the Chancellorship of the Duchy of Lancaster and a seat in the Cabinet.

Restrictions had been removed from Dissenters in 1828 and the Catholics had been emancipated the following year. The suppression of colonial slavery and their full emancipation were to come very soon, but the Reform Bill was the most important issue facing the new Government, and during the debates Lady Holland met, for the first time, Macaulay, then a young man of thirty, newly-elected as a Whig member of Parliament, and invited him to dine at Holland House.

He described her as a 'large bold-looking woman, with the remains of a fine person, and the air of Queen Elizabeth'. As for Lady Holland, she had been told that Macaulay 'was not pleasant nor good to look at'. Moreover, he was the son of Zachary Macaulay, the abolitionist, and from Lady Holland's viewpoint, as a plantation owner, 'the bitterest foe to all W. India's concerns'. Nevertheless, she took to young Macaulay, despite his lack of aristocratic pedigree, and he mightily enjoyed his visit, the first of many. He hired a glass coach to take him to Kensington, approaching the house 'through a fine avenue of elms'. Holland House, he told his sister, consisted of 'a considerable number of very large and comfortable rooms, rich with antique carving and gilding, but carpeted and furnished with all the skill of the best modern upholsterers'. He admired the library, in which Lord Holland himself had collected 13,000 volumes, and where there was 'almost everything that one ever wished to read', with 'little cabinets for study branching out of it, warmly and snugly fitted up' and he enjoyed 'a most excellent dinner' in the Gilt Room.

Of Lady Holland, Macaulay said: 'She is certainly a woman of considerable talents and great literary acquirements. To me she was excessively gracious; yet there is a haughtiness in her courtesy which, even after all that I had heard of her, surprised me. The centurion did not keep his soldiers in better order than she keeps her guests. It is to one "Go", and he goeth; and to another "Do this", and it is done. "Ring the bell, Mr Macaulay", "Lay down that screen, Lord Russell; you will spoil it", "Mr Allen, take a candle and show Mr Cradock the picture of Bonaparte". Lord Holland is, on the other hand, all kindness, simplicity and vivacity . . .'

It was in 1832, the year that the Reform Bill became law, that Macaulay met Talleyrand at Holland House. He was, he said, 'the greatest curiosity I ever fell in with. His head is sunk down between two high shoulders. One of his feet is hideously distorted. His face is as pale as that of a corpse and wrinkled to a frightful degree. His eyes have an odd glassy stare, quite peculiar to them. His hair, thickly powdered and pomatumed, hangs down on each side as straight as a pound of tallow candles. His conversation, however, soon makes you forget his ugliness and infirmities . . .'

Between 1830 and 1834 William IV dined five times at Holland House and there were other grand occasions when the entire Whig Cabinet was entertained. In 1831 Louis Napoleon came to dinner, and both Charles Greville and Thomas Creevey were visitors during the thirties, but Macaulay became a personal friend of the Hollands, received informally and with unfailing warmth.

In 1834 Lord Grey retired and Lord Melbourne became Prime Minister, still the cynical and rather remote man he had been when he had first visited Holland House more than thirty years earlier, as William Lamb. He had been wonderfully loyal to Caroline through the years of her increasing insanity, and a regular visitor to Holland House, but it was not until after Caroline's death, in 1828, that he rose to true political eminence.

In 1837 the twenty-six-year-old Charles Dickens was taken to dine at Holland House and became a firm friend of the ageing Hollands. 'He is . . . very unobtrusive, yet not shy, intelligent in countenance, and altogether prepossessing', wrote Lord Holland to his sister Caroline, who two years later met Dickens herself and was 'much struck with him'. 'His countenance I think, beautiful, because blended with its intelligence there is so much expression of goodness,' she recorded.

The only notable musician in the Holland House circle was Tom Moore but it included many artists, notably Landseer, Wilkie, Eastlake, Callcott and Leslie.

Lord Holland was enchanted with the young Queen Victoria when he visited her at Windsor Castle, shortly after her accession, but Lord Melbourne had to warn Lady Holland that the Queen could not receive her because of the divorce, even though it was such ancient history by now. However, in 1839 the Hollands were delighted by a visit from Prince Albert at Holland House.

It was the last time they were to receive royalty, for in October 1840 Lord Holland died. 'This wretched day closes all the happiness, refinement and hospitality within the walls of Holland House,' wrote Lady Holland in the Dinner Book.

By this time her children were all married and she could not bear to stay in the house alone. She spent most of her time in London, first at her house in South Street and then in Great Stanhope Street. Sometimes she stayed with Caroline at Little Holland House and would stroll over to visit her old home, but she could not endure 'a *stillness* that strikes to the heart, and drives me away'.

After a while she opened the ground floor and stayed there for a month or two, entertaining some of her old friends, including Greville, Dickens, Macaulay, Dr Allen and a new friend, Brunel, but in 1843 Dr Allen died, in 1845 Caroline, and a few months later both Sydney Smith and his brother Bobus. She had no heart left to visit Holland House again, for she had lost too much, and in November of that same year, after a short illness, she died, and Holland House came into the possession of her son Henry, the fourth and last Lord Holland.

XV

Kensington in the Early Nineteenth Century

ALTHOUGH Kensington was to retain its air of an exclusive country town for many years to come, early in the nineteenth century it was beginning to spread.

By the time of Queen Victoria's accession, St Mary Abbots Terrace, Upper and Lower Phillimore Place, to the north of the High Street, and Edwardes Square and Pembroke Square to the south had been built, as well as the villas to the east of the Addison Road and St Barnabas Church, which had gone up in 1826. The large, detached houses on Campden Hill, called the Dukeries because of the many titled and aristocratic residents, were standing and in 1825 Sir James South, one of the founders of the Royal Astronomical Society, had established his observatory there. Cam House was originally Bedford Lodge, the Kensington home of the Duke and Duchess of Bedford, Argyll Lodge the home of the Duke and Duchess of Argyll and Bute House the residence of the Duke of Rutland. On the east side of the hill, Macaulay was to make his home at Holly Lodge from 1856 till his death in 1859.

By 1840 more houses, cottages, streets and squares were being built round Notting Hill, Campden Hill, Kensington Gore and Earls Court and streets such as Peel Street, Campden Street and Bedford Gardens were linking Campden Hill and Church Street.

Rutland Gate was built in 1830, about the same time as Addison Road, and the nursery gardens of Brompton Park and Little Chelsea began to disappear as the Brompton Road, Brompton Square and Brompton Church were built.

In 1843 Palace Green was laid out and by the 1850s the building of the mansions in Kensington Palace Gardens had begun. The first Knightsbridge barracks had gone up in 1794 and the charming little houses in Yeoman's Row, which were still standing until the 1960s, were built for some of the officers' quarters. Parts of Montpelier Square, Montpelier Place and Montpelier Walk were also built about this time, though others did not go up until the Regency or a few years later.

Yet Kensington High Street remained narrow and winding, still keeping its eighteenth-century air, with its little Georgian houses and shuttered shops and the twenty-two public houses in between. In 1819 William Cobbett, the champion of radicalism, returned from America with the bones of Tom Paine and settled here, in a house standing just about where Kensington High Street station now lies. He established a small seed farm and it was from here that he set forth, a year or two later, on his 'Rural Rides', the accounts appearing at first in the *Weekly British Register*. At number 32 in the High Street, Breeze and James, linen-drapers, had been established in 1810 and 'enjoyed the distinguished patronage of H.M. the Queen when she was Princess Victoria and made her home at Kensington Palace'. By the time Joseph Toms had established his small shop in the High Street, in 1854, as a 'Toy and Fancy Repository', Breeze and James, renamed Coburg House after the Queen's marriage, had changed hands and was eventually to become John Bell and Company, but it was not till 1862 that Joseph Toms took as a partner Charles Derry.

In Knightsbridge Benjamin Harvey opened a small linen draper's shop in 1813 and was still in business on his own till the late 1850s, while in 1849 Henry Charles Harrod took over a little grocery business in the Brompton Road.

In 1800 the population of Kensington was 8,600 but by 1841 it had risen to 27,000, for as well as members of the aristocracy, writers, artists and the more successful members of the acting profession were settling in its peaceful surroundings, away from the fog and noise of London.

One of its most interesting residents at this time was Elizabeth Inchbald, the actress, novelist and dramatist. She was the daughter of a Roman Catholic farmer, born near Bury St Edmunds in 1753, and when she was eighteen she left home for London, with few possessions and very little money, determined to become an actress. After many adventures she sought the advice of the actor, Inchbald, whom she had once met, and he straightway asked her to marry him, for she was a beautiful and intelligent girl. She agreed and was thereby launched on the stage, but seven years later Inchbald died. She continued to act in London and Scottish theatres until 1789, when she left the stage and concentrated on writing.

She was always hard-pressed for money but she was thrifty, as well as being a kind and generous soul, and at great personal sacrifice she managed to support an invalid sister for many years. The two novels which brought her fame were *A Simple Story*, published in 1791, and *Nature and Art*, which came out in 1796, but she also wrote a farce, *The Mogul Tale*, produced in 1784, and within the next eleven years nine more plays and farces.

Mary Shelley, Godwin's daughter, wrote of her: 'Living in mean lodgings, dressed with an economy allied to penury, without connections, and alone, her beauty, her talents, and the charm of her manners gave her entrance into a delightful circle of society. Apt to fall in love and desirous to marry, she continued single because the men who loved and admired her were too worldly to take an actress and a poor author, however lovely and charming, for a wife.'

One of the men with whom Elizabeth was secretly in love was her doctor, the elderly Doctor Warren, and at one time she was said to pace up and down Sackville Street purely for the pleasure of seeing the light in his window.

In 1816, the year that the body of Shelley's first wife Harriet, who had deserted him, was taken from the Serpentine and carried to the old Fox and Bull Inn in Knightsbridge, Elizabeth Inchbald was seeking lodgings in Kensington. She called first at a small house in the Gore near Kingston House, but disliked what was offered her. 'The furniture was crazy', she said. She would not have accepted the first floor, had it been offered her for nothing, and one of her big trunks would have taken up half the bedroom.

For the next year or two she moved from one boarding-house in Kensington to another. In 1818, by which time she was sixty-five, she arrived at Mrs Voysey's in Leonard's Place. 'All the old widows and old maids of this house are stretched upon their beds or sofas, with swollen legs, nervous headaches, or slow fevers; brought on by loss of appetite, broken sleep, and other dog-day complaints; while I am the only young and strong person among them, and am called upon to divert their blue devils from bringing them to an untimely end,' she wrote. 'I love to be of importance; and so the present society is flattering to my vanity.'

She then moved to number 4 Earl's Terrace, so that, like the residents of Edwardes Square behind it, she would have been entitled to a key of the gardens, but she did not stay there long. She ended up at Kensington House, from which the Jesuits had departed and which was now a Roman Catholic boarding-house: and here on 1 August 1821, she died, her death being attributed to tight lacing. She had felt the first symptoms of illness in 1819 when 'after undressing for bed, she felt a sensation of tightness in her waist, which she naturally enough attributed to the habit of drawing rather too closely the strings of her under apparel', and the resultant inflammation 'awaited only the excitement of a cold to render her recovery impracticable', wrote her biographer.

William Wilberforce lived with his family at Gore House until 1823 and during the fifteen years of his residence it became the centre of many philanthropic movements, besides the cause of the slaves, and there was a host of famous names among the constant stream of visitors, including James Stephen, his brother-in-law, who lived close by, Zachary Macaulay, Clarkson and Pitt.

Before he moved to Brompton, for reasons of economy, Wilberforce had enlarged Gore House, so that it contained a dining-room, drawing-room, library, two studies, a long gallery and ten bed and dressing-rooms. After 1823 it was occupied by the Honourable T. Windsor for some time but from 1833 it stood empty until the arrival of Lady Marguerite Blessington in 1836.

Born in 1789, Marguerite was the daughter of Edmund Power, a small Irish landowner who forced her into marriage, at the age of fourteen, to a drunken army captain called Farmer, who was as brutal and ill-tempered as her own father. The beautiful Marguerite soon left him and when, in 1817, he fell from a window and was killed, it left her free to marry her lover, the Earl of Blessington, who was an ostentatious and rather stupid man but a distinct improvement on the other two men in her life.

Marguerite had already begun to write and when she and her new husband embarked on a long European tour they visited Byron in Genoa. Accompanying them on their travels was Blessington's fifteen-year-old daughter by an earlier marriage and also Count Alfred d'Orsay, a young French aristocrat who had survived the Revolution. Lord Blessington was so fond of d'Orsay that he persuaded him to marry the daughter, so that he might acquire some of the Blessington fortune. This d'Orsay obligingly did, in Naples, in 1827, to the annoyance of the daughter, who disliked him.

Two years later Lord Blessington died in Paris of apoplexy. Marguerite decided to return to London and the Count went with her, his young wife preferring to remain in Paris.

With the money inherited from Blessington, Marguerite and d'Orsay set up house together, first at Seamore Place and then at Gore House, by which time Marguerite was forty-four and the Count thirty-three. Shocked comments and scandalous rumours buzzed through London society, but they survived them all and proceeded to hold court at Gore House, attracting into their circle distinguished poets, novelists, journalists, actors, artists and French exiles.

As at Holland House, there were more men than women visitors, because of the unorthodox ménage, but they included Lord Holland, the Duke of Wellington, Lord Brougham, Lord Douro, Sir Edwin Landseer, Thomas Campbell, Tom Moore, Samuel Rogers, Walter Savage Landor, Bulwer Lytton, Thackeray, Dickens, John Forster, Byron's mistress, the Countess Guiccioli, and Prince Louis Napoleon.

Louis Napoleon dined there the night before his abortive landing at Boulogne in 1840 and puzzled the guests, who knew nothing of his immediate plans, by inviting them all to dine with him at the Tuileries a year hence: and it was not until several days later, when they heard of his failure at Boulogne, his capture and imprisonment at the fortress at Ham, that they understood. On the first day of his arrival in London, after his escape from Ham, in 1846, Louis Napoleon dined again at Gore House with Lady Blessington and Count d'Orsay, the company including Walter Savage Landor and John Forster, whom he entertained with an account of his adventures.

Neither Marguerite nor the Count had any sense of the value of money. They entertained lavishly and enjoyed their life of luxury. In the library, with its dark green carpet, its deep-fringed green damask curtains and damask-covered chairs, they had collected ten thousand volumes, and Marguerite had strips of mirror glass placed between the tiers of bookshelves and on the panels of the door to give the room lightness and make it one of the most beautiful in Kensington.

She had inherited £2,000 a year from Blessington and made a fairly good income from her writing. Her first novel appeared in 1833 and by 1847 she had published nearly a dozen more: and she edited the annual *Book of Beauty* and *The Keepsake*. Nevertheless, her reckless expenditure was soon far exceeding her resources.

D'Orsay was a very handsome and elegant man and without much justification laid claim to being an artist and sculptor. He was inordinately fond of dress and was known as the 'grand master of the dandies'. He was 'one of the padded men who wear the stays', sporting the skin-tight trousers and cut-away, tailored coats with high-standing collars, which were men's last sartorial fling after the Regency, before they settled down to the sober black clothes of mid-Victorian times.

Jane Carlyle records a visit of d'Orsay to Cheyne Row in 1839. He arrived in a blue and silver coach, with prancing horses and attendant flunkeys, wearing 'a skye-blue cravat . . . with white French gloves, light drab surcoat lined with velvet of the same colour, invisible inexpressibles, skin-coloured and fitting like a glove . . . two glorious breast-pins attached by a chain and length enough of gold watch-guard to have hanged himself in . . .'

And Thackeray's daughter recalled a visit he had made to her father when they were living close by, in Young Street. 'Count d'Orsay was the most splendid person I ever remember seeing,' she wrote years later. 'He appeared to us one Sunday morning in the sunshine . . . he seemed to fill the bow window with radiance as if he were Apollo; he leant against his chair with one elbow resting on its back, with shining studs and curls and boots. We could see his horse looking in at us over the blind . . .'

The bills mounted. D'Orsay gambled heavily at Crockford's and usually lost. He earned small amounts with his portrait sketches but Marguerite lost a valuable source of income when the publisher who produced *The Book of Beauty* and *The Keepsake* went bankrupt.

By 1845 d'Orsay's debts alone were estimated at £120,000. They held on for another year or two but by 1849 the bailiffs had arrived. D'Orsay fled to Paris and Marguerite, after arranging for the sale of all her possessions at Gore House, joined him a few weeks later. They sought help from Louis Napoleon, who by now had become President of the Second Republic, but to their shocked dismay he was not interested and a few weeks later Marguerite died, perhaps of grief and despair.

Barry Cornwall, in the epitaph he wrote for her tomb, said: 'In her lifetime she was loved and admired for her many graceful writings, her gentleness, her kind and generous heart', but a French servant, writing to her shortly after she had left for Paris, about the people who had come to view the contents of the house at the time of the sale, said: 'Mr Thackeray was here and there were tears in his eyes as he left. He is perhaps the only person I have seen who was really affected by your departure.'

As for the Count, he survived for only another three years and according to Thackeray, 'he lived without any doubts or remorses, admiring himself in the most horrible pictures which he has painted, and the statues which he gets done for him'. Yet when he lay dying, d'Orsay whispered to a friend, as the tears streamed down his face: 'She was to me a mother! a dear, dear mother! a true, loving mother to me!'

Thackeray had moved to Kensington with his two surviving daughters in 1846, when he was thirty-five. His much loved wife had been incurably insane for several years and the two little girls had spent their early years with their grandparents in Paris. But now, after much house-hunting, he had found a place where they could be together again. Number 13 Young Street, just off the High Street and at the corner of Kensington Square, was a double-fronted Georgian house after Thackeray's heart, with deep bow windows on the ground and first floors, an attic floor and a basement, the front door approached by a neat little flight of steps running up from the pavement: and the High Street at this time his daughter described as 'a noble highway, skirted by beautiful old houses, with scrolled iron gates, behind which were glimpses of big gardens and shady trees.'

Thackeray, in a letter to his mother about the house, said: 'There's a good study for me downstairs and a dining room and a drawing room, and a little court or garden and a little greenhouse: and Kensington Gardens at the gate, and omnibuses every two minutes. What can mortal man want more?'

It was not until late in the autumn that the children came from Paris to join their father. 'It was a dark wintry evening. The fires were lighted, the servants were engaged. Eliza – what family would be complete without its Eliza? – was in waiting to show us our rooms,' wrote Anne Thackeray, who was to become Lady Richie. 'He was away, he had not expected us so early. We saw the drawing room, the empty study; there was the feeling of London – London smelt of tobacco, we thought; we stared out through the uncurtained windows at the dark gardens behind; and then climbing the stairs, we looked in at his bedroom door, and came to our own rooms above it. There were pictures already hung on the walls of the school-room, and of the adjoining fire-lit nursery . . . and the picture of himself as a child he had hung up with his own hands, Eliza told us.'

'My father used to write in his study at the back of the house in

Young Street, said Lady Richie. 'The vine shaded his two windows, which looked out upon the bit of garden, and the medlar tree, and the Spanish jessamine of which the yellow flowers scented our old brick walls. . . . The top schoolroom was over my father's bedroom, and the bedroom was over the study. . . . I liked the top schoolroom the best of all the rooms in the dear old house, the sky was in it and the evening bells used to ring into it across the garden, and seemed to come in dancing and clanging with the sunset. . . . And then there was a mystery – a small trap-door between the windows which we never could open. Where did that trap-door lead to! It was the gateway of paradise, of many paradises to us.'

The house is still standing but today it looks sadly grimy and neglected, engulfed by Barker's store which reaches up to its front railings on the north side, while the little garden where the vine and jessamine grew is now a goods yard, through which the delivery vans, so huge that they seem to dwarf the charming old house, trundle backwards and forwards all day long.

Yet through that forlorn-looking doorway the little Thackeray girls used to set out, in their father's bright blue brougham, for Dickens' Christmas parties. Charlotte Brontë passed through it, 'a tiny, delicate, serious little lady, pale, with fair straight hair, and steady eyes. She may be a little over thirty; she is dressed in a little *barège* dress with a pattern of faint green moss. She enters in mittens, in silence, in seriousness.' Among the guests invited to meet the authoress whose books had set all London talking were Jane and Thomas Carlyle, but the party was not a success. 'It was a gloomy and silent evening. Everyone waited for the brilliant conversation which never began at all. Miss Brontë retired to the sofa in the study, and murmured a low word now and then to our kind governess, Miss Truelock. The room looked very dark, the lamp began to smoke a little, the conversation grew dimmer and more dim, the ladies sat around still expectant, my father was too much perturbed by the gloom and the silence to be able to cope with it at all.'

'Do you like London, Miss Brontë?' ventured one of the guests at last.

Another silence, a pause, then Miss Brontë answers, 'Yes and No', very gravely.

Soon afterwards she left and poor Thackeray, unable to endure any more of that disastrous evening, silently slipped away to his club, leaving the other guests to make the best they could of the rest of the party.

A guest who was always gay and ever welcome, however, was John Leech, the *Punch* artist, who had a house in the High Street.

The Thackerays lived in Young Street until 1855 and during these years Thackeray wrote *Vanity Fair*, *Pendennis* and *Henry Esmond*, much of the action of *Esmond* being set in Kensington Square.

John Stuart Mill was a near neighbour, living at number 18 Kensington Square, and it was in this house, in 1835, that the manuscript of the first volume of Carlyle's *French Revolution* was accidentally burned by the housemaid, who used it to light the fire.

Caroline Fox was one of John Stuart Mill's visitors and in 1840 she was writing of his little garden and charming library, his distinguished appearance and beautiful voice. This was the year that Leigh Hunt and his family moved from Upper Cheyne Row to 32 Edwardes Square, where they were to live for the next eleven years, until they moved to Phillimore Terrace for a brief spell and then to Hammersmith, where he died in 1859.

Hunt was happy in Kensington and although he was never well off he was a good deal more affluent than he had been in Upper Cheyne Row.

Lady Richie described meeting him when she was a small girl. 'We were walking across Kensington Square early one morning, when we heard someone hurrying after us and calling my father by his name. A bright-eyed, active old man, with long, wavy white hair and a picturesque cloak flung over one shoulder. . . . I can see him still. . . . My father, stopping short, greeting him kindly and bringing him home with us. . . . There was a sort of eagerness and vividness of manner about the stranger which was very impressive. . . . We wondered at his romantic, foreign looks, and his gaiety and bright eager way. Afterwards we were told that this was Leigh Hunt.'

It was not until he was living in Phillimore Terrace that Leigh Hunt wrote his history of Kensington – *The Old Court Suburb* – which appeared in Dickens' *Household Words* between August 1853 and February 1854, and many of the places he described were to vanish soon afterwards, while a good many had recently been cleared away and replaced by new buildings. Kensington Palace Gardens, for example, he described 'as gradually filling with mansions, some of which are in good taste and others in bad'.

The old church was to remain until 1869, however. Leigh Hunt did not think much of it. 'It is remarkable, as an edifice, for nothing but the smallness and homeliness of its appearance,' he said, 'but it has this curious additional claim to consideration; namely, that what with partial rebuildings, and wholesale repairs, it has been altered, since the year 1683, nearly a dozen times. . . . What were improvements or requirements in some respects, became defacements in others, or things to be wished away. The painted window was meagre; the galleries clogged up a space already too little, and looked as if they would slide into the pews; the pews themselves were too tall, and aggravated that sense of closeness and crowding, to which the increasing population naturally tended, and which is still the first thing that strikes a visitor to the church.' And he noted that, as he wrote, the church was undergoing yet another repair and the pews were being altered and lowered.

As late as 1850 there were still people living in Kensington who remembered the days when pedestrians from London to Knightsbridge went 'in bands sufficient to ensure mutual protection, starting on their journey only at known intervals, of which a bell gave due warning': but during the 1840s many of the old shops and houses at the eastern end of Knightsbridge had been cleared away, including the tobacconist's shop which once stood at the corner, where Wilton Place now runs. It was owned by an old woman called Mrs Dowell who had a passion for the Duke of Wellington and was for ever sending him pies and cakes and similar offerings, which his servants felt it simpler to accept than refuse, and in the end, harmlessly dotty by now, she took to laying a place for him at her table each day, in the hope that he might call on her.

Behind her shop, where Lowndes Square was built in the late 1830s and during the 1840s, were the Spring Gardens, which had been in existence since the seventeenth century.

With the appearance of the first railways in England, there was wild speculation for a time in railway shares. By the autumn of 1845, 357 new schemes were being advertised in the newspapers. George Hudson, who started life as a Yorkshire linen-draper's apprentice, invested a small legacy in North Midlands Railways, made money, extended his holdings and was soon so rich that he was able to buy the magnificent new mansion, number 58 Knightsbridge, which Thomas Cubitt had recently built.

Here George Hudson entertained so lavishly that he gained entry into London society for a few years, but the boom did not last. Many of the railway companies failed and one of the biggest casualties was Hudson. He had to sell his house, which became thereafter the French Embassy, and here, only a few years later, Louis Napoleon, now Emperor of France, entertained Queen Victoria and Prince Albert.

There were no Royal residents at Kensington Palace at this time and there was talk of pulling down some of the older parts and establishing a new National Gallery there, but Queen Victoria wanted the palace to remain as it was. Maintenance became increasingly expensive but the palace was kept in as good order as possible until the next members of the Royal Family went to live there in the late 1860s.

In 1845, when Lady Holland, widow of the third Lord Holland, died, their only surviving legitimate son, Henry, was Minister Plenipotentiary in Florence and happily married to Lady Augusta, a daughter of the Earl of Coventry. They had made their home a social and artistic centre in Florence and it was here that they met the young artist G. F. Watts, Lord Holland becoming his patron.

Lord Holland who, apart from his lameness, was a sick man and, like his father, a sufferer from gout, retired from the diplomatic service in 1846 and he and Lady Holland returned to Holland House. In 1850 he granted the lease of Little Holland House, vacant after the death of Caroline Fox, to Thoby Princeps, a friend of G. F. Watts, and here Watts joined the household and established himself as a fashionable portrait painter, the arrangement being only slightly disturbed by Watts' disastrous marriage, which lasted for barely a year, to Ellen Terry, when he was middle-aged and she only sixteen.

Lord Holland could not stand the English climate for more than two or three months at a time and he found Holland House 'piteous cold' but he loved the old house and strove to maintain it as he had remembered it in his childhood. The expense was enormous. He had to sell a few acres in the Addison Road region to building contractors but arranged mortgages rather than sell land nearer the house which he felt would affect its sheltered seclusion. He closed Nightingale Lane, a right of way which passed in front of the south terrace, and in exchange, in 1848, created Holland Walk, a public path running from the High Street to Notting Hill.

Between 1847 and 1848 he remodelled the east wing, where he made a new entrance hall. The old hall in the middle of the south front was turned into a magnificent breakfast room, its Jacobean panelling being replaced by tapestries and allegorical paintings. Watts restored the panelling of the Gilt Room and painted two staircase ceilings. The library in the west wing was given a new roof and ceiling and on the ground floor an additional room was made, leading to the Dutch garden, while in the garden itself he built an orangery and a garden ballroom.

During his brief spells of residence at Holland House, Lord Holland entertained in the old style. Brougham, Palmerston and Macaulay were visitors and also Thackeray, but Dickens and his work he had never cared for. French visitors were always welcomed and in 1849 and 1850 Queen Victoria and Prince Albert attended Scottish fêtes held in the grounds.

The Hollands had no children but in 1851 they adopted Marie, a little French girl, who later married Prince Louis Liechtenstein and wrote a history of Holland House.

Lord Holland died in Naples in 1859, and by that time there were great changes in Kensington, which came about after the Great Exhibition of 1851.

XVI

The Great Exhibition

THERE was consternation among many residents of Kensington
when it became known, in 1850, that twenty acres of Hyde Park, the
space between Rotten Row and Kensington Road, opposite the entrance to Prince's Gate, was to be given over to a great International
Exhibition, sponsored by Prince Albert, as President of the Society of
Arts. The idea had been brought to him by Henry Cole, an assistant
keeper of the Record Office who was also an artist, devoted to the
cause of good design in industry, and the editor of the *Journal of
Design*. He had visited the Paris Exhibition in 1849 and returned to
England full of ideas for an even more splendid exhibition in London
which should be international.

Prince Albert was enthusiastic, seeing it as a 'living picture of the
point of development at which mankind has arrived, and a new
starting-point from which all nations will be able to direct their
further exertions'.

Not so the opposition. People living in the new houses facing the
Park and in Belgravia foresaw a constant stream of hooligans disturb-
ing their expensive exclusiveness. Though it was made clear that the
Exhibition building would be only temporary, there were protests
that the public would be cheated of the amenities of London's largest
open space, blandly ignoring the fact that it would take only twenty-
one acres of the stretch of 515 acres comprising the Park and Kensington Gardens. The Protectionists protested that the country would be

flooded with cheap goods brought in by thieves and anarchists. There were stories whispered around of secret societies on the Continent, making plans to assassinate the Queen. Clergymen said the scheme was so arrogant that it would inevitably bring down the wrath of God. Doctors wrote to *The Times* warning that the invasion of foreign visitors would cause widespread venereal disease and, at the least, an epidemic of plague.

By June 1850, *The Times* was criticising the Prince for choosing the Hyde Park site and reporting that aliens were already renting houses near by to be used as brothels: and in August Prince Albert was writing despairingly to his brother Ernst: 'Now our Exhibition is to be driven from London. . . . We shall probably be defeated and have to give up the whole Exhibition. You see that we do not lie on a bed of roses.'

However, the site was eventually allowed, after Colonel Sibthorpe had made his protest about the felling of a few elm trees and denounced the whole enterprise as 'one of the greatest frauds, greatest humbugs, greatest absurdities ever known . . . an exhibition of the temporary and trash of foreign countries!'

Designs for the building were invited by the committee and after months of argument Brunel's plan was rejected in favour of Joseph Paxton's glass palace. Paxton had been head gardener at Chatsworth, and in the construction of many magnificent new glasshouses had become both an engineer and an architect. He solved the problem of enclosing the huge space of nineteen acres by using prefabricated sheets of glass and prefabricated iron girders, all of which could be quickly dismantled and used again. The idea was revolutionary and many said it would never work. It would be insufferably hot. The sun's rays through so much glass would set everything alight and the building would be a death-trap. Condensation would drench both the exhibits and the visitors. The Astronomer Royal agreed that the glass would never withstand wind, rain or snow.

Paxton's calm confidence prevailed. He had made provision for all contingencies, even agreeing to build round two large elm trees, in order to placate Sibthorpe and his agitators. In the autumn of 1850 the site was cleared and building began. It took 900,000 square feet of plate glass – a third of the country's yearly output – and two thousand men were employed on the building which was to house the wares of 15,000 exhibitors.

As the Crystal Palace took shape, even the critics paused to marvel and admire, though some were dubious at the sight of the miles of new-fangled gas-piping being installed, to light the place at night-time.

By the end of 1850 the building was almost completed and on 18 February 1851, Prince Albert was writing again to his brother: 'The goods for the Exhibition are being brought into the building. I am fully occupied with this work. The building itself is truly a work of marvellous art. It will be eleven miles going all round the tables.'

The only serious problem arose from Sibthorpe's elms, for as they put forth their leaves in the spring they became the home of count-less sparrows, which very quickly presented a serious nuisance. With so much glass around, they could not be shot. Netting was of no avail. At last the Queen had to be told and, as C. Hobhouse puts it so neatly: 'The Queen knew that there was only one thing to be done; she sent for the Duke of Wellington. . . . The Duke attended: very nearly stone deaf, he heard from the Queen's own lips of the awful problem.

' "Try sparrow-hawks, ma'am", he said.'

And the sparrows, who had respected not even Prince Albert, at last met their match.

Opening day was on 1 May 1851. Half a million people were watching in the Park and 25,000 season-ticket holders poured into the Crystal Palace to await the arrival of those taking part in the opening ceremony, which included the Duke of Wellington – it was his eighty-second birthday – the members of the Cabinet and the Corps Diplomatique and, arriving punctually at midday, the Queen and Prince Albert, with their two eldest children, the Prince of Wales and the Princess Royal, the Queen wearing a dress of pink-watered silk, embroidered in silver and diamonds, and a feathered head-dress set with diamonds.

'On the day of the opening of the Great Exhibition (held in what is now the Crystal Palace) I went into the park instead of the inside,' wrote Greville in his diary, a few days later. '. . . It was a wonderful spectacle to see the countless multitudes, streaming along in every direction, and congregated upon each bank of the Serpentine down to the water's edge: no soldiers, hardly any policemen to be seen and yet all so orderly and good-humoured. The success of everything was complete, the joy and exultation of the Court unbounded. The Queen wrote a touching letter to John Russell, full of delight at the success of her husband's undertaking and at the warm reception which her subjects gave her. Since that day all the world has been flocking to the Crystal Palace, and we hear nothing but expressions of wonder and admiration. The *frondeurs* are all come round, and those who abused it most vehemently now praise it as much.'

One of the visitors, describing the scene inside the palace, wrote: 'Its vastness was measured by the huge elms, two of the giants of the park, which rose as free and unconfined as if there was nothing between them and the open air. The plash of fountains, the luxuriance of tropical foliage, the play of colours from the choicest flowers, carried on into the vistas of the nave by the rich dyes of carpets and stuffs from the costliest looms, were enough to fill the eye and mind with a pleasure never to be forgotten, even without the vague sense of what lay beyond in the accumulated results of human ingenuity and cultivated art.'

Describing the general effect of the Exhibition, C. Hobhouse writes: 'The endless avenues were filled with such a richness of colour and variety of scale that the exhibits melted into tiny components of a vast mosaic. In the gallery hung carpets and chandeliers of a size only fit for royal palaces; in the transepts palms waved, fountains played, and statues gesticulated; in the naves there jostled an incredible variety of objects – lighthouses and rood-screens, organs and bridges, even the bombastic Godfrey de Bouillon; but all of them were swallowed up and harmonized by the size and perfection of the building. . . . Whether it was the shindy of machinery in motion, or the rich melancholy of the medieval court, or the gaudiness of the Indian tent, they blended with each other beneath, and blended with their great canopy of glass and iron.'*

At the opening ceremony, speeches were made, the Archbishop of Canterbury offered a prayer, the Hallelujah Chorus thundered forth from the mighty organ, fortified by a massed choir of six hundred voices, and then a long procession formed to tour the west and east naves, after which the Queen declared the Exhibition open.

Lord Macaulay described it as 'beyond the dreams of Arabian romance: it was more overwhelming than one's first entry into St Peters'. Lord John Russell said that it was 'astonishing in the extreme', while Dickens found it all too much, confessing that he was not sure that 'he had seen anything but the Crystal Fountain and The Amazon', but Thackeray wrote a special May-Day ode for the occasion and Lord Tennyson was also moved to verse.

The Queen in her diary described it as 'a glorious and touching sight, one which I shall ever be proud of for my beloved Albert and

* C. Hobhouse, *1851 and The Crystal Palace*, John Murray, 1937.

my country. . . . The tremendous cheers, the joy expressed in every face, the immensity of the building, the mixture of palms, flowers, trees, statues, fountains – the organ . . . and my beloved husband the author of the 'Peace-Festival' which united the industry of all nations of the earth – all this was moving indeed, and it was a day to live for ever': while the Prince Consort reported to Mr Cole, in more sober vein, that the opening day had been 'quite satisfactory'. It was an understatement. It had been an overwhelming success and was to remain so until the closing day on 15 October, during which time there were more than six million visitors.

Anyone who has studied the three volumes of the catalogue, each of five hundred pages, can see how comprehensive the Exhibition was, ranging over the whole commercial, industrial and cultural life of a large part of the civilised world. Foreign exhibits were displayed in the eastern half of the building, arranged by countries. There were jewelled weapons from Madrid, watches, clocks and carved cabinets from Switzerland, quantities of terracotta, majolica and lacquer work, carpets, silks and damasks, jewellery and precious stones, and the Rajah of Travancore sent an ivory throne.

The British exhibits were in the western part of the palace, grouped into four sections, minerals and raw materials, machinery, manufacturers and fine arts.

The first two gave a picture of British engineering skill at a time when the Industrial Revolution had made Britain the leading manufacturing country of the world, a position she was to hold until about the end of the century. Here was displayed the first gas cooker, but it was considered far too dangerous a contraption and the Victorians, for the most part, remained faithful to their kitchen ranges.

In the manufacturers section, textiles predominated and there was a magnificent display of English silks from the Spitalfields weavers and from Samuel Courtauld's company. There was lace from Honiton, embroidery and quilting from Heal's, linen from Belfast, tapestries and carpets from Axminster, gloves from Yeovil.

The Wedgwood, Copeland and Minton factories showed china, porcelain and earthenware.

The furniture section was the least successful, for a good deal of it was hideous – cumbersome, heavily carved and over-ornamented – a pitiable decline from the elegance of the work of the great cabinet-makers of the late eighteenth century and the Regency, but much of it set the fashion for the mass-produced furniture which was to clutter the homes of the late Victorians.

Pianos were much in evidence, including 'a collapsible piano for gentlemen's yachts' and a silent piano which 'resembles the ordinary piano in appearance, but when acted upon is perfectly silent'.

There were plenty more oddities, including 'railroad caps' for men, which served as crash-helmets in the event of a railway accident, and a 'Patent Ventilating Hat' with a valve fixed to the top of the crown 'which may be opened and shut at pleasure to allow perspiration to escape'.

One bright idea was a carriage drawn by kites instead of horses, which was called a charvolant, but even the most naïve were dubious about the medical walking-stick, containing medicine, surgical in-struments and an enema, all of which, as someone had the temerity to point out, could have been carried far more easily in a small tin case in the pocket. The craziest idea of all came from America, for among the Colt revolvers and the products of the new Goodyear Rubber Company they sent a floating church for seamen, complete with tower and steeple and stained-glass windows, which was presumably built for cruising among the shipping of the high seas.

Attached to the English furniture section was the Medieval Court, which was under the care of Pugin, the medievalist who had recently turned Roman Catholic. He and his craftsmen had created some beautiful stained glass and medieval, ecclesiastical furnishings for the Exhibition, as well as secular furniture with an ecclesiastical flavour, much of it too large and overpowering for an ordinary home but nevertheless of impeccable workmanship.

Pugin set the taste for the Gothic revival. He died the following year but his successor in the medieval tradition was Gilbert Scott, whose work was shortly to be seen in Kensington.

One interesting exhibit was Prince Albert's design for a Model Dwelling for a Working Man, which was put up to the east of the main exhibition, near the Knightsbridge barracks. It was a block of four flats for artisans, arranged two on each floor, approached by an entrance lobby and covered stairway. Each flat had a living-room and a scullery, equipped with a sink, a meat safe, a coal bin and a rubbish chute. There were three bedrooms, a heated linen cupboard and a water closet. The cost of the block was under £500, which meant that each flat, costing initially about £120, could have been let profitably at a rent of 3s. 6d. to 4s. a week: but unfortunately no capitalist willing to develop the idea was forthcoming.

The Queen visited the Exhibition at least three times a week during that happy summer of 1851, and apart from all the foreign visitors, people flocked in from the country, particularly on the days when admission was only one shilling. On Saturdays it cost five shillings, but was just as crowded.

Lady Blessington's old home, Gore House, was turned into a restaurant by the famous chef of the Reform Club, Alexis Soyer, where he organised a 'Gastronomic Symposium of All Nations'. He was living at number 3 Young Street at this time and his assistant was George Augustus Sala, who was responsible for some remarkable décor.

A few days after the Exhibition closed, the Royal Commissioners were able to announce that it had made a profit of £186,000 and that the money was to be used for the encouragement of the arts and sciences.

The time had come to move the Crystal Palace. Some did not want to see it go, but Paxton, knowing that it could not remain, formed a company to buy the building and a site for its re-erection at Sydenham, where it was moved in 1852 and stood until it was accidentally destroyed by fire in 1936.

Leigh Hunt, writing a year or two after all trace of it had disappeared from Hyde Park, said that 'as soon as it was determined that the structure should reappear in another quarter . . . we felt as glad to have the old trees and turf back again, undisturbed, as the most sequestered of the suburban aristocracies . . . we began to own, that there certainly had been a *dust* and *kick-up* about the once quiet approaches to Kensington, a turmoil of crowds, and omnibuses, and cabs, of hot faces and loud voices, of stalls, dogs, penny trumpets, policemen, and extempore public-houses, which, for the sake of the many themselves, one could hardly have wished to see continued, lest they also should ultimately have missed their portion in the tranquil pleasures of the few'.

A certain measure of tranquillity certainly returned to the Court Suburb, but it was never to be the same again, for now began the development of South Kensington, the materialisation of Prince Albert's vision of a 'university city' of museums and colleges.

The greater part of the Gore, lying back from the main road, was still market gardens and open fields, and, as a first step, the Commission bought a stretch of land lying partly in the Gore and partly in Brompton. This included the Gore House estate of twenty-one acres and another forty-eight acres belong to Baron de Villars, on which Queen's Gate, part of the Cromwell Road and the Natural History Museum were to be built: and seventeen acres of the Harrington estate, part of which became the site of the Victoria and Albert Museum.

Twenty acres of open space which still remained were offered to the Horticultural Society for new experimental gardens. The society was given a new charter, making it Royal, and developed the land at considerable cost, but an exhibition held there in 1862, the year after the Prince Consort's death, was a financial failure, and despite subsequent more successful exhibitions the society was not able to maintain the grounds and they were eventually given over to more building.

The Victoria and Albert Museum began as the Museum of Manufactures and was first opened in 1852 at Marlborough House. In 1857 it was transferred to a hideous building in Brompton, now demolished, known officially as the South Kensington Museum, but more familiarly as the Brompton Boilers, because of its two iron cupolas. The old South Kensington Museum combined both scientific and art exhibitions, the former Museum of Manufactures now being named the Museum of Ornamental Art, established to illustrate the 'application of fine art to objects of utility'.

There were endless discussions and false starts, in the midst of which Prince Albert died, but under the creative drive of Henry Cole the scheme developed.

The College of Art had come about as a result of the report of a Select Committee on Arts and Manufactures, which had sat as early as 1835 and 1836, and had been opened in 1837 in rooms at Somerset House. This was transferred to South Kensington in 1857 and in 1896 granted the title of the Royal College of Art.

The building of the Albert Memorial, designed by Sir George Gilbert Scott, began in 1864, a shrine of marble and mosaic symbolising Britain's Victorian achievements in the arts and sciences and empire-building. Its carved reliefs and statuary and the Gothic pinnacled canopy were completed by 1872, but it was not until 1876 that Henry Foley's seated statue of the Prince, holding a catalogue of the Great Exhibition, was placed in position.

The Albert Hall, built between 1867 and 1871, on the site of Gore House, was designed by Fowke, an impressive elliptical brick building, with a glass and iron dome, large enough to seat eight thousand people, though many a musician has had cause to complain of the acoustics, and many experiments have been made to try and improve them.

The romanesque Natural History Museum was designed by Alfred

Waterhouse and built between 1875 and 1881, and here the early eighteenth-century collection of Hans Sloane was moved from the British Museum. Today the museum has departments of zoology, entomology, palaeontology, mineralogy and botany. It is a wonderful collection, which includes half a million butterflies in the entomology section and six hundred British wild flowers in the botanical gallery.

The Royal College of Organists opened in 1875, the Royal College of Music in 1876, to which was added the Donaldson Museum of musical instruments, including Handel's spinet and Haydn's clavichord.

The Imperial Institute was designed by T. E. Collcutt and went up between 1887 and 1893 as a salute to Queen Victoria's jubilee. Until the Colonial Institute was built in the 1960s it was used for exhibitions of Imperial and Colonial activities, but its purpose was never particularly clearly defined and the London University took over a good deal of it, using part as an examination hall, but most of the building has now been demolished.

In 1897 it was decided to split the arts and science departments of the old South Kensington Museum. The Victoria and Albert Museum, in the Cromwell Road, built on the site of old Cromwell House, was designed by Sir Aston Webb and opened as the National Museum of Fine and Applied Arts, the foundation stone being laid by Queen Victoria in 1899 – her last public engagement – and the opening ceremony being performed by King Edward VII in 1909.

The Victoria and Albert Museum has become one of the major museums of the world. Its exhibits cover every branch of applied art, ranging from ceramics to furniture, costume to musical instruments. It holds the national collection of miniature paintings and watercolours and also of post-classical sculpture, apart from the moderns. It has some fine Constables and nineteenth-century English painters and among its most valuable possessions are the Raphael cartoons.

It also houses the National Art Library, the largest in the world on its subjects, which is open to the public.

The science and engineering departments of the original South Kensington Museum were established on the same site, in 1909, as the Science Museum, with the Geological Museum adjoining it: and the Science Museum has recently been extended.

The Imperial College of Science and Technology, 'for the most advanced training and research in Science, especially in its application to Industry', was opened in 1907 in Prince Consort Road. This was rebuilt in the 1960s and today comprises the Royal School of Mines, the Royal College of Science, founded in 1851, the City and Guilds College, established by the Corporation and Livery Companies of the City of London in 1878, and a centre for Computing and Automation.

The Royal College of Art in Kensington Gore has also been reconstituted and rebuilt and now comprises the faculties of Fine Arts, Graphic Design and Industrial Design, as well as a department of general studies: and since its Royal Charter of 1967 it grants its own degrees.

Between 1841 and 1861 the population of Kensington rose from 27,000 to 70,000, but during the years of the development of South Kensington it increased so quickly that by 1881 it had reached 163,000, for between the museums and colleges arose the terraces of large private houses for the upper middle-class Victorians who now found this a fashionable place in which to live.

In place of old Kensington House, which in the end became a lunatic asylum, and Colby House next to it, there arose in 1872 a new Kensington House, in 'hideous magnificence', with grounds so large that they reached as far as Kensington Square and overran the Rookeries, which were swept away, the inhabitants migrating to Notting Hill. The new Kensington House, with its marble halls and granite pillars, cost £250,000 to build and in the end its owner, Albert Grant, could not afford to live in it, so after ten years it was all pulled down again. The building materials fetched £10,000 and in its place rose Kensington Court.

Tower Cressy, built in 1854 by Thomas Page, was another Victorian folly, but it survived until it was destroyed by a flying bomb in 1944.

In 1873 Norman Shaw built Lowther House in the Gore, which was to become the home of the Royal Geographical Society, with its excellent library and wonderful map collection, and in 1879 he built Albert Hall mansions.

In 1872 Sir Gilbert Scott built the new St Mary Abbots church, a Gothic revival, to house a congregation of 1,800. Few regretted the disappearance of the seventeenth-century church, which Bishop Blomfield had described as 'the ugliest in his diocese', and in the new building William III's pulpit was placed and a few of the old memorials, including one to Thomas Renshaw, a member of the household of Charles II, James II and William III. Another is to Mrs Jael Boscawen, sister of the Earl of Godolphin, and the statue of the young Earl of Warwick and Holland, who became Addison's stepson, was placed in the south aisle.

The Brompton Oratory, with the house of the Oratorians and St Wilfred's Hall, was built in 1882. The Congregation of the Oratory was an order of secular priests founded by St Philip Neri in the sixteenth century and the Oratory is built in the style of sixteenth-century Italian baroque. The order was introduced into England by Cardinal Newman in 1847 and they moved from King William Street off the Strand to Brompton in 1854.

The Oratory contains the gigantic marble statues of the Apostles, carved by Mazzuoli in the 1680s, which once stood in the cathedral at Siena, and a statue of St Peter which is a replica of the one at St Peter's, Rome.

St Barnabas Church, in Addison Road, had been consecrated in 1827 and Holy Trinity, Brompton, in 1829, but twenty-six more churches were to be built in Kensington during the rest of the century.

In 1865 Tattersalls was moved from Grosvenor Place to the corner of Brompton Road and Knightsbridge, and in 1879 the eighteenth-century Knightsbridge barracks were rebuilt.

XVII

The Victorians in Chelsea

IN 1836 the Reverend Charles Kingsley arrived at St Luke's rectory from Clovelly, to succeed the Reverend Dr Wellesley, brother of the Duke of Wellington. He was rector of Chelsea until 1860. Of Charles Kingsley's four sons, Charles became a clergyman and author and George a doctor, whose daughter was that remarkable Victorian spinster, the fearless Mary Kingsley. 'After Clovelly . . . the change to Chelsea came hard,' wrote Mary Kingsley, 'for it was then a dismal suburb'.

Parts of the old town were undoubtedly running down. Carlyle complained that the house next door, number 6, grew shabbier every year and the garden had become a sordid patch of rubbish and weeds.

The Stadium at Cremorne House, a financial failure, was closed in 1841 and in 1845 the Cremorne Gardens were opened, a pleasure-ground of twelve acres with a theatre and a concert room, a marionette theatre, a platform for four thousand dancers, a circus, a maze and a gipsy's tent. There were refreshment bars, a dining-room and tiers of boxes where couples could take supper in seclusion, and in the gardens were grottoes, coloured lights and a fountain, made alluring with the plaster figure of the Stooping Venus. The proprietors offered a programme of concerts, dances, fireworks, balloon ascents, galas and all the rest, and the garden could be approached either by the King's Road or the threepenny steamer from the City to Cremorne Pier. But Cremorne never achieved the distinction of the best days of Ranelagh. It began where Ranelagh ended, raffish and noisy and a place of assignation.

The promenading and tea-drinking of the eighteenth century were little to the taste of mid-Victorian Londoners, suffering from the worst evils of the Industrial Revolution, and the surrounding public houses were enlarged to accommodate visitors needing quicker and stronger stimulus. Even as far away as Cheyne Row, Carlyle suffered from the noise of Cremorne, but Whistler and Rossetti were fascinated by the surging life of the garden, the cockneys who came to escape into a spuriously gay world of dancing, music and merry-making, and the lights which transformed the blackening, industrial buildings, steadily encroaching from Fulham, into shadowy beauty against the moonlit sky. However, by 1875 the gardens had become so rowdy and disreputable that they were closed, as being a 'nuisance to the neighbourhood'.

With the astonishing increase of population in England during the nineteenth century – it rose from 14,000,000 in 1837 to 32,500,000 in 1901 – London spread in all directions, and Chelsea was engulfed by the builders who pressed on through Fulham, Chiswick, Richmond and Twickenham. Hans Town disappeared as the red-brick mansions of Norman Shaw's Sloane Street, Cadogan Place, Cadogan Square and Hans Place were built. In the King's Road, the Duke of York's school became the Duke of York's Territorial Headquarters. Whitelands House became Whitelands Training College for School Teachers, an institution in which John Ruskin took an interest, inaugurating a May Day festival.

Among Victorian architects the battle between a modified Palladian and neo-Gothic was raging. In the labyrinth of small houses in the side streets north and south of the King's Road, which came into existence at this time, a simple Classical style of brick covered with stucco prevailed, but the town hall, built in 1860 by J. M. Brydon, was in the 'Italian' style: and about the same time he also designed the public library in Manresa Road.

The heart of Chelsea, along the river-front, did not escape the changes which were afoot. The pollution of the river by the discharge from gasworks, sewage works and factories had killed off all the fish and driven the fishermen from Chelsea very early in the century, and in 1874 the Chelsea Embankment was built. Old Chelsea was rudely divorced from the river, for the embankment was wide and the river considerably narrowed. Many old landmarks had to go, the taverns with their balconies overhanging the water, the rickety water-steps and little jetties, the boatsheds and barges which littered the fore-shore. The Physic Garden suffered, for the gardeners had used the land bordering the river for the cultivation of many water plants. Now it was drained and in place of the water-steps and the river stretched a broad expanse of pavement and roadway. The old boat-house was left high and dry and the soil in this part of the garden underwent a change which entailed many adjustments. The grounds of the Royal Hospital had already been mutilated when the Queen's Road, later to be known as the Royal Hospital Road, had been cut straight across its front courtyard, thereby separating Burton's Court from the rest of the grounds. Now they lost their magnificent river approach, as well as Sir Robert Walpole's summer house and Admi-ral Russell's gazebo, but by way of compensation, it was about this time that the old Ranelagh Gardens were acquired for the Hospital and replanted by the Office of Works.

In 1885 the old Battersea bridge was demolished and the new iron bridge was completed by 1887. The Albert Suspension bridge, built in 1873, linked Oakley Street with the Albert Bridge Road in Battersea.

Late in the century, by which time Chelsea and Kensington had become the acknowledged artists' quarters of London, the large studio houses in Tite Street were built, with their top and north lights, as well as the studios in Glebe Place and many other parts of Chelsea.

In the borough, the population increased as steadily as in other parts of London. In 1801 it was 12,000; in 1841, 40,000; in 1881, 88,000 and by 1901 it had risen to 95,000.

After the building of the Embankment, the Embankment Gardens were planted, a poor substitute for the haphazard charm of the old days, although many Victorians, including Carlyle, thought them a vast improvement. Yet with all the new building, the essential character of Chelsea did not change.

In 1862 Dante Gabriel Rossetti came to live in Chelsea at Queen's House, number 16 Cheyne Walk, and was to be there for the next twenty years. He had been born in London in 1828, the eldest son of an Italian political exile and a mother who was half Italian, half English. His art master at King's College school had been John Cotman and when he went to the Royal Academy school he met Holman Hunt and John Millais. All three had a love of the early Renaissance Italian painters, and under the persuasion of the domi-nant Rossetti they formed the Pre-Raphaelite Brotherhood, their aim being to attempt to capture, in their work, the religious and emotional intensity of feeling of the old Italians and also their minute attention to detail.

Rossetti was a poet and romantic, at odds with the materialism of nineteenth-century industrial England. He dreamed of the days of medieval chivalry when goodness and beauty, as he fondly believed, still prevailed over ugliness and wickedness. The Brotherhood was extended to include Thomas Woolner, a sculptor and worshipper of Shelley, James Collinson, Gabriel's brother, William, and Frederick Stephens. Ford Maddox Brown was also invited, but declined.

The aims of the Pre-Raphaelites were nebulous – a renouncement of the horrors of industrialism and a return to the days when people lived more simply, naturally and happily – and the paths of its members soon diverged, but their influence on English painting was considerable. During the late 1840s the group remained close friends and were warmly supported by Ruskin, the arbiter of nineteenth-century artistic taste. Rossetti worked hard and successfully at both painting and poetry, though he did not publish a great deal of his poetry at this time.

In 1850 the friends found a new model in Elizabeth Siddal, a work-girl at a milliner's shop off Oxford Street. She was intelligent and very beautiful in an ethereal, emaciated way, and had a mass of glorious auburn hair. She posed for Holman Hunt and for Deverell. For Millais she was the drowning Ophelia, lying in the bath at his home in Gower Street, 'her clothes spread wide and mermaid-like'. She sat for Rossetti and before long they were in love. He adored her and wrote some of his most beautiful and romantic poems for her. She was, said Ruskin, 'Beautiful as the reflection of a golden mountain in a crystal lake . . . which is what she was to him'.

They became engaged, but Elizabeth was consumptive. Ruskin was kind and on one occasion at least helped by sending her to Nice, to try and recover her health.

The first serious rift in the circle of friends came when Ruskin and his beautiful wife Effie parted, after a deeply unhappy marriage which had never been consummated. After the divorce, Effie married Millais and their marriage was long and very successful. Ruskin appeared to be not unduly concerned, however, for his marriage to Effie had been arranged by his mother and he had never shown much enthusiasm for it: and his friendship with Rossetti remained as warm as ever.

Millais was elected an ARA and became high fashion. Holman

Hunt went off to Palestine, to find the exact background for his religious paintings. Rossetti remained cheerfully busy in London.

In 1856 he met two young men just down from Oxford, Edward Burne-Jones and William Morris, who had been drawn into a close friendship by their mutual love of medieval art and culture. Burne-Jones joined the Pre-Raphaelites but Morris had other interests besides painting – poetry, translation and the designing of furniture and fabrics, for he deplored the decline in craftsmanship which had come about with the mid-century mass production from the factories.

For a while, Burne-Jones and Morris shared a studio, with Rossetti a constant visitor. When Morris married and moved to the Red House, which Philip Webb had planned and built for him at Bexley Heath, he decided that he would design every piece of furniture and every yard of curtain fabric for it himself. The result of this decision was that in 1861 he opened his studio and business at 8 Red Lion Square. The company called itself *Fine Art Workmen in Painting, Carving, Furniture and the Metals* and Morris' partners were Burne-Jones, Rossetti, Ford Maddox Brown, Philip Webb, P. P. Marshall and C. J. Faulkner.

They built a small kiln for firing glass and pottery and announced to the world that they would undertake mural decoration, carving, stained glass, metal work, including jewellery, as well as embroidery, stamped leather work and the making of furniture.

Morris had a genius for every kind of craftsmanship and the company prospered. Their first furniture was of solid oak, rather massive and unwieldy – 'Intensely medieval – tables and chairs like incubi and succubi' said Rossetti, but he happily painted scenes from the medieval romances on some of the panelled chests and cupboards.

He had married at last – about the same time as William Morris and Jane – but Elizabeth was a desperately sick woman. 'She had seemed ready to die daily and more than once a day,' he wrote. 'It has needed all my own strength to nurse her through this dreadful attack . . . it makes me feel as if I had been dug up out of a vault, so many times lately has it seemed to me she could never lift her head again. . . . I assure you it has been almost too much for me . . . indeed, it hardly seems as if I should ever work again.'

Elizabeth became passive and listless. A still-born child left her frailer than ever. She was subject to long fits of melancholia and began taking laudanum to relieve the pain from bouts of acute neuralgia.

When she stayed with the Morrises at the Red House she was 'like a ghost in the house of the living', silent and remote, rising from the dinner table and 'gliding away silent and unobserved as she had come'.

How deeply Rossetti was in love with her at the time of their marriage it is hard to tell. He had certainly had other attachments since their engagement and the one Elizabeth almost certainly knew about was with Fanny Cornforth, another model, comely but earthy, and a complete contrast in every way to Elizabeth's ethereal loveliness.

John Middleton, who knew Rossetti at this time, said that 'Rossetti was addicted to loves of the most material kind both before and after his marriage with women, generally models, without other soul than beauty. It was remorse at the contrast between his ideal and his real loves that preyed on him and destroyed his mind.'

Hall Caine, who was his companion during his last years, said that Rossetti confessed to him that he had fallen out of love with Elizabeth before they married and was in love with another woman whom he did not name. This was probably Jane Morris, for whom he was reputed to have an abiding but secret love, but Fanny Cornforth remained a friend till the end of his life, although they did not often meet and the rest of his circle regarded her as an evil influence.

Elizabeth and Rossetti lived for the first few months of their marriage at his studio in Chatham Place, Blackfriars, which he had taken a few years earlier with such enthusiasm. 'You cannot imagine what delightful rooms these are for a party,' he had written to Woolner, 'regularly built out into the river, and with windows on all sides – also a large balcony over the water, large enough to sit there with a model and paint – a feat which I actually accomplished the other day for several hours in the teeth of the elements.'

But the murky, foggy Thames-side was no place for Elizabeth and they soon moved to Highgate. One evening in 1862, only two years after the marriage, Rossetti gave a lecture at the Working Men's College, leaving Elizabeth alone at Highgate. When he returned, she was dead, with an empty bottle of laudanum by her side. Years later, Rossetti confided to Hall Caine that she had left a brief suicide note, though it was not produced at the inquest and no one knows what it said.

Rossetti was distraught with grief and remorse, torn by conflicting emotions. He had failed Elizabeth. Yet perhaps, through no fault of her own, she had failed him. Into her coffin he placed the book of unpublished poems which he had written for her during their happy days together – poems which had been inspired by the rapture of their first love, a strange, mystical, exalted love, on a plane which it was almost humanly impossible to maintain.

It was soon after Elizabeth's death that he moved to the Queen's House at number 16 Cheyne Walk. The house was very large, with an acre of garden. There was a legend that it had once been the home of Charles II's queen, Catherine of Braganza, but it had not, in fact, been built until 1717, and by the time Rossetti came there it had been very much altered. The main staircase had been removed, making of the house a maze of dark corridors, but there was a large room over-looking the garden, which he used for a studio, and in the front of the house a drawing-room 40 feet long, with a magnificent view of the river.

Soon after he moved in, he began to assemble his famous mena-gerie, partly in cages, partly roaming freely in the garden. It included owls, rabbits, squirrels, doormice, hedgehogs, wombats, kangaroos and wallabies, salamanders and lizards, armadillos, a jackdaw, a raven, a deer and some peacocks.

He installed a cook-housekeeper and two housemaids, and then set about finding companions to share the large number of unoccupied rooms he had on his hands. Swinburne lived with him for a while and then Theodore Watts Dunton. His brother William also had rooms there until his marriage with one of Ford Maddox Brown's daugh-ters, when he settled close by. Meredith agreed to move in and drove over one morning from his lodgings in Mayfair to inspect his new apartments. 'It was past noon,' he recorded. 'Rossetti had not yet risen, though it was an exquisite day. On the breakfast table, on a huge dish, rested five thick slabs of bacon, upon which five rigid eggs had slowly bled to death! Presently Rossetti appeared in his dressing-gown with slippers down at heel and devoured the dainty repast like an ogre!'

Meredith said that he promptly changed his mind about living in Queen's House, wrote a cheque for a quarter's rent and departed, but Rossetti's version of the story is that after an argument and a warning, he threw a cup of tea in Meredith's face.

During his first years at Chelsea, Rossetti, still only in his thirties, entertained all his old friends, Burne-Jones and his wife, William and Jane Morris, the Ford Maddox Browns, as well as new friends, in-cluding Robert Browning and Augustus Sala and his new neighbour in Cheyne Walk, James Whistler.

Yet with all the gay parties and nights at Cremorne, Rossetti worked steadily at his painting and maintained his earlier success. With the passing years, he began to think increasingly of the poems he had buried with Elizabeth in Highgate cemetery. He felt they represented some of his best work and he wanted to see them again. At last, seven years after her death, he decided to seek permission for them to be recovered from her grave. Once the Home Office agreed, he tortured himself with agonies of self-reproach. Was he committing a sacrilege? They were hers and she had had so little.

On the night of the exhumation, he sat alone, while his friends watched the coffin being raised, in the light of a large bonfire in Highgate cemetery. The book of poems, still entwined in a lock of Elizabeth's beautiful hair, was intact, and in 1870 it was published.

The volume, entitled simply *Poems*, was an immediate success. It was enthusiastically reviewed and quickly ran into six or seven editions. Rossetti was happy and began writing again with renewed inspiration. But in 1871 an article by Robert Buchanan appeared in the *Contemporary Review*, entitled *The Fleshly School of Poetry*. In it he condemned the poems of Swinburne, William Morris, and in particular, Rossetti. He accused them of extolling 'fleshliness as the distinct and supreme end of poetic and pictorial art', implying that 'the body is greater than the soul, and sound superior to sense'. Rossetti's poetry was, the article said, 'charged with gross animalism and vapid affectation', and he was accused of demoralising the public mind.

Rossetti was mortally wounded. His reply in the *Athenaeum*, entitled *The Stealthy School of Criticism*, pointed out that in his sonnets, 'if they be not garbled by malice' it was made clear that 'all the passionate and just delights of the body are declared – somewhat figuratively, it is true, but unmistakably – to be naught if not ennobled by the concurrence of the soul at all times'.

There was no reply and in the end Rossetti fell silent. He never recovered from the venom of the attack and became increasingly melancholic. He dropped all his friends and turned into a recluse, resorting to chloral, which he took at first for insomnia. Years later Buchanan confessed, in a private letter, that he had been 'most unjust' when he 'impugned the purity and misconceived the passion of writings, too hurriedly read . . .' He sent a short poem of his own to Rossetti, which was intended as a graceful apology, but by then it was too late. The chloral had become an incurable addiction and Rossetti was haunted by delusions that he had been cursed for desecrating Elizabeth's grave and that all men were against him.

It was in 1880 that Hall Caine first called on Rossetti, after several years of correspondence. Rossetti was by then fifty-two, though he looked older, and Hall Caine a young man of twenty-seven. 'Cheyne Walk was unknown to me at the time of my first visit to Rossetti,' he wrote, 'except as the locality in which men and women eminent in literature were residing . . . the embankment and the gardens that separated it from the main thoroughfare had already taken something from its quaint beauty; but it still possessed attractions, among them a look of age . . . which contrasted agreeably with the spick-and-span newness of neighbouring districts.

'The house itself was a plain Queen Anne erection, much muti-lated by the introduction of unsightly bow windows, the brick work falling into decay, the paint in need of renewal, the windows dull with the dust of months, the sills bearing more than the suspicion of cobwebs, the angles of the steps to the porch and the untrodden flags of the little court leading up to them overgrown with moss and weeds, while round the walls and up the reveals of doors and win-dows were creeping the tangled branches of the wildest ivy that ever grew untouched by shears.'

'The hall,' he continued, 'had a puzzling look of equal nobility and shabbiness, for the floor was paved with white marble, which was partly covered by a strip of worn out cocoanut matting. Three doors led out of the hall, one at each side and one in front, and two corri-dors opened into it, but there was no sign of a staircase; neither was there any daylight, except the little that was borrowed from a fan-light which looked into the porch . . . It was a house inhabited by a man who had once felt a vivid interest in life, but was now living from day to day.'

A warm friendship sprang up between the two oddly-assorted characters and Hall Caine spoke rapturously of Rossetti's beautiful voice when he read to him some of his poems, a deep, rich baritone voice with an infinite variety of tone and intensely moving.

Caine talked to him of the Pre-Raphaelite Brotherhood but Rossetti assured him it had long ceased to exist. 'Pre-Raphael-ites,' laughed Rossetti. 'A group of young fellows who couldn't draw !'

'As for all the prattle about Pre-Raphaelites', he said later, 'I confess to you I am weary of it and long have been. Why should we go on talking about the visionary vanities of half-a-dozen boys? We've all grown out of them, I hope, by now'.

That night, as they went to bed, they 'took candles from a table in the hall and went up a narrow and tortuous staircase, which was otherwise dark, to a landing from which many rooms seemed to open, so large was the house in which Rossetti lived alone, except for a cook and two maid-servants.'

Hall Caine's description of that strange household reads like a Victorian melodrama; the bedrooms dark with velvet hangings and black furniture; the musty, unused drawing-room in which hung Elizabeth's paintings, for during her short life she had learnt much from Rossetti and showed no mean talent; the little green dining-room; the wild, unkempt garden, with its weeds and long dank grass and moss-covered paths, utterly silent now, for the birds and animals had all gone; the anxious, perplexed housekeeper; and Rossetti, the recluse, who never left the house except to walk six times round the garden each day, slowly killing himself with chloral, yet still producing his masterpieces, and appearing to the young Hall Caine 'the most fascinating, the most inspiring, the most affectionate, and the most magnetic of men'.

When, a few months later, Caine went to live with Rossetti, for the last year or two of Rossetti's life, their circle of friends, though small, slowly widened again, to include William Rossetti and his family, Theodore Watts-Dunton, Ford Maddox Brown and Fiona Macleod, as well as Mrs Rossetti, Gabriel's mother, and his sister Christina. At rare intervals, a 'certain woman – the evil influence' came to dine, but on those occasions Rossetti intimated that he wished to be alone with her, and Hall Caine never met her.

Rossetti's health was declining, but Hall Caine's company revived him a little and he was induced to take occasional evening walks along the Embankment, where on one occasion they caught sight of the plaid of the aged Carlyle, trudging briskly along Cheyne Walk for his nightly exercise, with his devoted niece trying to keep up with him.

It was about this time that George Eliot came to live in Cheyne Walk, at number 4. At sixty-one, she had only recently married her second husband, John Cross. They moved to Chelsea in the early December of 1880, but less than three weeks later she had caught a chill and died.

Rossetti had known most of the famous Victorian writers and artists. He had stories to tell Hall Caine of Tennyson and the Brownings, Longfellow and George Eliot, Swinburne and Whistler. When Ruskin's wife left him for Millais, it was Rossetti who took care of Millais' portrait of her, to save it from being destroyed by Ruskin's outraged father. Yet of the friends of his youth, William Morris, Holman Hunt and Burne-Jones, he hardly ever spoke.

In 1881 Rossetti suffered a stroke and was desperately ill for weeks. So completely had he cut himself adrift from his old Pre-Raphaelite friends, that only Burne-Jones came to see him. Rossetti recovered a little and early in 1882 Hall Caine took him to Birchington. He was never to see Chelsea again, for on Easter Sunday he had another seizure which was fatal and he was buried at Birchington.

The Pre-Raphaelites and their associates had many other connections with Chelsea. Holman Hunt had been working there since the 1850s, first at a studio in Prospect Place, where the Children's Hospital was later built, and it was here that he did some of his most famous work, including *The Light Of The World*. Many years later, he was painting in a studio in Manresa Road, though late in the century he moved to the new artists' colony in Melbury Road, Kensington. He survived all the Brotherhood, for he did not die until 1910, at the age of eighty-three.

William Morris' firm in Red Lion Square still prospered and until his death, in 1896, apart from his poetry, romances, translations and lectures, he devoted himself to designing and organizing the production of furniture, wall-papers, tapestries, carpets and fabrics.

Burne-Jones designed some of the Merton tapestries and also much of the firm's stained glass, including the beautiful east window in Holy Trinity Church, Sloane Street, which had been built in 1830.

Philip Webb, who had designed William Morris' Red House at Bexley, also had a hand in some of the new Chelsea building, including number 35 Glebe Place.

In the early days, the firm had produced painted tiles depicting scenes from the medieval legends and romances, but they soon formed an association with William de Morgan, who was a great admirer of Morris and the arts and crafts movement. During the 1860s, while still in his twenties, de Morgan began experimenting with stained glass and pottery, at his studio in Fitzroy Square. By 1872 he was producing tiles with patterns adapted from the lovely sixteenth- and seventeenth-century Persian and Damascus tiles, and, encouraged by William Morris, he moved to number 30 (then number 8) Cheyne Row, built a small kiln at the end of the garden, and set up business as a potter, the Morris firm taking much of his work.

By 1876 he was able to enlarge the business by renting Orange House, a few doors up the Row, where the Church of the Holy

Redeemer now stands. In the coach-house at the side he built a larger kiln and he installed his two painters, Charles and Fred Passenger, on the first floor, using the ground floor for a store and show-room.

De Morgan was a perfectionist. At first he had bought plain tiles from Wedgwood and other pottery firms and concentrated on the decoration, but at Orange House he made his own tiles, as well as plates, plaques, bowls, dishes and vases. He not only designed the decoration, but superintended every stage of the work, from the preparation of the clay, to the throwing and firing of the biscuit ware, the preparation of the glaze and the painting. He also experimented successfully in lustre work, using silver and copper lustre in his decoration.

He took infinite pains to reproduce the deep, rich colouring of the Eastern potters and his designs were beautiful and romantic – fabulous beasts and birds, grotesque monsters, proud ships in full sail and wondering, winsome, curling fishes – all painted on vessels of simple satisfying shapes.

In 1882, owing to a problem of the lease of Orange House, he moved his kiln to Morris' headquarters at Merton for a while, but in 1887 he married. He moved his pottery and his two painters again, this time to Sandy End, Fulham, and took on a new partner and designer, Halsey Ricardo.

De Morgan and his wife lived at number 1 the Vale, a charming little cul-de-sac off the north side of the King's Road, built on part of Lord Wharton's deer park, which has long since been redeveloped. A. M. W. Stirling said their house was 'a quaint, rambling dwelling, shrouded in creepers with a veranda back and front . . . full of unexpected nooks and irregularities, spruce with gay Morris papers and decorated with De Morgan pots and rich-hued paintings'.

At Sandy End they employed eventually fifteen painters, eight women and seven men. Two of the biggest pieces of work the firm undertook were the tiled walls of the Bishop Selwyn mortuary chapel at Lichfield Cathedral and the Arab hall of Lord Leighton's house in Holland Park Road.

De Morgan invented an ingenious method of transferring his designs on to pottery by paper transfers and, towards the end of his life, when he spent his winters in Florence, he established a tile-painting industry there, the Italian artists painting his designs on paper, which were sent to England for transfer to the tiles.

After the partnership with Ricardo was dissolved in 1898, De Morgan carried on the firm for a while, but by 1907 it was not paying its way and he was forced to close. He was already in his late sixties but it was now that he began his successful career as a novelist, while the two Passenger brothers opened a pot-decorating trade in the Brompton Road, which survived until 1911.

In 1909 the three residents of the Vale were told they must go, as the houses were to be demolished. De Morgan made the leave-taking the occasion for a party, as yet another piece of old Chelsea was doomed to extinction. 'The guests wandered into an unexpected Fairyland. Old Chelsea Pensioners in their scarlet coats guarded the lane, which was festooned with glowing lanterns. The three houses (those of de Morgan, Professor Oliver and Stirling Lee, the sculptor) and their respective gardens were open to the guests of all . . . in one, a band played softly while nymphs drifted over the turf in pictur-esque dances . . . in de Morgan's garden choral singing was inter-spersed by the song of a living dryad among the bushes, hard by where the head of Pan looked out wickedly from a grove of grass-green lamps . . . in the flower-scented dimness. . . . Then, by and by, there was supper and song in the old deer-park beneath the doomed trees wreathed with fairy lamps . . .'

To many that party must have become a bitter-sweet memory of the innocent pleasures which were never to return, after the 'carnage incomparable and human squander' of the First World War, which broke out only five years later.

The De Morgans moved to number 127 Church Street, Chelsea, where they lived until De Morgan's death in 1917.

Even more controversial, in his day, than the Pre-Raphaelites was James Whistler. He was an American of Irish descent, born in Massa-chusetts in 1834. As a child of eight, he was taken by his family to St Petersburg, where his father had been asked to advise on the railway being built between St Petersburg and Moscow. Already Whistler was showing remarkable gifts for drawing, and it was during these years in Russia that he learnt to speak French fluently.

When his father died of cholera in 1849, his mother took her family back to America, and in due course Whistler, following the family tradition, was sent to West Point, but his tastes lay in a very different direction and he failed. A few months later he arrived in Washington as a draughtsman in the Government Coast Survey. He found the restrictions of regular employment intolerable and the only work he did was to draw exquisite maps. In those days maps were reproduced by etching, and Whistler learnt to etch and engrave, producing some delightful work which was of more interest to him than the Survey. In 1855 he resigned and persuaded his family to send him to Paris to study art. Here, with a small allowance, he arrived by the end of the year.

Life in Paris during the Second Empire was at its gayest, and Whistler, just twenty-one, already a dandy and something of a gourmet, with gay, charming manners and a quick American wit, plunged riotously into the student life of the Left Bank, soon meeting the young English students Du Maurier, Poynter and Armstrong, with whom he enrolled as a student of Gleyre.

He learned little from Gleyre and he varied the Bohemian round of cafés, student dances, debts, pawnshops, models and grisettes, with sallies into Parisian social life and balls at the Tuileries, to which he was invited through friends at the American Embassy.

However, he worked hard, in his own fashion and in his own time, either in his own room or in the boulevard cafés, both at painting and etching. For two years he lived with Éloise, the pretty little *modiste* with the fiery temper, whom he called Fumette, but when she tore up all his drawings, in a fit of jealous rage, it took him only one evening's drinking to recover, forget her and seek consolation with Finette.

He left Gleyre and went to study with Courbet, the apostle of 'realism' – not the meticulous, detailed realism of the Pre-Raphaelites, but the realism which accepts life as it is, in everyday surroundings. In Courbet's teaching, Whistler found what he had been seeking, and by the following year he felt ready to begin work professionally. About 1859 he came to England and stayed with his step-sister and her husband, Seymour Haden, at their home at 62 Sloane Street. Here Whistler produced his first important painting *At the Piano*, a study of his step-sister and her small daughter. The Salon in Paris refused it, but in 1860 it was exhibited at the Royal Academy and sold.

The Thames fascinated Whistler and for a few months he lived in a waterside tavern down at Wapping, producing one or two paintings, but in particular, delicate copper-plate etchings of the murky, mid-Victorian Thames, with its barges and lighters, ships and tugs, water-front inns and squalor and teeming life.

His attractive, red-haired model – Jo Hefferman – became his mistress, and in 1863, after staying for a while in Paris and Blooms-bury, they settled at number 101 Cheyne Walk, where the friendship with Rossetti became so close. Three years later Whistler and Jo moved to number 96 Cheyne Walk, the east wing of the old Lindsey House and part of Lindsey Row, and here they remained for the next twelve years.

It was not until the 1850s that Paris became familiar with the Japanese artists of the earlier part of the century and then the enthusiasm for their work quickly spread. Whistler was intrigued by the satisfying simplicity of their form and colour and inspired Rossetti with his passion for Oriental art. William Rossetti began collecting and the cult spread, so that before long Lazenby Liberty was setting up his shop in Regent Street for the sale of Oriental wares, including Japanese prints and Chinese porcelain.

In Chelsea, Whistler was known as the 'Japanese' artist, and when he moved to Lindsey Row his taste for simplicity in interior decorating was startling to his guests at the house-warming party, accustomed as they were to the crowded rooms of mid-Victorian England, cluttered with bric-à-brac and potted palms and the over-elaborate, heavily carved furniture which had become popular since the 1851 Exhibition. They found a dining-room with painted blue walls, on which were a few purple Japanese fans, the paintwork and door being painted a deeper blue. The drawing-room had flesh-coloured walls hung with a few strips of Japanese embroidery, and the doors were painted yellow and white, while the studio had plain grey walls with black paint.

The two sons of Charles Greaves, the boat-builder, lived in a cottage close by and, like Turner, Whistler employed them to row him about the river. They both became artists and Walter, who was Whistler's faithful disciple for several years, achieved fame. His picture *Boat Race from Hammersmith Bridge*, which is now in the Tate Gallery, was painted when he was only sixteen, but he made little money from his work and died in poverty.

During the early 1860s Whistler's success in London seemed assured. He and Jo were happy in their charming white house, with its patch of lawn in front and the straight, flagged path leading to the simple, arched doorway. There were gay nights at Cremorne, parties at the Queen's House and the exhilaration of success. Jo obligingly overlooked Whistler's infidelities and brought up his son by some unknown woman as well as her own child, her sister being introduced to the household as nursemaid.

Jo was his model for his *Symphony in White Number II*, which was exhibited at the Academy in 1865, but it received a good deal of hostile criticism. Whistler followed it with *Symphony in White Number*

III, but the critics could make nothing of it and were even more
hostile, while Whistler grew ever angrier at their lack of perception.
It was about this time that Jo disappeared from the scene and was
replaced by Maud Franklin, who called herself Mrs Whistler, a more
sophisticated and elegant young woman than the placid, good-
natured Jo. In 1872, Whistler's painting of his mother, then living in
London, which today is considered one of the world's masterpieces
of portraiture, was nearly rejected by the Royal Academy. Shortly
afterwards he painted his portrait of Carlyle, who proved an impatient and difficult sitter, for he always referred to Whistler as 'the
creature' and regarded him with amused contempt.

Whistler's income began to fall, but by 1877 Sir Coutts Lindsay
had built the Grosvenor Gallery, and at the first exhibition Whistler
showed seven paintings, including four of his beautiful nocturnes,
two in blue and silver, one in blue and gold, and one in black and
gold. As Turner had caught the sunset light on the river, Whistler
now captured the evening light of sky and water: but to most of the
critics, the nocturnes were incomprehensible, for they had never seen
painting like it before.

Several years later, in his 'Ten O'Clock' lecture, Whistler tried to
describe what he saw as he painted the nocturnes: 'When the evening
mist clothes the riverside with poetry, as with a veil, and the poor
buildings lose themselves in the dim sky, and the tall chimneys become campanili, and the warehouses are palaces in the night, and the
whole city hangs in the heavens, and fairyland is before us – then
the wayfarer hastens home; the working man and the cultured one, the
wise man and the one of pleasure, cease to understand as they have
ceased to see, and Nature, who, for once, has sung in tune, sings her
exquisite song to the artist alone, her son and her master, her son in
that he loves her, her master in that he knows her.' But in 1877 many
people regarded Whistler as a charlatan, among them Ruskin, who
in July of that year wrote in *Fors Clavigera*: 'For Mr Whistler's own
sake, no less than for the protection of the purchaser, Sir Coutts
Lindsay ought not to have admitted works into the gallery into
which the ill-educated conceit of the artist so nearly approached the
aspect of wilful imposture. I have seen, and heard, much of cockney
impudence before now; but never expected to hear a coxcomb ask
two hundred guineas by flinging a pot of paint in the public's face.'

'Flinging a pot of paint' was the same expression that a critic had
once used about Turner's work and, less than thirty years after Ruskin
had written those damaging words, one of Whistler's 'wilful

impostures' – the *Nocturne in Blue and Gold*: – *Old Battersea Bridge* –
was bought for two thousand guineas and presented to the nation, but
in 1877 the denunciation affected Whistler disastrously.

When he exhibited at the Grosvenor Gallery the following year his
sales were so low that he decided to take action against Ruskin for
libel. It was in this same year, 1878, that he planned to build himself a
house. He had very little money, as his sales had been so reduced
under the lash of the critics, and although he had always shown a fine
disregard for bills, they were mounting disconcertingly. Nevertheless, Edward Godwin, his friend, designed a studio house for him in
Tite Street, large enough to be a school for pupils as well as a private
residence. The White House had a large studio at the top of the
house, a studio drawing-room, five bedrooms, a dining-room and
a kitchen, and the predominating colour of the interior decoration
was a light yellow.

He moved into the White House in October 1878 and a few weeks
later his case for libel against Ruskin was heard. Whistler's plea was
that he was an accepted artist, whose paintings had been exhibited in
the Royal Academy and whose etchings had been bought both by
the British Museum and for the Royal collection at Windsor Castle,
and Ruskin's criticisms had seriously affected the sale of his work.

The defence was that Whistler was a lazy and unsuccessful artist,
who spent only a day or two painting a picture and then offered it for
sale at an exorbitant price. William Rossetti and Albert Moore appeared in defence of Whistler and Burne-Jones, Frith and Taylor, the
art critic of *The Times*, in support of Ruskin, who was too ill to come
to court.

Whistler explained to the judge that to him 'a picture was not the
imitative delineation of natural objects, but an arrangement of light,
form and colour'. When the judge asked him if *The Blue and Gold
Nocturne* was 'a correct representation of Battersea Bridge', Whistler
confounded him by replying that it was never intended to be anything but a moonlight scene. Burne-Jones admitted that the picture
had fine colour and atmosphere, but said it lacked 'finish'. In order to
try and explain to the judge what this meant, Taylor produced a
Titian, which was passed to the jury. The argument was far above
their heads, and the story goes that one of them, mistaking the Titian
for a work of Whistler's, exclaimed: 'We've had enough of this
Whistler' and refused to look at it.

In the end, Whistler was awarded a farthing damages and both
sides had to pay their own costs, which amounted to £385 each. A

subscription list was opened and Ruskin's costs were quickly contributed, but Whistler received not a penny. He was now in grave straits. The new house had involved greater expense than he had anticipated and he had many other debts. In May 1879 he was declared bankrupt. He had to leave the White House, which was bought by Harry Quilter the art critic for £2,700, and all his possessions were sold to pay his debts.

Whistler was not a particularly likeable personality. He was egotistical, vain and self-absorbed, but these traits carried him safely through the following months of outrageous ill-fortune. Sick at heart, he must have suffered agonies of bitterness and disappointment, but he showed a brave and gallant face to the world, spiced by his acid wit.

When the outlook was at its bleakest, Ernest Brown of the Fine Art Society arranged for him to be sent to Venice to do a series of etchings. Whistler departed, and shortly afterwards Maud joined him. He was desperately poor but his work was brilliant and by 1880 he was back in England again, re-establishing himself. A few critics were still hostile but his position gradually improved, as his work at last began to receive the appreciation it so richly deserved.

In 1881 he and Maud, who by this time had had a child by him, settled at number 13 Tite Street, close to the White House he had lost. At number 16 was living a young man of twenty-five, just down from Oxford, who had already made a name for himself – Oscar Wilde.

At Oxford, Wilde had read Ruskin and Swinburne avidly. He had attended Ruskin's lectures and absorbed much of Walter Pater's philosophy of 'art for art's sake'. He had studied Whistler's new ideas of interior decoration and claimed to be the leader of the new aesthetic cult, the symbols of which were peacock's feathers, sun-flowers and blue and white china. He was eccentric in dress, had long hair and wore velveteen breeches.

Whistler was excessively irritated by Wilde. In some ways they were too much alike, and when Gilbert and Sullivan presented *Patience* at the Savoy in 1881, there was even some confusion at first as to whether Bunthorne was intended for Wilde or Whistler.

Whistler considered himself a dandy, but his dress at this time was far too eccentric for conventional good taste. He habitually wore a well-cut but over-long frock-coat, a silk hat much taller than most, with a wide flat rim, white trousers, black patent leather pumps with coloured bows – sometimes pink – a very tall cane and a monocle.

Yet when he saw Oscar Wilde in a long green overcoat, heavily frogged, he sent him a note telling him to 'restore those things to Nathan's; and never again let me find you masquerading the streets of my Chelsea in the combined costumes of Kossuth and Mr Mantalini'.

By this time Spy, the cartoonist, was living in Leigh Hunt's old house in Upper Cheyne Row, so was finding excellent material almost on his doorstep.

In 1886 Whistler and Maud moved to the Vale, becoming neighbours of the de Morgans. Mrs Godwin, whose husband had been flagrantly unfaithful to her for years, became a frequent visitor at the studio and Whistler was fascinated by her. The situation with Maud became explosive and on one occasion, when the two women broke into a violent quarrel, Whistler pushed them both out into the street to cool off, but Maud burst a blood vessel and he had to fetch a doctor.

The triangle was resolved when Godwin died. Maud was discarded and in 1888 Whistler and Mrs Godwin were married.

Two years later they moved to number 21 Cheyne Walk, but by 1892 they had settled in Paris, in the rue du Bac. They had a few gay, triumphant years together. Recognition and honours came quickly to Whistler now. His portrait of his mother was bought for the Luxembourg and he received the Legion of Honour. After an exhibition at the Goupil Gallery in Bond Street, where many of his most famous pictures were assembled, he was made President of the International Society of Sculptors, Painters and Gravers.

Whistler was only sixty and his wife many years younger, but her health began to fail. He brought her back to England but it was soon discovered that she was dying of cancer. After her death in 1896 Whistler was desperately unhappy and restless. He eventually returned to number 74 Cheyne Walk, where his mother-in-law and sister-in-law kept house for him, but in 1903 at the age of sixty-nine he succumbed to a heart attack.

He was buried with his wife at Chiswick, but the funeral service was held at Old Chelsea Church, and among the congregation was an elderly woman whom few recognized, his faithful Jo.

Oscar Wilde, born in Dublin in 1856, was the son of Sir William Wilde, the distinguished eye surgeon, and of Lady Wilde, the poetess who wrote under the pseudonym 'Speranza'. After Trinity College, Dublin and Magdalen College, Oxford, Oscar Wilde came to London. In 1884 he married Constance Lloyd and they lived at number 16 Tite Street. By this time Sir William had died and Lady Wilde had established herself in Oakley Street, where the circle of friends she gathered round her, poets and admirers of her work, Irish Nationalists and devotees of Oscar, soon created a brilliant salon.

Whistler, living at number 13 Tite Street from 1881 to 1886, disliked the particular brand of aestheticism which Wilde affected, although so much of it had derived from his own preaching, and was soon openly antagonistic.

'What has Oscar in common with Art?' he wrote in a letter to *The World*. 'Except that he dines at our tables and picks from our platters the plums for the pudding he peddles in the provinces. Oscar – the amiable, irresponsible, esurient Oscar – with no more sense of a picture than of the fit of a coat, has the courage of the opinions . . . of others!'

The charge of plagiarism, which others besides Whistler were to make, was unjust, for Wilde had a mind of outstanding originality and a brilliant command of language.

His wife shared his enthusiasm for the aesthetic cult and was also leader of the movement for drastic reform in women's dress, favouring the flowing Classical draperies of the Pre-Raphaelite women in place of the tight waists, rigid corsets, bustles and long, encumbering skirts of the 1880s. Their house in Tite Street, with its fresh white and yellow paint, its framed etchings and Japanese prints, was elegantly and simply furnished, despite Whistler's jibes. During the eleven years they lived there they had two sons.

Wilde's first volume of poems, published in 1881, was well received but made little money, and he earned his living by journalism, editing *The Woman's World* for a time.

In 1888 he published his first collection of short stories, *The Happy Prince and Other Tales* and, in 1891, a second volume, *Lord Arthur Savile's Crime and Other Stories*. This was the year that his one novel appeared, *The Picture of Dorian Gray*. And that same year 'fate knocked at the door of 16 Tite Street, in the person of Lionel Johnson, old Wykehamist, poet, distinguished Oxonian and homosexual, bringing with him Lord Alfred Douglas'.*

The story of Wilde's downfall begins with this meeting with Lord Alfred Douglas, the selfish and exacting little Bosie, but the trial was not until seven years later.

* *Oscar Wilde and the Black Douglas* – by the Marquess of Queensberry, in collaboration with Percy Colson, London, 1949.

His four successful comedies appeared in quick succession. The first was *Lady Windermere's Fan* in 1892, followed by *A Woman of No Importance* in 1893. His next play *Salome*, which Sarah Bernhardt was anxious to play, was refused a licence by the Lord Chamberlain, but was published in 1893, with illustrations by Aubrey Beardsley.

It was about this time that William Rothenstein first met Wilde. 'I expected to meet someone pale and slender,' he said. 'Great was my surprise at seeing a huge and rather fleshly figure, floridly dressed in a frock coat and a red waistcoat. I was not at all attracted by his appearance. He had elaborately-waved, long hair, parted in the middle, which made his forehead appear lower than it was, a finely shaped nose, but dark-coloured lips and uneven teeth, and his cheeks were full and touching his wide-winged collar. His hands were fat and useless looking, and the more conspicuous from a large scarab ring he wore. But before he left I was charmed by his conversation, and his looks were forgotten. . . . There was certainly something florid, almost vulgar, in his appearance; and his manners were emphasised. But he was not only an unique talker and story-teller – I have never heard anyone tell stories as he did – but he had an extra-ordinarily illuminating intellect. His description of people, his appreciation of prose and verse, were a never-failing delight. He seemed to have read all books, and to have known all men and women. . . . He was remarkably free from malice. . . . He had a quality of sympathy and understanding which was more than mere flattery, and he seemed to see better than anyone else just what was one's aim; or rather he made one believe that what was latent perhaps in one's nature had been actually achieved.'*

By the 1890s, Wilde was neglecting his wife and two sons and was seen more and more in the fashionable West End resorts with Bosie, who kept Wilde poor by borrowing money from him, wasting his time and insisting on the most lavish and expensive entertainment, to which he contributed not a penny.

In 1894 Bosie's father, the Marquess of Queensberry, called on Wilde at Tite Street and threatened to ruin him if he did not break with his son immediately. He was shown to the door and the relationship continued. Early in 1895 *The Ideal Husband* was presented at the Haymarket Theatre. Rehearsals for his fifth play *The Importance of Being Earnest* began. Wilde took Bosie on holiday with him to North Africa. Here they met André Gide, who described the impression the pair made on him. Bosie he disliked intensely, finding

* *Men and Memories*, William Rothenstein (Faber & Faber, 1931).

him cynical and selfish. Wilde, in spite of his sparkling conversation, seemed to him 'full of forebodings'. 'People do not always realize how much truth, wisdom and seriousness were concealed under the mask of the jester,' observed Gide.

Wilde came back to London for the first night of *The Importance of Being Earnest*. Then he went into the country for a few days, and when he returned he found Lord Queensberry's card with the insulting message. It was Bosie, hating his father, and caring nothing for the possible effect on Wilde, who persuaded him, against the advice of his real friends, to take action against Lord Queensberry for criminal libel: and when it failed, he was arrested, found guilty and sentenced to two years' imprisonment with hard labour. Many Victorians did not know that the practice of homosexuality existed and the scandal shook London society. The run of his two plays continued but his name was removed from the theatre bills. John Lane removed his books from circulation and the bailiffs took possession of his house. All his possessions were put up for sale and the prurient and the curious fell upon them, snatching bargains from the ruins, at far below their worth.

For the first six months he was in Wandsworth Prison, but his friends managed to arrange a transfer to Reading gaol, where conditions may have been a little easier for him. Here he wrote the letter to Bosie which was later called *De Profundis* and it must have been little consolation to him to hear that *Salome* was being produced in Paris at last. Lady Wilde died while he was in prison and when he was released, in May 1897, he went to France. A few weeks later he was writing to William Rothenstein: 'I have not come out of prison an embittered or disappointed man ... but I *am* really ashamed of having led a life unworthy of an artist ... a life of definite and studied materialism, and philosophy of appetite and cynicism, and a cult of sensual and senseless ease, are bad things for an artist; they narrow the imagination, and dull the more delicate sensibilities.'

Wilde wrote *The Ballad of Reading Gaol* during the first months of his release and then asked Bosie to join him. Together they went to Naples, but when Wilde's money was exhausted, Bosie left him. Wilde made his way back to Paris, and here he spent the last two years of his life, a lonely and tragic exile. He died in November 1900, at the age of forty-four, after being received into the Roman Catholic Church.

XVIII

The Late Victorians in Kensington

AFTER the death of the last Lord Holland, in 1859, Lady Holland entertained in the grand manner of the house during the month or two of each year that she lived there, but before long she became worried over money and began to sell parts of the estate. By 1873 she was in real difficulties and, in return for an annuity, handed the estate and its management to her heir, the fifth Earl of Ilchester, while retaining the use of the house for her lifetime. Already much of the land on the west side of Addison Road had gone for building and also many acres giving on to the Uxbridge Road, by now known as Holland Park.

Lord Ilchester embarked on further necessary developments, including the pulling down, in 1875, of Little Holland House, which was, in any case, very dilapidated: and on this land Melbury Road gradually took shape, soon to become Kensington's artists' colony.

Earlier in the century many artists had lived in Kensington, Sir David Wilkie in Lower Phillimore Place and then at Maitland House in Church Street, the Redgraves in Kensington Square, Richard Ansdell at Lytham House and Samuel William Reynolds in Holland Street. Sir Augustus Callcott lived in the Mall, off Church Street, and William Mulready in Linden Grove, near the Linden Gardens. John Leech drew his pictures for *Punch* in his home in the High Street and W. P. Frith painted *Derby Day* and the *Railway Station* at a house in

Swan Walk, Chelsea, *c.* 1890

Turk's Row, Lower Sloane Street, Chelsea, 1888

Dante Gabriel Rossetti's house in Cheyne Walk, *c.* 1890

Holland House, *c.* 1900
Lady Holland's sitting-room

Kensington High Street in the 1890s

Crosby Hall, Cheyne Walk, Chelsea, *c.* 1910

Kensington House, Kensington Gore

Kensington Square, west side

Sir Thomas More's Chapel, Chelsea
Old Church, after the bombing of 1941

Chelsea – in the 1970s

The shopping precinct off the King's Road, Chelsea

Pembridge Villas which has now disappeared with new building developments.

While G. F. Watts had been living with the Princeps in Little Holland House their circle of friends had included Thackeray, Richard Doyle, Tennyson, Rossetti, Burne-Jones and Frederic Leighton. Now the first house to be built in Melbury Road was a new Little Holland House, today number 6, where G. F. Watts moved in 1876. Round the corner, in Holland Park Road, at that time a narrow country lane, lived Frederic Leighton: and eventually Valentine Princeps was to live at number 1, Holland Park Road, in a house built for him by Philip Webb.

Leighton, having spent many years of his youth in Italy, had introduced the classical revival into Victorian painting. Under his direction, George Aitchison had built Leighton House in 1866, a large red-brick studio house, the studio occupying the whole of the first floor on the north side.

In 1878 he was to be elected President of the Royal Academy and given a knighthood, while in 1896 he was raised to the peerage, but he died the following day.

The fascination of Leighton House is the Arab Hall, leading from the inner hall on the ground floor. It is an authentic copy of an Arab hall in Moorish Spain. The dome is inlaid with stained glass, the walls are faced with thirteenth-, sixteenth- and seventeenth-century tiles collected by Leighton and his friends Sir C. Purdom Clarke and Sir Richard Burton from Rhodes, Persia, Damascus and other parts of the Middle East, the carved wooden screens and the screens in the windows and the zenana came from Cairo. In the centre is a little fountain which tinkles gently into a black marble pool.

The hall took several years to complete and many of his friends made their contributions. Sir Edgar Boehm carved the alabaster caps of the marble columns supporting the dome with fabulous birds which had been designed by Caldecott. Walter Crane, living in the delightful Old House close by, designed the mosaic frieze, in brown, blue, silver and gold.

The inner hall of the house and the walls of the white stone staircase leading to the domed landing are also hung with Damascus tiles as well as many made by William de Morgan, which are of outstanding beauty in colour and design.

It was in this exotic setting that Leighton delighted to give his famous musical parties.

Lady Holland was dismayed at the sight of the new houses. She disliked 'the fantastic erections of Watts and Leighton' and more particularly 'the tall red house' of Luke Fildes, now number 11 Melbury Road, designed by Norman Shaw in 1877. Shaw also designed number 8 for Marcus Stone. Both Thomas Thorneycroft, the sculptor and his son Sir William Hamo Thorneycroft lived in Melbury Road and William Burges, the architect, built number 9, the Tower House, a Gothic fantasy on which he lavished years of care, adding painted ceilings, sculptured marble fireplaces, mosaics and bronze doors, to create an atmosphere of medieval splendour.

At number 18 Melbury Road Holman Hunt, an old friend of G. F. Watts', came to live. It was Holman Hunt who had designed Ellen Terry's wedding dress when she married Watts. By the time he moved to Melbury Road the Pre-Raphaelite Brotherhood had ended, and Rossetti was living alone in Cheyne Walk. Hunt remained good friends with Millais but Ruskin had turned against Hunt as well as Millais, though remaining a loyal supporter of Rossetti.

Burne-Jones had been living in Kensington Square during the 1860s and Millais at Cromwell Place, but in 1878 Millais moved to Palace Gate, near the house where his old friend Thackeray had lived.

In 1855, when Anne Thackeray was eighteen and Minny fifteen, friends had persuaded Thackeray to take them from Young Street to the new and fashionable district of South Kensington, and for the next eleven years they had lived at 36 Onslow Square, but Thackeray's health was failing and it was decided that the higher ground of Kensington might suit him better. He therefore bought an old house, now number 2 Palace Green, which he hoped to adapt. However, as Anne recorded: 'The old house which my father had intended to alter and live in was found to be tumbling to pieces and not safe to knock about. After some demur it was pulled down and the Queen Anne building was erected in which he took so much pleasure.'

'The house is delightful,' Thackeray wrote to a friend. 'I have paid 5,000 on it in two years out of income – but there's ever so much more to pay I don't know how much. . . . Well upon my word it is one of the nicest houses I have ever seen . . . there is an old green and an old palace and magnificent trees before the window at wh. I write. I have the most delightful study, bedroom, and so forth.'

Thackeray loved his new house, but he was not to enjoy it for long, for two years later, in the early morning of Christmas Eve, 1863, when he was only fifty-two, he died, quite suddenly, and the orphaned girls later moved to Onslow Gardens.

Thackeray had been greatly loved by all his friends in Kensington. Anne, writing the following autumn, said: 'Minny is going out for a drive with Mrs Carlyle this afternoon – we met old Thomas the other day on his horse and he suddenly began to cry. I shall always love him in future, for I used to fancy he did not care about Papa.'

Millais, who had become wealthy as a fashionable portrait painter, had greatly admired Thackeray's house on Palace Green and when he moved to Palace Gate in 1878 he designed for himself a magnificent mansion, the architect being Philip Hardwick. It was, said Millais, 'a great plain square house, with none of the thought-out quaintness of the Anglo-Dutch revival'. The marble hall was 35 feet square and on the landing of the wide staircase a fountain played, while the lofty first-floor studio was 40 feet long.

Holman Hunt's house in Melbury Road had none of this palatial grandeur. Holman Hunt took immense pains with his work and his granddaughter Diana Holman Hunt describes in her book *My Grandmothers and I** the desperate difficulties he encountered with his picture *Flight into Egypt*, which was afterwards called *The Triumph of the Innocents*. He had gone to Palestine to work on it but back in Melbury Road he was dissatisfied with the anatomy of the ass. He went to a knacker, hoping to buy a dead donkey, but the knacker could produce only a large, dead horse, the tail of which he had already sold. It duly arrived in a cart outside the large red-brick house, with its dignified pillared porch. 'The carcase was cut into huge red joints which we carried through the drawing room, down the steps, and laid on the grass in the garden,' recounted Grandmother Hunt.

Holman's idea was to burn the body till the flesh fell off the bones and reassemble the skeleton in his studio, but this presented difficulties for which he had not bargained. He and his devoted wife 'went out and bought some bricks, and a large old copper, which we found abandoned in a builder's yard. Holman borrowed a barrow and we wheeled everything home, causing some consternation in the streets – dear Holman was quite unselfconscious. We carried jug after jug of water out of the house.'

But the fire wouldn't burn and the water wouldn't boil. It poured with rain. The sticks were damp and the fire went out. That horse just wouldn't cook. Day after day they tried, the smell growing hourly worse, until at last the whole neighbourhood complained and the police arrived.

* Diana Holman Hunt, *My Grandmothers and I*, Hamish Hamilton, 1960.

Living in fashionable Bolton Gardens in South Kensington were friends of the Millais', Mr and Mrs Potter, their son and their daughter Beatrix: and after all poor Holman Hunt's troubles, it is sad to read the entry Beatrix made in her diary during March 1885. 'Holman Hunt's picture of the *Flight Into Egypt* is at the Fine Arts in Bond Street, creating a certain languid excitement. He has been working on the subject for seven years . . .': and the following week she wrote: 'Saw Oscar Wilde and his wife just going into the Fine Arts to see the Holman Hunt . . . a very interesting picture, but the execution is rather disappointing in places. It does not look finished in parts and does not show seven years work. Had it not shown this crude look in parts, and had the donkeys and some of the children been more true to nature, it would have been a most splendid work . . .'

Mrs Holman Hunt disliked Rossetti intensely. 'He was dirty and horrid,' she said, 'his hair was always greasy and he spilt his soup and spaghetti all down his clothes. They weren't even his. He borrowed everyone else's, even Bruno's (Ford Maddox Brown). He never gave them back, and what's more he was a cheat. He was Grandpa's pupil and never paid the rent and sent his picture – Grandpa had painted most of it – to an exhibition, without telling him and Johnnie Millais, although he'd said he wouldn't until theirs were ready too. He ate Grandpa out of house and home and gave noisy parties and shouted at the models. . . . Poor Grandpa got thrown out because he hadn't any money and Mr Ruskin turned against him because he was Johnnie's friend. Everything went wrong and it was all Rossetti's fault . . .'

Feelings ran high in Kensington about its painters. At the end of 1882 Beatrix was writing: 'Mr Whistler is holding an Exhibition somewhere, termed an Arrangement in white and yellow. The furniture is painted yellow and the footman is dressed in white and yellow, someone said he looked like a poached egg. . . . It's quite disgusting how people go on about these Pre-Raphaelite aesthetic painters.' And two years later she is confessing that she had never been a great admirer of Leighton and 'Dislike is a mild word for my feeling towards Burne-Jones. Some of the papers say his pictures ought to go to the National Gallery. But for their praise he would be below contempt and notice.'

Holman Hunt died in 1910 at the age of eighty-three, but his widow lived on for many years at Melbury Road, growing odder every year, though in an endearing way. She had worshipped Hol-

THE LATE VICTORIANS IN KENSINGTON   217

man and nearly every Sunday took a bus to St Paul's Cathedral to visit his tomb and gaze at *The Light of the World.*

The house has been turned into flats and today looks well cared for and prosperous, but to Diana Holman Hunt, visiting it as a child, in the 1920s, it was a gloomy and alarming place. 'In the inner hall one jet of gas burned low and blue on an iron bracket, casting a glinting light on the brass plates, copper trays, daggers, scimitars and swords that dotted the walls, between oil paintings . . . Christs, virgins and saints . . . at the Burmese gongs, supported by gilded dragons . . .' In the sitting-room there was 'a leafy Morris wall paper. The Della Robbia, covered with dust, over the fireplace, vases of honesty and peacock feathers, spindly bamboo tables.' A purple taffeta curtain was pulled across the Van Dyck crucifixion, a curtain of faded orange silk over the Bellini. In the day time the more precious pictures were also covered to prevent their fading by the sun and the Byzantine black Madonna with her jewelled crown was shrouded in a muslin veil.

And every night Helen, the only servant, helped the old lady fix trip wires, booby traps and bells in the ground-floor rooms, in case of burglars. 'Helen stood there, puffing as usual. Lengths of wire, with sharp prongs at each end, were wound round her neck, and bells and metal rings were hanging from her arms. In one hand she held a hammer and in the other a basket full of tins.

'Grand stretched the wires across the room and hammered the sharp pegs in the floor between the Persian rugs. She made piles of tins here and there about the rooms and hooked the bells over the doors.'

The unlighted stairs leading down to the basement kitchen, which, according to Helen, was 'a living mass of black beetles' at night, the cockroaches in the larder, the sinister weapons, glinting on the walls, were bad enough, but worst of all were the Friday bath nights.

When they reached the bathroom Grandma lit the gas and turned it very low. 'Stand well back!' she ordered, approaching the geyser, 'just in case it explodes.'

A sinister hissing was followed by a violent bang and a roar. 'Keep well away till the water runs. You never know.' She held up a warning finger.

'I cowered in the doorway. A thin stream of boiling, rusty water cascaded into the bath, filling the room with steam. She shouted out of the fog: "Stay where you are! Shut your eyes! I'm going to get in when I've turned off the cold."

'I sank to the floor coughing. I couldn't see a thing but I could hear a dragon snorting and then a long agonised sigh, followed by sudden pandemonium: the pipes thumping and banging and invisible water gurgling in torrents.

' "Look alive!" she cried. "Your turn next. The water isn't dirty: it's only lather from the Castile soap".'

As she lay dying, poor Edith Holman Hunt was increasingly troubled by the fact that her dear Holman had first married her younger sister, who had died young, and she was now faced with the insoluble problem of how the three of them would manage all together in Heaven, where Fanny and Holman had already been united for so many years, 'perhaps as they never were before'.

And Diana, trying to comfort her, said: 'I'm sure Grandpa Holman has been here in this house with you, far more than he's been in heaven with great-aunt Fanny. I know he's here, he always has been.'

XIX

Kensington Before 1914

WHILE the artists turned their backs on the materialism of the nineteenth century, it escaped them by becoming the even harsher and infinitely more crowded twentieth century.

In 1867 the Kensington Improvement Scheme had been launched and Kensington High Street was widened, to form a 'noble roadway' in place of the 'inadequate and cramped approach to Town'.

On the north side, the town hall was built in 1878, next to the Vestry hall which had gone up in 1852.

On the south side, shops were planned and by 1870 fifty-five houses and shops had been built in the High Street, opposite St Mary Abbots, in a block bounded by Young Street in the east and what is now Derry Street in the west. John Barker leased numbers 91 and 93 and opened as a general draper, with such success that within twelve months he had bought two more shops and by 1872 had also acquired 87 High Street. The business expanded steadily and in 1877 Sam Beeton's magazine *The Queen* was recommending Barker's as 'the best establishment in London for Drapery at moderate prices'.

Samuel Little and Company also opened in the High Street in 1870, as Silk Mercers, Linen and General Drapers, and were very successful for a time but did not stay the course, succumbing before the growing might of Derry and Toms, who soon acquired seven shops, with two hundred living-in assistants.

The next arrivals were the Ponting Brothers, who opened in 1873, first at 125 High Street, and by 1900 had acquired 123, 123a and 127 High Street and also the ancient Scarsdale House in between, which was preserved for a time but eventually pulled down to make way for a new Pontings store. In 1906 the firm had to go into liquidation and was taken over by Barker's, and in 1971 the business was transferred entirely to Barker's and the old Pontings store has been demolished.

In Knightsbridge Benjamin Harvey's store flourished until his death in the late 1850s, when his daughter took Colonel Nichols, the silk buyer, into partnership, and as Harvey Nichols it became exclusive and fashionable. Harrods, a few yards away down the Brompton Road, steadily expanded throughout the nineteenth century from the little grocer's shop of 1849, and by the late 1880s had added carpets and furniture to its departments and finally drapery and clothing, the sumptuous terracotta store, which quickly became world famous, being built in 1901 to 1905, while behind it the tall, dark red houses of High Victorian Kensington rose in dignified solemnity.

Beatrix Potter's diary records much of the building which took place round her own corner of Kensington during the last twenty years of Queen Victoria's reign. On 31 October 1882, she wrote that 'every patch of land is being built up', and in June 1883: 'They cut down the old walnut up the new road. Poor tree. I remember it almost as long as I remember anything here abouts. They are cutting a road across the field, preparatory to building. It is the last bit of orchard left.' On the 15th, 'they cut down the big mulberry bush on the left at the bottom of Gloucester Road, and most of the other trees except the big plane. I wonder how the rooks know, they left these trees a very short time before they were felled, and they left the rookery in Kensington Gardens the autumn before the trees went.'

Less than three years later, John Hunter's old house and gardens in Earls Court, which had become a private lunatic asylum, were put up for sale as building land. 'The house has been done up, but the grounds seem to be in the same state as when John Hunter kept his leopards, and the Princess Charlotte played with the Albemarle children,' wrote Beatrix. 'Independent of sentiment, it is a pity the fine ilex and horse-chestnut cannot escape.'

The following year the first Earls Court exhibition was held – Buffalo Bill's Wild West show – but the present Exhibition building was not built until 1937.

In Kensington Palace Gardens the building of the Italianate mansions, begun mainly in the 1850s, continued, to form a beautiful avenue, shaded by great plane trees, running from Palace Green to Notting Hill and Bayswater, and today many of these houses, each standing in its own garden, are occupied by embassies, including those of Russia, Japan, Norway, Nepal, Syria, the Lebanon and the Philippines.

In 1862 Campden House which, after years as a girls' boarding-school, had become a private residence again, was burnt to the ground, one of those dubious fires which occurred only a year or two after a heavy insurance, and by 1900 a block of flats, Campden Hill Court, stood on the site. Bullingham House was pulled down in 1892 to make way for Bullingham Mansions but Little Campden House survived until it was destroyed by a flying bomb in 1944.

Lady Holland died at Holland House in 1889 and those who had watched the disappearance of rural Kensington with growing sadness were relieved to hear that Lord Ilchester proposed to live there and so preserve the last 'cuckoo haunted wilderness' of the Holland estate. He and Lady Ilchester moved in in 1890 and began a complete renovation of Holland House, which had once more fallen into a state of neglect. Electric lighting was installed and a new room, called the Swannery, was added to the south-west corner. New drainage was installed, the roof was repaired and much of the stone of the arcades and balustrades restored or replaced.

Lord and Lady Ilchester began to entertain, the first important function being a masked ball, in 1891. All through the last years of Queen Victoria and the early Edwardian years the parties and entertainments at Holland House were important events in London society, but in 1905 Lord Ilchester died.

Lady Ilchester survived her husband for thirty years and during this time, until her death in 1935, she remained at Holland House, living in the east wing, preserving the house and its contents and lavishing infinite care on the gardens, which became some of the finest in England. Here, only a few hundred yards behind the growing bustle of Kensington High Street, throughout the first forty years of the twentieth century, woodpeckers, cuckoos, jays, willow wrens and blackcaps were nesting.

Lady Ilchester still entertained a little, but on nothing like the old scale. Her son, the sixth Earl of Ilchester, did not join her, living with his wife in Dorset, but he did most valuable work in his study of the Holland House papers, writing many memoirs, and in 1937 his important history of Holland House was published.

The maintenance of the house was a constant financial burden.

During the thirties a staff of eighteen were employed in the grounds alone. More land was sold. In 1926 the flats of Melbury Court were built in the High Street, occupying part of the frontage of the grounds, and in 1928 Ilchester Place, north of Melbury Road. In 1936 the Holland House Properties Company was launched and Abbotsbury Road, in which a few houses had been built in 1900, was extended northwards, to link Melbury Road and Ilchester Place with Holland Park.

Holland House was gradually being surrounded, but cuckoos still sang in the grounds and herons hovered over the fountain pool, and it was still to see one or two grand occasions, the last being a dance given by the Honourable Roland Cubitt and Mrs Cubitt for their daughter, on 7 July 1939. Before the dance King George VI and Queen Elizabeth dined with Lord and Lady Ilchester, the last sovereigns ever to visit the old house, for early in the Second World War incendiary bombs fell on it and before the staff and firemen could get to them, from attending another fire, the roof was alight and nothing could save it. Only the east wing and parts of the west wing survived. Fortunately most of the valuable pictures, books and furniture had been removed at the outbreak of war, but the ruined shell remained derelict for the next seventeen years, and then the greater part of it had to be demolished.

At Kensington Palace, Prince Franz of Teck and his bride, Princess Mary Adelaide of Cambridge, a cousin of Queen Victoria, were granted apartments at Kensington Palace, occupying the rooms used by the Duchess of Kent, who had died in 1861: and there their daughter, Princess May, who was to become the future Queen Mary, wife of George V, was born in 1867.

Their neighbour at the palace was the Duchess of Inverness, the surviving second wife of the Duke of Sussex, who lived on until 1873.

The Tecks were far from wealthy, but they maintained a splendid household at Kensington Palace, and in 1870, thinking that the proximity of the Round Pond was not good for their children, they moved to White Lodge, Richmond Park, while retaining their rooms at the palace.

In February 1882 Beatrix Potter recorded that 'Mr Millais is going to paint the portrait of one of the Duchess of Edinburgh's children. The Duchess is staying with Princess Mary at Kensington Palace. Mr Millais went to see her yesterday. . . . She offended him greatly. She enquired where his "rooms" were, evidently doubtful whether a

Princess might condescend to come to them. "My *rooms*, ma'am, are in Palace Gate," he said ... and he told Papa afterwards, with great indignation, he daresay they were much better than hers. He is right proud of his house.'

And in order to maintain his dignity and prestige, Millais took on an extra butler for the occasions of the Princess' visits.

The following year the Tecks, hard-pressed for money and heavily in debt, had to move from Kensington Palace. They retired to Florence for a year or two and Princess May never lived there again.

In 1873 Princess Louise, Queen Victoria's sixth child, went to live at the palace, after her marriage to the Marquess of Lorne, occupying first the rooms of the late Duchess of Inverness and later, after her return from Canada, apartments in the south-west corner. Here she had her studio, where she worked on the statue of her mother, which was placed on the Broad Walk and unveiled by the Queen in 1893.

The palace was in constant need of repair and once more there were suggestions that it might be pulled down, but Queen Victoria saved it. By an arrangement whereby she yielded other Crown properties, Parliament agreed to restore Kensington Palace, provided the State Rooms were opened to the public, and on 24 May 1899, the Queen's eightieth birthday, with the apartments cleaned and many of the pictures returned from Hampton Court, they were opened: while at the end of 1901, the year of her death, Kensington became, at her wish, a Royal Borough.

The London Museum was first established at the palace in 1911. Two years later it was moved to Lancaster House but it is now back temporarily at the palace, until it goes to its ultimate home in the Museum of London in the City of London's Barbican, in about 1974. It now occupies twenty rooms on the ground floor and semi-basement of the main building, which is the site of the original Nottingham House, and since 1956 it has also administered the State Apartments above.

Princess Beatrice, the last survivor of Queen Victoria's children, was given an apartment at the palace after the Queen's death and lived on until 1944. Prince Philip often stayed there as a boy, with his grandmother, the Dowager Marchioness of Milford Haven, who had apartments in the north-west corner of Prince of Wales' Court, and he spent the night there on the eve of his wedding to Princess Elizabeth.

Marina, Duchess of Kent moved to the palace in 1955 and since her death her children have retained apartments there.

Princess Margaret and Lord Snowdon moved there after their wedding in 1960, first to number 10, the rooms of the Maids of Honour in the north wing, and then to apartments on the south side of Clock Court, which had been occupied by the Duke of Sussex.

During the Second World War there was damage from incendiary bombs and a flying bomb, most of which has been repaired, but the north and east sides of Prince of Wales' Court are still in need of attention.

All through Victorian times and on into the present century Kensington Gardens have been popular. All the babies of Kensington who could boast nursemaids – and that is a very high proportion – have been wheeled there for their daily airings, and complaints that the nursemaids spent more time flirting with the soldiers from Knightsbridge barracks than looking after their wealthy little charges have never been taken very seriously. And as the babies grew up, they sailed their boats on the Round Pond.

At the turn of the century, J. M. Barrie was living at 133 Gloucester Road. He had no children of his own but was great friends with Arthur Llewelyn Davies and his wife, Sylvia, daughter of George du Maurier, and often played with their small sons in Kensington Gardens. For them he wrote *The Little White Bird*, published in 1902, and two years later the play *Peter Pan*, adapted from it, was produced at the Duke of York's theatre, after which he published *Peter Pan in Kensington Gardens*, which was, in the main, a reprint of part of *The Little White Bird*. It was made extremely successful with Arthur Rackham's illustrations, and in 1912 George Frampton's statue of Peter Pan was placed on the south bank of the Serpentine, at the point where Peter first landed from his boat.

New generations of artists and writers came to Kensington as the mid-Victorians died away, Andrew Lang at number 1 Marloes Road, until his death in 1912, E. F. Benson at number 25 Brompton Square, John Galsworthy at South House, Campden Hill, G. K. Chesterton at number 11 Warwick Gardens. Ford Maddox Brown, editor of *The English Review*, lived at South Lodge, Campden Hill Road with Violet Hunt, and among their circle of friends were Henry James, Joseph Conrad, H. G. Wells, Arnold Bennett and Ezra Pound.

Sir John Lavery had his studio at Cromwell Place, Sir William Orpen in The Boltons, Philip de Laszlo at West House, a Norman Shaw house in Campden Hill Road, and Percy Wyndham Lewis at number 27a Notting Hill Studios, until his death in 1937.

XX

Chelsea Before 1914

CHELSEA is 'a gilded desert to those who knew it in the seventies' wrote William Morris' daughter sadly, during the early years of the twentieth century, yet a good deal of the eighteenth-century village still remained. When William Rothenstein came to Chelsea in the last years of the nineteenth century, he wrote: 'I was at first disappointed with the long King's Road, a shabbier Oxford Street, with its straggling, dirty, stucco mid-century houses and shops. But the river-side along Cheyne Walk was beautiful; what noble houses! and there was Lindsey Row and Cheyne Row and Paradise Walk, and the Physic Garden and the Vale.

'The Vale was then really a vale, with wild gardens and houses hidden among the trees. Oscar Wilde had taken me to the Vale to see Ricketts and Shannon before I came to live in Chelsea, when I was charmed by those two men and their simple dwelling, with its primrose walls, apple-green skirting and shelves, the rooms hung with Shannon's lithographs, a fan-shaped water-colour by Whistler, and drawings by Hokusai . . .'

This was the house where Whistler had lived with Maud Franklin for a few stormy years and where he had 'cultivated his delphiniums', and it was here that Ricketts and Shannon set up their Vale Press. On the occasion of Rothenstein's visit, Walter Sickert was living in William de Morgan's house, presumably while de Morgan was in Italy.

Rothenstein borrowed Jacomb-Hood's studio in Tite Street for a while, a house which, like Whistler's White House, had been built by Godwin, and at this time Oscar and Constance Wilde were still living at number 16 Tite Street.

Walter Sickert did not work in the Vale. He rented a small room at the western end of the Embankment, beyond Beaufort Street. 'Needless to say,' says Rothenstein, 'the room was in one of the few ugly houses to be found in Cheyne Walk. . . . Walter Sickert's genius for discovering the dreariest house and most forbidding rooms in which to work was a source of wonder and amusement to me. He himself was so fastidious in his person, in his manners, in the choice of his clothes. . . . He was a famous wit. . . . As a talker he could hold his own with Whistler and Wilde.'

Born in 1860, Sickert had been an actor in his youth, playing with Ellen Terry and Henry Irving, and he never lost his love of the theatre and theatre people. He took to painting and was one of the young disciples of Whistler, in company with the Greaves brothers. The 'followers' were not exactly pupils, writes Rothenstein, 'for Whistler was too selfish to trouble himself about them. "You must occupy yourselves with the Master," said Whistler, "not with your-selves. There is a great deal to be done." They ran his errands, they helped to print his plates, but (more important from Whistler's point of view) they formed a bodyguard when he walked abroad. In restaurants and in the streets they made him the centre of a noisy crowd. They advertised him everywhere. They were terribly bad for him, and terribly necessary.'

As Sickert's work developed and he drifted away from Whistler's influence, Whistler seems to have turned a blind eye on his talent, and when Pennell brought an action against Sickert for the article in the *Saturday Review*, in which he suggested that Pennell's work was not true lithography, Whistler, for the plaintiff, referred to Sickert as 'an absolutely unknown authority' and an 'insignificant and irresponsible person'.

Sickert went to Paris, where he lived for several years and studied the work of the French Impressionists, particularly Degas. He helped to introduce Impressionism to England. At de Morgan's house in the Vale he opened a school for a short time, two of his pupils being

oger Fry and William Rothenstein, who was to become Director of the Kensington School of Art. Sickert loved to paint the squalor of London slum life – dim interiors of poverty made beautiful by soft twilight – Victorian music-hall galleries, subtly lit by reflected light from the stage – costermongers and flower girls in the misty, grey murk of a London winter.

'Night after night, Sickert would go to the Bedford or Sadler's Wells, to watch the light effects on stage and boxes, on pit and gallery, making tiny studies on scraps of paper with enduring patience and with such fruitful results,' wrote Rothenstein.

One day, when Sickert and Wilson Steer were passing a rag-and-bone shop, Sickert remarked: 'That's how I should like my pictures to look.' 'They do,' replied Steer.

Born in the same year, the two men were close friends. Wilson Steer had also studied in Paris and come under the influence of the Impressionists. He came to Chelsea in 1898, settling at number 109 Cheyne Walk, where he remained until his death in 1942. Sickert never settled anywhere for long, but he was frequently in Chelsea, visiting Steer and his other artist friends.

Steer's house was late eighteenth century, but it had been altered a great deal and the windows gave it a Victorian air. Even today it seems to symbolise the solid comfort of those late Victorian and Edwardian days before the First World War, the days of lamplighters and muffin-men and trim parlour maids, German bands and Italian organ-grinders, lavender sellers and hot potato men, hansoms and growlers. Here Steer lived in bachelor contentment, painting in his first-floor drawing-room studio, looked after by a faithful house-keeper and entertaining his friends, collecting pictures and antiques, coins and bronzes and a good deal of Chelsea porcelain, which pro-voked Rothenstein into telling him he had the worst good taste of anyone he knew.

Wilson Steer was not a close imitator of the French Impressionists but developed a style of his own, in which the English tradition of Gainsborough, Constable and Turner mingled with the later French manner, but he was a founder of the New English Art Club which helped to introduce the Impressionists to England. They held their first exhibition at the Marlborough Galleries in Pall Mall in 1886 and Sickert, Charles Furse, William Orpen and Augustus John were all members.

Wilson Steer, whose landscapes and portraits were equally brilli-ant, was a revolutionary painter in his day, but in his private life he was intensely conservative. 'His habits were simple,' wrote Rothen-stein. 'He was extremely matter of fact; in life, for him, there was little romance. Without a brush in his hand, he was indifferent to most things save dry feet and freedom from draughts.' He hated change and was 'content to meet the same people every day. He liked, too, to hear the same jokes; with a little gossip, a naughty story or two, the evenings passed pleasantly. Sickert and George Moore, Tonks and Harrison, MacColl, Frederick Brown, Sargent and myself formed his regular circle.'

Sargent, who, like Whistler, was of American parentage, was born in Florence in 1856 and, by 1885, after studying painting in Paris, he had come to Chelsea, taking a studio in Tite Street, first at number 13, where Whistler had lived for a time, and then at number 31. He became a member of the New English Art Club but he was never in England for more than four months at a time and his fashionable portraits were painted during that short period each year, the rest of his time being spent in Italy, France or America. His sister and mother lived in Carlyle Mansions close by and it was here that the three entertained their Chelsea circle of friends, which included Wilson Steer, Henry Tonks, who was to succeed Professor Brown at the Slade School, and later Henry James, as well as visiting American artists.

After leaving Jacomb-Hood's studio, Rothenstein found rooms and a studio for himself in Glebe Place, which Sickert had once used. His neighbours were James Guthrie, living in the Philip Webb house, who was to become President of the Royal Scottish Academy, and Derwent Wood, who had been a Slade pupil under Legros, Professor Brown's distinguished predecessor. Rothenstein had met Henry James in Paris during his student days. Born in 1843, James had left his native America in 1869 and settled in England, though frequently crossing to France in the early days.

'He was charming to all of us; he liked young people and all his life had been closely associated with painters and sculptors,' wrote Rothenstein. 'I was amused by his slow and exact way of speaking. He was not in those days so massive as he became later, either in person or manner, but he was already elaborately precise and correct. He always carried his silk hat, stick and gloves into the room when he paid a call, laying hat and gloves across his knee.'

Henry James was a great admirer of Sargent. Oscar Wilde, on the other hand, he considered a 'fatuous cad' and *The Importance of being Earnest* he dismissed as 'miserable trash'.

He spent the first few years of his time in England at Rye, but in 1911, already an elderly man, he came to live in Chelsea, taking rooms in Cheyne Walk at first but ultimately settling at 21 Carlyle Mansions. Here, overlooking the river, he found great peace and contentment. 'I sit here, with my big south window open to the River, open wide and a sort of healing balm of sunshine flooding the place,' he wrote in a letter to his sister-in-law.

Most of his important work had been written, including *The Ambassadors*, which he considered his best novel, but in Chelsea he wrote his autobiographical studies *A Small Boy and Others* and *Notes of a Son and Brother* (1913–14) and *The Middle Years*, which was published after his death.

The circle of artists and writers in Chelsea during these years was outstanding. As well as in fashionable Cheyne Walk, Tite Street and Glebe Place, there were studios available in many other parts of Fulham and Chelsea, including those in Manresa Road, near the library and where the Chelsea Art School was to be built, and it was at a studio in Manresa Road that Brangwyn first worked.

There were not many restaurants and cafés in Chelsea where artists could meet and talk, nor did they appear to have much taste for the late Victorian public houses of the King's Road and Fulham, apart from the Six Bells, where Rossetti, Whistler and their friends used to drink. In 1891 they remedied this by forming the Chelsea Arts Club. Their first headquarters were at number 181 King's Road, but in 1902 they moved to number 143 Old Church Street, with its beautiful garden. Although membership was restricted to artists engaged in one or other of the visual arts, it was a purely social club. Whistler, Sargent and Wilson Steer were among its ninety founder members and the first chairman was the sculptor, Thomas Stirling Lee. Their annual fancy dress party grew yearly more elaborate, eventually developing into the Chelsea Arts Ball, which was first held at the Chelsea Town Hall and the following year, in 1908, at the Albert Hall. The Albert Hall ball took place each year, with the exception of the war years, until well into the 1960s, by which time it had become too popular and unmanageable for real enjoyment. It had begun in the tradition of the best days of Ranelagh and finished sadly, as Cremorne had ended. An unpleasant, rowdy element destroyed its long gay history and the balls were no longer held.

From the 1890s until the outbreak of the First World War life in the artists' Chelsea was never more vigorous and rich with achievement, but elsewhere in Chelsea the story was different. By 1901 the population of the borough had risen to well over 60,000 and, as in most other parts of London, there was dire poverty and overcrowding. Many of the small eighteenth- and early nineteenth-century houses had become appallingly neglected and dilapidated: and clearance and demolition were considered a better answer to the problem than restoration.

The saddest casualty was Paradise Row. In 1906, despite a few lonely voices of protest, the lovely old houses, so full of memories, with their elegant front doors and fan-lights, carved porticoes and corniced eaves, deep sash windows, wide stairways and carved balusters, their neat front courts and dignified, pillared gateways were pulled down to make way for the present buildings in Royal Hospital Road.

These were the days of flat building. Blocks of large flats, on the lines of those appearing in Europe, arose in many parts of London – in Kensington, Westminster and Bloomsbury – and also in Chelsea. They were roomy and comfortable, with the servants' quarters discreetly hidden at the end of the kitchen corridors, but they were a poor substitute for the charm of the old houses.

And in the unfashionable parts of Chelsea arose blocks of flats and tenements, like those of the Peabody Trust, which served a real need but were stark and grim, with never a hint of a flower or a shrub to maintain Chelsea's tradition of beautiful gardens.

Along the Embankment many new houses were built. Norman Shaw had built Swan House, where the Old Swan Inn had once stood, in 1875, as well as Cheyne House, the Clock House and numbers 9, 10 and 11 Chelsea Embankment. Godwin built numbers 4 to 6 and G. F. Bodley number 3, known as the River House. C. R. Ashbee built numbers 37, 38 and 39 Cheyne Walk and in 1894 he rebuilt the old Tudor tavern, the Magpye and Stump, which had been burnt down in 1886.

At the beginning of the twentieth century Crosby Hall still stood in Bishopsgate. It had been built in 1470 by Sir John Crosby, grocer and woolstapler. A stone and timber building, it was 'very large and beautiful, and the highest at that time in London', according to Stow. Sir John's widow sold the mansion to Richard, Duke of Gloucester. 'There he lodged himself, and little by little all folks drew unto him, so that the Protector's Court was crowded and King Henry left desolate,' wrote Sir Thomas More, in his history of Richard III, and it was here that the mayor of London and a deputation of citizens offered Richard the crown of England.

Richard left Crosby Hall for the palace of Westminster and by the early sixteenth century another mayor was living there and entertaining Katharine of Aragon, on the eve of her wedding to Prince Arthur.

By 1576 Sir Thomas More was living at Crosby Hall and when he moved to Chelsea he sold it to his 'dear friend', the Italian merchant Antonio Bonvici. Bonvici bequeathed it to a cousin by marriage of Sir Thomas Gresham, whose house was opposite the hall, and it passed through the years to a succession of wealthy London merchants, many of whom held office as Lord Mayor of London, but during the Civil War, like Gresham College, Lambeth Palace and Chelsea College, Crosby Hall became a temporary prison for 'malignants' and was never again used as a private dwelling-place.

It became a chapel for a time. In 1678 a sale was announced there of 'tapestry, a good chariot and a black girl about fifteen'. The Withdrawing Room and the Throne Room became warehouses for the East India Company and by 1831, about the time that the East India Company came to an end, Crosby Hall seemed doomed. But the public conscience was stirred and by 1836 it had been partially restored by public subscription. It became a literary and scientific institute for some years but by 1860 it had been turned into a restaurant.

In 1908 the Bank of India acquired the land in Bishopsgate where the ancient Gothic hall still survived and it was decided to remove what was left of it to Chelsea. The work was undertaken with infinite care and the interior of the hall today, with its lovely oriel window and magnificent timbered roof, is much as More knew it when it had been the great hall of his home in Bishopsgate. It was placed on the Embankment, on the site of his old Chelsea garden, and later it was incorporated in the headquarters and hostel of the British Federation of University Women, forming one side of their quadrangle, but the view of the superb old building from the Embankment has now been sadly ruined by additional buildings to the hostel.

At the Royal Hospital, the stream of life proceeded evenly, as the Crimean veterans died away to make room for those who were to suffer in the Boer War. The year 1852 had seen the lying-in-state, in the Great Hall, of the Duke of Wellington. On the first day of mourning, Queen Victoria and the Prince Consort had attended, but on the following day, when the Great Hall was open to the public, the crowds streaming into Chelsea to pay their last respects to the Duke were so great that several people were crushed to death.

Four years later, the Hall was the scene of an enquiry into the causes of the muddles and disasters of the Crimean War. 'The conclusion reached,' writes Captain C. G. T. Dean, in his history of the Hospital, 'was that the breakdown in the administrative services was due to the Treasury's failure to dispatch a particular consignment of pressed hay at the right moment, a travesty of a verdict that provoked much ridicule at the time.'

By the end of the century, the Physic Garden was in grave trouble. For many years the Apothecaries' Society had been finding difficulty in providing the money for the maintenance of the garden. By 1853 the lectures had been discontinued. To save the expense of fuel, no plants were cultivated in the hothouses. One of the hothouses was dismantled and sold and many exotic plants had to be sold or exchanged for hardier ones. The garden was left in the sole charge of a curator, but the financial situation deteriorated so gravely that there seemed no future for it.

In May 1900 the Secretary of the Trustees, Mr Howard Batten, was writing to Reginald Blunt: 'The Apothecaries' Society applied to the Charity Commissioners for a Scheme, expecting the Garden would be sold and the proceeds of the sale applied in advancement of the study of botany or pharmacy; and as there were no funds applicable to the maintenance of the Garden out of their corporate funds, the sale appeared to be the only solution.

'The Charity Commissioners asked the Treasury to hold an enquiry as to the value of the Garden for educational and botanical purposes. The enquiry was held; evidence was taken, and a report was made that the Garden, if properly administered, would still be of value for scientific purposes. But where was the money to come from?'

In the end, the Trustees of the London Parochial Charities offered £800 a year, the Treasury another £150 a year. The Charity Commissioners appointed a committee of management for the garden, consisting of members appointed by the Trustees, the Treasury, the Lord President of the Council, the Technical Education Board of the London County Council, the Royal Society, the Society of Apothecaries, the Royal College of Physicians, the Pharmaceutical Society, the Senate of London University and the heir to Sir Hans Sloane.

The garden was given a new lease of life, although it had lost its unique library, which the Society of Apothecaries had transferred to the Apothecaries' Hall in 1832, and was not to have it back until 1953. With the proceeds of the sale of a strip of the garden along its northern boundary with the Queen's Road, and a loan from the City Parochial Foundation, the old buildings, by now in a ruinous state, were demolished and a new lecture room, laboratory and curator's house were built. A new glasshouse and pits were installed, with more modern heating apparatus, and under the direction of the new curator, Mr William Hales, who was given three assistants, the large plant beds were changed to long, narrow ones, which were more suitable for study.

In 1903 the last of the four famous cedar trees had to be cut down, but the garden was now in good hands and has remained so ever since, its purpose being 'the promotion of the study of botany, with special reference to the requirements of general education, scientific instruction and research in botany, including vegetable physiology, and instruction in technical pharmacology, so far as the culture of medicinal plants is concerned'.

The Royal Court Theatre in Sloane Square had been built in 1871, the same year as the Chelsea Hospital for Women. The theatre replaced a chapel which had been built in 1818, on the site of an earlier theatre, and it was here, from 1904 onwards, that many of the plays of George Bernard Shaw, the first British exponent of social realism in the theatre, were presented. The critics had condemned some of his earlier work, although they soon changed their minds. Yet *Mrs Warren's Profession* was banned by the censor for a number of years and the 'bloody' in *Pygmalion* was received by Edwardian theatre-goers with delicious and excited horror and discussed with bated breath.

XXI

Chelsea During Two World Wars

BY 1914 most of the Pre-Raphaelites and those who had worked
with them so closely were dead. William Morris, who towards the
end of his life had turned socialist, died in 1897. The Social Democratic Federation had been launched in Britain in 1884 by followers
of Karl Marx, the same year that the Fabian Society had been
founded. The following year a group called the Socialist League had
broken away from the Social Democratic Federation, with William
Morris as one of its strongest supporters. He died contented with the
achievements of his company of Fine Art Workmen and with his
literary work, which filled twenty-five volumes, but disillusioned
with his dream of a social revolution which would make the world
'a beautiful and happy place', a dream which he had come to realise,
as had Sir Thomas More centuries earlier, was unlikely of achievement until men and women could cure themselves of their own short-
comings. The beautiful Jane Morris survived him for many years,
dying in 1914.

With the outbreak of the First World War, most of the artists of
Chelsea and Kensington disappeared on war service. Among those
appointed official war artists were William Orpen and Frank Brangwyn, both of whom were later knighted.

Along with the beginning of the social revolution in the pre-war
years, there had been a revolution among artists, as the Post-Impres-
sionists, the Cubists and the Vorticists began their experiments, but

with the grim horror of the war, *avant-garde* Vorticists, such as P. Wyndham Lewis, returned for a while to stark realism in their painting.

Henry James was still living in Carlyle Mansions when the war broke out and, more devoted to England than ever, became a naturalised Englishman. He did what he could to help Belgian refugees who arrived in Chelsea, but he was a sick man and in 1916 he suffered a fatal stroke. As he lay dying, Edmund Gosse was able to bring him the news that he had been awarded the Order of Merit.

The following year, William de Morgan died at his house in Old Church Street.

The most serious damage to Chelsea during the First World War was in February 1918, when a 500-pound bomb fell on the Royal Hospital, destroying the north-east wing of the Light Horse Court, one of the two courts which had been added in the seventeenth century, yet the number of casualties was surprisingly light. After the war the wing was rebuilt, at a cost of £10,000.

With the end of the war, Chelsea like the rest of the country tried at first to rebuild its life on the pattern of 1914, but this was not to be. Too much had happened and the changes had been too fundamental. The 'timeless lyricism' of the Georgian poets of the early twenties showed a yearning for the pre-war life which, seen from the troubled years between the wars, seemed so uncomplicated and sweet, but the mood did not last long. As people faced the years of economic depression and unemployment, they quickly realised that the slow-moving days of horses and carts, hansoms and carriages had gone for ever in the new world of motor-cars and movies, radio and jazz, short skirts and bobbed hair, plus-fours and Oxford bags. Many, however, awakened to a keener perception of the charm of Georgian and early Victorian architecture and in Chelsea there was a growing awareness of how much was being destroyed. It came too late to save a great deal which should have been preserved, but the Chelsea Society has done much good work since.

Throughout the twenties and thirties, Chelsea did not change a great deal in appearance. The belching chimneys of the new Battersea Power Station, added to those of the Lots Road Power Station, which had been built in 1904 to supply power to the Underground, ruined the river view, but Chelsea was still the home of London's artists.

John Sargent was at number 31 Tite Street and Augustus John at number 33. In 1925 Sargent gave a farewell party at Carlyle Mansions on the eve of his departure for America. Afterwards he returned to his Tite Street studio, but in the morning the maid found that he had died in his sleep.

Doctor (later Sir Alexander) Fleming was living in Danvers Street. While studying septic wounds during the First World War he had found that the antiseptics then in use, while killing the bacteria were sometimes toxic to the body tissues. In 1928, when working at his laboratory at St Mary's Hospital, he discovered an antiseptic which doctors had been waiting for since the days of Lord Lister – one which was innocuous to the body cells. He called this penicillin.

In a very different sphere, these were the years of triumph for Bernard Shaw. *St Joan* was produced at the New Theatre, with Sybil Thorndike as St Joan, there was a Shaw season at the old Regent theatre at King's Cross, and in Chelsea, Barry Jackson presented *Back to Methuselah* at the Royal Court, Sloane Square, with the Birmingham Repertory Company.

In 1926 there was a splendid exhibition at the Chelsea Town Hall of Chelsea porcelain from the Sprimont factory. Also on view was some of de Morgan's pottery and that of later Chelsea potters, including the *School for Scandal* figures by Gwendolen Parnell, from her studio in Glebe Place. There were exhibits by Reginald Wells, who had been making bowls and pots, animal and human figurines since 1910, first at Elystan Street and then in the King's Road, pieces by Charles Vyse, who had begun making his delightful figures of flower-sellers, gypsies and the like at 14a Cheyne Row since 1919, and some by Harry Parr who also began making his figures and figure groups soon after the war. Other exhibitors were Kate Kitching, who began as Gwendolen Parnell's assistant in 1919 and later modelled her tiny animals and birds on her own account, and Madeline Roper, who founded the Glebe pottery in 1924, specialising in inns and cottages.

At the Royal Hospital a concession to changing fashion was the replacement, in 1920, of three bathrooms near the Great Kitchen, with twelve new ones near the Choir vestry, which meant that the Pensioners could now have a weekly bath. A few years later lifts were installed and central heating fitted in the wards. By 1932 every bunk had wireless headphones and an electric reading lamp. The number of in-pensioners varied very little from the original 476 non-commissioned officers and men.

The population of Chelsea declined between the wars – 1911 being the peak year with 66,000 inhabitants – but by 1921 it was down to 63,000; in 1931 it was 59,000 and in 1939 only 56,000.

During the Second World War it fell even more sharply and by 1942 it was only 27,000, while for a short time during the worst of the air-raids it was estimated at 16,000.

Chelsea suffered grievous damage and many casualties from air-raids during the Second World War, from Sloane Square station in the east (although Peter Jones was miraculously unscathed) to Ash-burnham Mansions in the west. Night after night during the winter of 1940–1 the darkening sky turned luridly crimson and the slow ripples of the black river gleamed ominously blood red in the light of the flames which encompassed human lives and ancient buildings. Being so close to Westminster and also the two important power stations, Chelsea was in a perilous position, and for its size was one of the most heavily bombed boroughs of London.

When war seemed imminent in September 1938, arrangements were made to evacuate all the Chelsea pensioners to a group of country houses near Ross-on-Wye, but the plans were dropped during the following months of false hope. In September 1939 about fifty pensioners were sent to Rudhall, Ross-on-Wye, where they remained until 1946, and the pictures and other valuables were re-moved from the Hospital to Montacute House in Somerset, for safe keeping.

The rest of the pensioners and the staff remained in Chelsea. There were enough shelters for about half of them and the others slept on the ground floor, either in bunks or on mattresses. The old men suffered greatly from the discomfort and exposure, and, apart from air-raid casualties, the mortality rate doubled during the grim winter of 1940–1.

On 28 August 1940, two bombs fell on the open space of Burton's Court, causing no casualties. In September 1940, a bomb dropped near the stable yard, breaking the gas and water mains and also the public sewer. In October, the Infirmary had a near miss and two other bombs fell close by without exploding.

Ten days later, a stick of four bombs fell on the hospital and the grounds, destroying the main staircase of the east wing. On 8 March 1941, the hospital was hit by sixty incendiary bombs, but the fires they caused were quickly contained and extinguished.

On the terrible night of 16 April 1941, 450 German bombers at-tacked southern and central London for nearly eight hours. Over a thousand people were killed and two thousand seriously injured.

In Chelsea, thousands of incendiaries fell and numbers of high
explosive bombs, including five parachute mines. About half past
eleven, a land-mine destroyed the east wing of the Infirmary. Four
nurses, the ward-master and eight pensioners were killed outright
and there were another thirty-seven casualties, who were taken to
civilian hospitals. A few hours later there was another land-mine in
Franklyn's Row close by and a bomb which did further damage to the
hospital.

The headquarters of the wardens guarding Chelsea Old Church
was at the adjoining Petyt House, in Old Church Street, a house
which had been built as the parish school during the reign of Queen
Anne and was subsequently used as the Church House and a Sunday
School. About one o'clock in the morning, two enormous explosions
shook that end of Chelsea. Two wardens on patrol told how, as they
turned the corner from Glebe Place into Upper Cheyne Row, they
saw lights streaming from the houses, where windows and window
frames, complete with blackout, had been sucked out into the road
or pushed into the room. Tiles, broken slates, lath and plaster, bits of
wood and glass littered the roadway. Justice Walk was blocked half-
way in from Lawrence Street. 'As they ran round the corner into
Cheyne Walk they were brought down by a length of garden railing.
Near Danvers Street in a shallow crater in the road a gas main was on
fire. And then it came to them both: "The Old Church has gone!"'
In place of the massive square tower was a jagged stump of brick-
work and broken timbers.

Beyond the church, in Cheyne Walk, some houses were completely demolished, others were hanging shells, blasted through from
back to front. In one of them a woman was crying for help.

Another warden described looking down Old Church Street to
where Petyt House and the church should have been on the left and
the tall Cheyne Walk houses on the right. Petyt House had disappeared altogether, dissolved into a pile of rubble, and so had the west
end of the church, with jagged broken beams sticking up from where
the chancel had been. The blast had 'lifted the old bricks and blown
out the powdery mortar like a winnowing fan . . .'

Half blinded by the thick fog of the dust, dazed by the fury of the
night, the thudding of guns, the explosion of bombs, the brilliance of
the flares hovering in the sky, the light of the fires and the hundreds
of incendiaries which fell incessantly, the wardens began searching
for people sheltering in the basements of the little houses around
Petyt Place and bringing out the bodies from the shattered remains

of the brave new Café Lombard. An elderly artist ran by, clutching the fragments of a half-finished portrait, crying distractedly: 'She's in ribbons! She's in ribbons!' A parachute mine exploded in a corner of Chelsea Square – another on Cranmer Court, just behind the police station. At the Cross Keys in Lawrence Street, one wall was blown into the bar.

In the morning, fires broke out again. Demolition workers, crunching on broken bricks and shattered glass, began to shovel away the debris of the church tower which was blocking the end of the street. The sanctuary stood open to the weather. The beautiful altar rails were broken, the altar and cross badly damaged by a fallen beam. The More tomb was in pieces. The figures on the Stanley Memorial protruded from a heap of broken masonry. The Bray tomb, protected by its arch, remained intact.

Then they discovered that the More Chapel and the pillars with the capitals, ascribed by many to Holbein, which supported the entrance arch were unscathed. Eagerly the incumbent, the architect and the verger searched the wreckage and they found more than they had dared hope for. The salvaged treasures were carefully stored in the crypt of St Luke's Church, and that, for the time being, was all that could be done.

The war went on. The Cheyne Hospital for Children, itself badly damaged, offered a ward as a place for worship. The candlesticks and cross were set up on a Credence table which served as an altar and here, for several years, the services of the Old Church were held, so that the continuity of worship of the congregation remained unbroken.

There was a lull in the bombing for the next year or two. Wilson Steer was still living and working at number 109 Cheyne Walk and he died there in 1942, at the age of eighty.

In June of 1944 the flying bombs arrived. When Sloane Court was wrecked, the Royal Hospital suffered from blast, but worse was to come. In January 1945, a long-range rocket destroyed the north-east wing in Light Horse Court, the wing that had been destroyed by bombing in the First World War, killing four and injuring nineteen.

This was the last serious bomb damage to Chelsea, for a few months later, the war was over.

XXII

Chelsea After 1945

THE war was over and people came flocking back to Chelsea. By 1945 the population had risen to 35,000, by 1946 to 45,000 and by 1947 to over 50,000, after which the figure remained fairly steady until 1963, when the Local Government Act joined her to her much larger neighbour. The title of Royal Borough of Kensington and Chelsea was conferred in 1964, perpetuating the distinction bestowed on the borough of Kensington in 1900.

In Chelsea, as elsewhere in London, new houses and flats were built on cleared bomb sites and slowly the buildings capable of restoration were put into order again.

At the Royal Hospital the number of in-pensioners had dwindled to just under three hundred during the war, compared with its average of four hundred and fifty to five hundred, but admissions were resumed and the work of rebuilding begun. Today the Hospital shows little of its past sufferings and its traditions are maintained in the informal orderliness of its organisation. Those who are fit enough may work in the hospital and the gardens if they wish, and so earn extra pocket money, but there is no compulsion. They have their pensions and their freedom, companionship and a comfortable home, and the ancient hospital with its beautiful riverside garden is one of the most peaceful places in London. The Grinling Gibbons statue of Charles II, without his wig and dressed as a Roman general, still stands in Figure Court, as it has for nearly three hundred years, and

Founder's Day is celebrated each year, as it has been since 1698. It is on 29 May – oak apple day, which celebrates Charles II's birthday and restoration – when the Governor and officers dine together and the pensioners receive double rations of food and beer. A member of the Royal Family or a distinguished soldier is the guest of honour and the pensioners parade before the assembled company, to the tune of *The Old Brigade*, wearing oak sprigs in their scarlet tunics.

And every year, in the late spring, the grounds are given over to the magnificent show of the Royal Horticultural Society, thereby maintaining Chelsea's long tradition as the home of beautiful gardens.

The congregation of Chelsea Old Church, which had continued to worship together through the war years and the bombing and devastation of their church, still had no permanent home and began a long campaign for its rebuilding.

There were many times of disappointment and they must often have been near to despair, but they never lost their faith and determination, and at last, after months of bitter controversy and a great deal of hard work, in which they were supported by the Chelsea Society, the Chelsea Borough Council, the Ancient Monuments division of the Ministry of Works, and the Chelsea incumbent, who had been serving as a Naval Chaplain, the Diocesan Reorganization Committee finally agreed that Chelsea Old Church should be rebuilt on its old foundations as a new parish church, and a stipend was assigned to the priest-in-charge.

The next problem to be solved was whether the new building should be a replica of the old one or an entirely new and modern design. In the end, a compromise was reached and it was built on the general plan of the old one.

In July 1950 the More Chapel was reopened for services. The chancel and the Lawrence Chapel were restored and rededicated a few years later and by May 1958 the new church was reconsecrated.

In July 1964 the More Chapel was refurnished and dedicated for use again, probably for the first time in 408 years, as a Lady Chapel.

Much of Chelsea Old Church as it stands today is therefore only a few years old, and the bricks still look very new, but entering it from the mad race of the Embankment traffic, there is a wonderful atmosphere of timelessness and of the presence of the past. It is a resurrection. The seventeenth-century altar and altar rails are there, the rails conforming to the regulations imposed three hundred years ago by the Bishop of Norwich, being 'neer one yarde in height, so thick with

pillars that dogs may not gett in'. The seventeenth-century font had
to have a new cover but the base is original; and the chained books
which Sir Hans Sloane gave to the church were recovered from the
destruction and are back in place – the Vinegar Bible (so called because the word 'vinegar' was printed in mistake for 'vineyard'), two
volumes of Foxe's *Book of Martyrs*, an early eighteenth-century
prayer book and the seventeenth-century *Homilies*. The bell
presented by William Ashburnham in 1679 hangs again in the
porch.

The monuments to the people who made Chelsea's history have
been beautifully restored and today, as they rest on the same little
patch of ground, it seems as though they have never been disturbed.

In the south-east corner of the More Chapel, with its pillared entrance, is the tomb of Jane, Duchess of Northumberland, mother-in-
law of Lady Jane Grey, mother of Queen Elizabeth's greatly loved
Earl of Leicester and grandmother of Sir Philip Sidney. The tomb is
battered and ancient but has that air of imperishable dignity which
the Duchess herself possessed. In the north wall is the memorial brass
of the Stanley family.

The memorial to Sir Thomas More stands on the south side of the
sanctuary. He had intended the tomb for his two wives, both of
whom he loved dearly, and also for himself, and wrote an inscription
which seems aimed at avoiding any possibility of an eternal triangle
in the next world: 'Ah! how well could we three have lived together,
did fate and religion permit. But the tomb shall unite us I pray, and
Death give us what Life could not.'

In drafting his own epitaph, More described himself as 'the
scourge of thieves, murderers and heretics' but Erasmus protested
against such intolerance, so More deleted the word 'heretics' and in
the final version left a blank which has remained ever since.

Opposite the More memorial is the tomb of the first Lord Bray,
heir to Sir Reginald Bray, who was the early Tudor lord of the
manor, and the Hungerford memorial hangs above it.

On the same side of the nave is the tomb of Lord Dacre and his
wife, who succeeded to the More estates. Their effigies lie side by side
on their massive tomb, Lord Dacre, bearded, and wearing Elizabethan armour, his wife, Ann, in starched ruff and farthingale.

In the Lawrence Chapel are the memorials to Sir Thomas Lawrence and John Lawrence, and at the east end is the magnificent
alabaster monument of Sir Robert Stanley, son-in-law of Sir Arthur
Gorges, who came into possession of the More estates later in the

sixteenth century. Here also is the tomb of his daughter, Sarah Col-
ville, who has been depicted in alabaster, rising in her shroud from a
black marble sarcophagus.

In the eastern end of the chapel is the triumphal arch commemo-
rating Sir Richard Jervoise, who lived in the old manor-house after
Lord Sandys had sold the manor to Henry VIII.

On the north side of the nave is the memorial to Charles Cheyne
and his first wife, Jane, who did so much for the church and the
village when they came into possession of the manor after the Civil
War. It is a large and impressive monument, made in Rome by Paolo
Bernini and Antonio Raggi.

There are memorials to William de Morgan and Henry James, and
among the famous Chelsea women commemorated in the tablet
erected by the Federation of University Women, we meet Mary
Astell again.

In the churchyard, the monumental stone urn in memory of Sir
Hans Sloane has remained unharmed.

Equally vigorous in its survival after the difficult war years has been
the Physic Garden. In 1953 it received back, on permanent loan, the
books which had been removed by the Society of Apothecaries, and
through grants from the Trustees of the London Parochial Charities
its original library has gradually been restored. Today these beautiful
books, including the lovely ancient, leather-bound volumes of John
Gerard's *Herball* and Elizabeth Blackwell's *Curious Herbal*, are kept in
five large oak presses, at least two of which are almost certainly the
original presses ordered by the Society of Apothecaries in 1739, for
books and herbals which had been bequeathed to them by Dr
Samuel Dale.

Today the gardens are in impeccable order, growing more than
5,000 species of plants. In the 'natural order' beds, close on a hundred
families are represented in the open ground. Medicinal plants and
culinary herbs are also grown and tropical and sub-tropical plants are
cultivated in the greenhouses.

Seeds are sent to other botanical institutions all over the world. In
1963, 4,686 packets of seeds were sent out and 1,400 received. That
year the garden supplied 34,000 specimens of plants for teaching and
examinations to twelve university colleges, six medical schools,
twelve training colleges and numerous schools, the University of
London alone receiving 10,000 specimens for examination, while
3,750 students visited the garden to study.

Evening lectures are held as part of the University Extension courses and students of the Imperial College of Science attend day-time lectures during the spring and summer terms.

The ground floor of the laboratory, with two of the greenhouses and certain parts of the garden are set aside for research into problems of plant biology, physiology and pathology, this work being undertaken by the Agricultural Research Council, the Natural History section of the British Museum, the Chelsea College of Science and Technology, the Medical Research Council and the Imperial College of Science and Technology.

The old Physic Garden is more active and useful than at any time in its history and plays its part in the scientific life of the twentieth century. This is no museum. It is a place of peaceful, progressive cultivation and research. Yet there are few places in Chelsea which evoke so vividly the village of three hundred years ago. Much of the ancient brick garden wall still stands. The boat-house is still here. The beautiful old lead water cistern, with its ornamental panels and the inscription, 'W. W. 1680' is still in use. Joseph Banks' plants still creep over the rockery, and Sir Hans Sloane, from his pedestal in the middle of the garden, still surveys it all, with an expression of serene contemplation.

It was about the time of the 1951 Exhibition that London began to smarten itself up, and today, with all trace of bomb damage removed, the houses in Cheyne Walk are as delightful as ever, in good order, immaculately painted and a little aloof behind their railings and iron gateways. Their large, secluded gardens are beautiful, as Chelsea gardens have ever been, with vines and fig-trees, wistarias and mulberry trees surviving from past glories.

The eighteenth-century houses in the streets between the south side of the King's Road and St Leonard's Terrace – Cheltenham Terrace, Royal Avenue, Wellington Square – are all painted and spruce. The smaller houses in the streets farther west, between the King's Road to the north and the Royal Hospital Road and Cheyne Walk to the south, are also renovated, as well as many of the Regency houses in the streets northwards, between the King's Road and the Fulham Road.

As houses have fallen vacant or their leases have expired, their value has soared, but there are also islands of property in this part of Chelsea and to the west – mostly mid-Victorian – which are far gone in dilapidation. Some have been given a coat of white paint and a brilliantly coloured front door, to preserve an air of prosperity, but inside they are miserably squalid, let off into small flats or single rooms: and in the dingy basements many an old woman lives out a lonely existence, preferring this last gesture of independence to the only alternative, the King's Mead old people's home in Dovehouse Street, which, admirable as it is, looks dauntingly bleak and grim from the outside.

Mostly these old people help each other, to the best of their ability, and the Meals on Wheels service is a boon they whole-heartedly welcome, but it is not unknown for one of the welfare visitors to find that some old man or woman has died in the night, in a solitary bed-sitting room – all alone and unnoticed by the neighbours.

Most of these houses are scheduled for demolition, but the value of better preserved and often much smaller properties continues to soar. When Whistler was forced to sell his White House in Tite Street in 1878, it brought him £2,700, and the price when it was sold in 1962 is said to have been £50,000.

In the late 1940s and 1950s, the artists came back to Chelsea, for nowhere else in London was there such a selection of excellent studios, but rising prices in the sixties and seventies have driven them away again, either farther west, beyond the World's End, or, if they are prospering though not yet wealthy enough for Chelsea prices today, northwards into Hampstead, although prices have now risen as quickly there as in Chelsea.

The tradition that Chelsea is the centre of the artists' colony in London still persists, but is growing very thin. One post-war venture is still in a flourishing state, however – the Chelsea Pottery, founded by David Rawnsley in 1952, in a delightful, ramshackle old building in Radnor Walk, converted from an eighteenth-century carriage builder's shop, overlooking a cobbled courtyard. It is very much like Sprimont's factory must have been, and de Morgan's Pottery in the coach-house at the end of Lawrence Street.

The Chelsea Pottery makes bowls, pots, tiles and figurines – some in terracotta but mostly glazed, in clear, brilliant colours, and has developed a flourishing export business, more than a third of its output being sent abroad. The designs are highly original, some with a Byzantine flavour, others reminiscent of some of de Morgan's work, but all strongly individualistic.

The Pottery is also a club where members can receive instruction, buy clay and glazes, and make their own pots on one of the four electric wheels or the kick wheel, having a free run of the ovens and other facilities. Within sight and sound of the blustering, commercial

King's Road, the Chelsea Pottery contentedly follows the tradition of the craftsmen potters of a bygone age – and prospers.

The old taverns for which Chelsea was once famous, most of which were set in delightful gardens, have nearly all disappeared. *Jenny's Whim*, situated about where Ebury Bridge now stands, lasted well into the last century. The old wooden bridge and the turnpike close by also bore her name. Tradition says that Jenny, the first landlady, 'caused the gardens round her house to be laid out in so fantastic a manner, as to cause the expressive little noun to be affixed to the pretty and familiar Christian name that she bore'. Another story is that the founder of Jenny's Whim was not a woman at all but 'a celebrated pyrotechnist who lived in the time of George I'. In various parts of the large garden were recesses, 'and by treading on a spring – taking you by surprise – up started different figures, some ugly enough to frighten you outright – a harlequin, a Mother Shipton, or some terrific animal', inducements 'to allure the curious to it by its amusing deceptions'.

And very disconcerting they must have been, too. But the customers were distinguished, Horace Walpole complaining that when Lord Granby joined his party at Vauxhall, he arrived 'very drunk from *Jenny's Whim*'.

Near by was the *Dwarf's Tavern* where Spring Gardens was later to appear, between Ebury Street and Belgrave Terrace. This was another garden inn, over which a dwarf from Norfolk named Coan presided, offering ham, collared eels, potted beef and 'sound old bright Wine and Punch like Nectar' to all who 'love to live well'.

The *Daily Advertiser* for 12 July 1762 reported that 'On Friday last the Cherokee king and his two chiefs were so greatly pleased with curiosities of the *Dwarf's Tavern*, in Chelsea Fields, that they were there again on Sunday, at seven in the evening, to drink tea, and will be there again in a few days'.

Close to the Dwarf's Tavern was the *Star and Garter*, renowned for its firework displays.

The *Old Swan* was the most famous of the riverside taverns. The *King's Arms* at 114 Cheyne Walk, has been going since the eighteenth century, and the *Magpye and Stump* where the Courts Leet used to meet, to impose fines on people who failed to take their share of repairing the river wall, or allowed their cattle to stray, was an ancient, timbered building before it was rebuilt, after the fire of 1886.

In the King's Road, the *World's End*, once deep in the countryside, was a garden tavern of doubtful repute, notorious as far back as Congreve's time, for in *Love for Love*, Mrs Foresight and Mrs Frail are equally disconcerted when they each discover that the other has been there. It has been rebuilt several times since those days but it still stands, large and ornate, grimly scowling upon the unlovely vista of the New King's Road.

The Six Bells, with its bowling alley, rebuilt in 1900, was once the haunt of Whistler and his circle. *The Chelsea Potter*, at 119 King's Road, is a large, mid-Victorian house. *The Lord Nelson* and the *Cadogan Arms* both have a loyal following. Church Street has its *Old White Horse* and also the seventeenth-century *Black Lion*, and Lawrence Street the *Cross Keys*.

During the 1950s the most popular pubs for the artists were the *Queen's Elm* and *Finch's* – the *King's Arms* – both in the Fulham Road.

The *Queen's Elm* was originally the tree under which Lord Burleigh and Queen Elizabeth took shelter from a shower of rain, when they were walking near his house. When the shower was over, Lord Burleigh said 'Let this tree be called the Queen's Elm', which it was, for as long as it survived. It was even described as such in the parish rate books and an enterprising and patriotic character called Bostock built an arbour round it, composed of nine elms, though the expense was charged to the parish.

XXIII

The Royal Borough in the 1970s

'Youth! Youth! There is absolutely nothing
in the world but youth.'
Oscar Wilde: *The Picture of Dorian Gray*

DURING the late 1950s and early sixties, strange things happened
in the King's Road, Chelsea. By that time the thousands of children
who had been born just after the end of the Second World War had
grown into a hitherto unnamed group of the human race, the teenagers. By 1962 there were 5,000,000 of them in Great Britain, a
greater number than at any time since the end of the First World
War. Eighty in every hundred of them were leaving school at fifteen
and earning high wages. They were not called upon to pay much at
home for their board and lodging, for with the mother usually working as well as the father, there was little necessity, and it was
estimated that, between them, these young people had about
£500,000,000 to spend each year on clothes and diversions – cigar-
ettes, alcohol, cinemas, discothèques, gramophone records, cafés,
magazines and motor-cycles or cars.

By the late 1960s the proportion of teenagers to the rest of the
population was not so high and a greater number were staying
longer at school and attending universities and technical schools, but
the wages of those who were working were considerably higher, in
relation to the cost of living, than they had been ten years previously,
so the commercial potentialities for their exploitation were much the
same. By the end of the sixties their collective spending power was
estimated at £900,000,000 a year, a quarter of the total amount spent
by the entire country on consumer goods: and a new industry to

cater for these young people, skilfully creating their tastes for them by devious methods of advertising, was soon under way.

The fashion revolution began in the late 1940s when women, weary of their wartime utility clothes, took to the curves and swirling skirts of the 'New Look'. Savile Row tailors determined that once men were out of uniform they too should become clothes conscious. They designed Edwardian suits with short, square jackets and very tight trousers to replace the old, pre-war lounge suits. However, before they had time to launch the new fashion among their customers, youths leaving school at fourteen or fifteen, to whom Savile Row and its fashions had hitherto been a remote and altogether unattainable world, found themselves with large pay packets and freedom to spend most of them as they wished. They saw the new Edwardian fashion and liked it.

It was these boys who were the first to become fashion conscious. They took to Edwardian suits and embellished them with velvet collars and colourful waistcoats. They grew their hair longer, to match their new clothes, and took to side whiskers, while the tailors of Savile Row, in the interests of exclusiveness, hastily modified their plans and for a time became conservative again.

The Teddy boys were immensely proud of their new elegance and, by way of contrast, the university students took to duffle-coats and loose, ungainly, bulky sweaters, though not for long. Many soon seceded and went Edwardian. The swing of fashion did not follow the usual course of beginning at the highest level of society and infiltrating downwards. This time it began at the top but, before it was fully fledged, plummetted to the depths and then slowly climbed upwards again.

In London the Edwardian cult centred first in Carnaby Street, where new shops were opened for men. They sold colourful clothing which became increasingly bizarre and heralded the dawn of the permissive and affluent society. Carnaby Street was so well advertised and grew so popular that before long it became a tourist attraction for overseas visitors and coach-loads of sightseers were being decanted all through the holiday season to view the strange-looking young people who were shaping the brave new world of the sixties. As the sexes gradually became almost indistinguishable in appearance, shops were opened which catered for both men and girls, as well as a few which were solely for girls.

Then came the invasion of the King's Road, Chelsea, where boutiques for both youths and girls, shoe shops, hairdressers and wigmakers, furriers and knackatories, to use old Don Saltero's expressive description, sprang up with bewildering speed. Some were branches of the Carnaby Street shops. A few were branches of existing chain stores. Others were independent. And as they prospered, one or two opened branches in Carnaby Street. All had arresting names, such as *Miss, The Westerner, All Kinds, Kleptomania, Kweens, The Village Gate, The Squire Shop, Take 6, Just Men, Lord Kitchener's Thing, Stop! The Shop, Skin* and *Quorum.*

For girls, these were the years of the mini-skirt, the topless dress and see-through blouse. For boys there was anything from purple velvet suits and skin-tight trousers to pink and orange silk shirts and baroque jewellery.

As the sixties progressed, an ever-increasing number of these boutiques were opened and while some failed, others prospered and made fortunes. In the scramble to gain a footing in this potential gold mine, the prices of property in the King's Road, particularly at the eastern end and on the favourite south side, soared astronomically.

In the first half of 1969, although there was no new building development, fifteen properties changed hands in the profitable stretch from Sloane Square to about Flood Street, the total value of which was close on £1,000,000. In January 1969, the freehold of a shop with a window space of thirty feet cost £100,000. A shop near by was bought for £75,000 and let a few weeks later for a yearly rental of £7,000. In February a chain tobacconist sold out to a woman's shoe shop for £125,000. Another shoe shop, worth £4,500 in 1950, was valued at £30,000 in 1967 and £45,000 in 1969.

The residents of Chelsea saw the old-established traders of the King's Road, which they and their families had used for years, quickly disappear, for greengrocers, butchers, bakers and wine-merchants, chemists and the like, who had been peacefully running small, family businesses, could not withstand the onslaught of the boutique invasion and the inflationary rise in the value of property. In their place appeared help-yourself supermarkets and branches of large provision firms, including, on the north side, the *Sainsbury* shopping precinct. The days of the delivery van and personal service were over.

Still more dress shops and boutiques opened, catering not for the local residents but for the whole of London and also for foreign visitors, and at one time it looked as though Chelsea's own High Street had become an international fair ground. When Mary Quant's first shop in the King's Road, *Bazaar*, became vacant, the agents are said to have been offered £13,500 a year rent for the premises, for in the late 1960s the demand for trading space in this part of the King's Road was estimated at twenty times the supply, and rents were shooting up by as much as £1,000 in six months.

Turnover has to be ten times the rent, for a safe margin of profit, so with an average rent for a small shop at between £4,000 and £5,000 a year, the weekly turnover had to reach £1,000. Despite a few failures, many, backed by the finance houses and insurance companies, prospered and a number are still flourishing.*

One of the success stories belongs to Ossie Clarke, the boy from Liverpool, born in 1942, who trained at the Manchester College of Art at the same time as David Hockney, with whom he has remained close friends. From Manchester he won a scholarship to the Royal College of Art in London and he is now regarded as one of the most talented of the young English fashion designers. With his partner, Alice Pollock, who is the same age to the day, they first opened their business in a little house in Radnor Walk, but later moved to the black-fronted *Quorum*, an austere, blind-looking but intriguing shop on the south side of the King's Road, from which they run a wholesale and boutique business.

Ossie Clarke is now immensely rich, though he has only the vaguest idea of what he earns and wears his success with an air of disconcerting nonchalance. Perhaps success has come too easily and too quickly. He has a deep love of beauty. 'I don't care how much anything costs as long as it's beautiful,' he says. Nevertheless, he is restlessly dissatisfied and quickly bored. 'Well, just clothes don't matter much, do they? But what can I do that matters?' he asks.

As for Alice, she once remarked: 'I haven't been anywhere but I've been round the world. Ossie took me round the world, but I haven't been anywhere else.'

On the corner of the beautiful, eighteenth-century Royal Avenue and the King's Road is the new *Chelsea Drug Store*, an oddly-shaped, high, narrow building, approached by a short flight of steps, which sells pretty well everything but drugs, which it is not allowed to do unless a qualified chemist is employed on the premises. It is equipped with a bar, a restaurant, a discothèque and innumerable boutiques, and here is the testimony of one of the sales girls, sixteen years old.†

*These figures are quoted from an article by Gwen Nuttall: 'The Swinging Cash-in Down The King's Road', *Sunday Times*, 17.8.1969.

† 'Look What It Means to be 16 in 1969' (edited by J. Hunter Davies), *Sunday Times*, 9.11.1969.

'As soon as I left school, I knew I wanted to work in the store. It's so lively and crazy. I just walked in one day and asked for a job . . .

'I love it here. There's never a minute still, you never know what to expect. I could live here, really. I love the music, in fact I couldn't work without it.

'I earn £14 a week, but we're just going to start getting commission on things as well. I give £2 to my mother and I don't have to pay out for much, so I never feel hard up. . . . I go out every night, but I don't have a regular boy friend. . . . We go to the *Speakeasy*, the *Revolution* or the *Pheasantry* usually.'

When the *Drug Store* first opened, young people streamed into it from all over London, particularly at weekends. Residents in Royal Avenue formed themselves into a Residents' Association for their mutual protection and threatened to withhold their rates if the council did not preserve them from 'Rubbish, noise and hippies'. Saturday evenings were the worst time, for the shops in the King's Road stay open on Saturday afternoons and the hippies parked their cars in the avenue and other residential roads near by, regardless of parking meters and residents' own parking places, and were completely unmoved when they were caught and fined.

The Chelsea Society also took up the cause of the residents of Royal Avenue, for matters grew intolerable. They were harried by the noise of the cars of the *Drug Store* patrons, seven days and nights each week, far into the small hours, and a one-way enforcement on each side of the avenue turned it into a race track. The residents demanded that the avenue should be closed at the King's Road end and this has now been done.

The quality of the new shops in the King's Road is varied. Some of the boutiques are beautiful and many have proved themselves attractive enough to stay the course, but during its brief spell of notoriety there have arisen some catch-penny establishments offering tasteless, over-priced goods which would have been a hard sell in pre-war Port Said. Inside they are dimly lit and so noisy with canned music that the customer is deafened and bemused from the moment of crossing the threshold.

The bookshops are splendid and the fascinating shops selling artists' equipment remind one that there are still artists living in Chelsea. There are some excellent antique shops and at the western end of the King's Road, opposite Carlyle Square, is the *Chelsea Antique Market*, which was opened in the late 1960s. From the outside it looks like an ordinary small shop, but it stretches back a very long way, and each 'stallholder' has his own alcove or open-fronted shop, as in a covered Oriental bazaar. It is infinitely more comfortable for browsing and shopping than an open market, for here is an abundance of books, prints, china and porcelain, glass, pictures, furniture, jewellery, mirrors and the usual bric-à-brac of an antique shop, all neatly displayed and priced. For a short time they also sold clothes, both the antique, second-hand variety and contemporary, 'way-out' ones, but, as the King's Road quietened down again, they dropped the idea and are again concentrating on antiques.

Another antique market *Antiquarius* has recently opened in the King's Road, similar in plan though under a different management, next to *The Village Gate*, just beyond Shawfield Street.

Along with the new shops in the King's Road, there opened innumerable cafés, bistros, coffee houses, steak houses, French, Italian and Chinese restaurants, as well as delicatessen shops and pastry cooks.

Of the restaurants, the expensive ones offer very good food and service. The rest differ little from other medium-priced and relatively cheap restaurants in other parts of London, the cooking and service not always attaining the standard of the elaborate décor. At one time some were made unbearable with a cacophony of the most terrible canned music that the human race ever contrived. Deafening and hideous, it streamed forth unceasingly, paralysing all rational thought, but the craze for noise subsided and now all one hears is an occasional muted and plaintive ballad.

Only a year or two ago, the crowds surged up and down the King's Road all day long, sightseers come to see other sightseers as well as to shop. Like the promenaders of Ranelagh, they went round the shops – and then they went round again. They drifted along in an endless procession, window-gazing and buying, dropping into cafés for odd meals, at even odder times, and drifting out again, a motley collection, some in the most outrageous fancy dress – girls wearing cowboy hats, Arab kaftans, Cossack boots and Minnehaha headbands, striding along in mini-skirts or tottering by in maxi-skirts, which after several years of the minis, they found difficult to manage. The boys, in their brilliantly coloured silks and velvets, affected the sinister, drooping moustaches of a Genghiz Khan or the straggling locks of an Indian fakir.

There were clever, sensitive faces among the crowds, who seemed to be at grips with the eternal problem of what life is all about, and blank, alarmingly stupid ones, apparently having no idea of what they were doing or where they were going. They all strove to be different and individual, but their very efforts to achieve visual distinction gave them a strange similarity.

With this invasion came a sharp increase in crime, drunkenness and drug addiction, and the Saturday night hooligans who stormed in from the distant suburbs were also sometimes guilty of deliberate and unforgivable vandalism, even attempting to rob the church offertory boxes: but with the changing mood of Chelsea, they seem to have retreated.

In 1970 the clothes being sold in the King's Road were so fashionable that many predicted that the street would become a second Knightsbridge or Bond Street, but the old-established London stores, particularly *Harrods*, with its *Way In*, and *Selfridges*, with its *Miss Selfridge*, were quick to establish their own boutiques, offering teenage clothes and accessories which compared favourably with those in Chelsea, so the market began to diffuse rather than to concentrate, reaching Oxford Street, Kensington and Hammersmith and then spreading into the provinces: and the noisy, self-conscious 'Swinging Chelsea' cult of the King's Road has abated.

Chelsea has a long history of visionaries and revolutionaries, of artists wearing odd clothes, of being misunderstood by the Philistines, even of drug addiction and sexual perversion.

Sir Thomas More had his own ideas of how life should be lived and he died for his convictions, though the Reformation he deplored was so long overdue.

Swift wrote to Stella about the strange garb of the inhabitants of Chelsea in a letter of 1711, when he complained that the 'haymaking nymphs are perfect drabs, nothing so clean and pretty as farther in the country. There is a mighty increase of dirty wenches in straw hats since I knew London.'

The Moravians tried to create Utopia in Chelsea. William Morris tried to induce his Chelsea friends to join a social revolution.

And, to quote Bernard Denvir, in his introduction to the catalogue of the Whistler Exhibition at the Chelsea Arts Club, in April 1968: 'Whilst Samuel Smiles and other improvers of morals were canonising respectability elsewhere in the Metropolis, down in Cheyne Walk, Dante Gabriel Rossetti, surrounded by his private menagerie and plump mistresses, was playing host to a selection of Victorian flower people whose antics make those of their successors seem like the carryings-on of a group of church elders. Rossetti himself consumed enough drugs in a day to keep a modern pop group stoned for a month. And he was not unique; there was the tiny red-headed figure of Swinburne lurching off to whipping orgies in St John's Wood; Oscar Wilde, camping it out in Tite Street with juvenile male prostitutes; Charles Augustus Howell concocting new and unlikely spiveries as he skirted the edges of criminality to help his friends, and in the dark eighteenth-century rooms of Cheyne Row Jane Carlyle watching over her melancholic husband as she mourned her life-long virginity.'

It is sad to think that for all Carlyle's agonies, as he grappled with his work, and for all Jane's vicarious suffering, he is no longer popular as an historian. Rossetti, long before his drug addiction killed him, had become impatient of the Pre-Raphaelite movement. And although Oscar Wilde, at the peak of his success, declared that 'there is absolutely nothing in the world but youth', just before he died, at the age of forty-four, he wrote to William Rothenstein 'I was all wrong, my dear boy, in my life . . .'

Whistler was described as 'eccentric in dress – though clean' during his student days, and remained so all his life, even though he complained that Oscar Wilde was despoiling Chelsea by wearing 'fancy dress'.

People found Turner's paintings incomprehensible and assumed he was mad. Whistler suffered an even more disastrous misunderstanding during his middle years, although he lived long enough to be acclaimed by his contemporaries for the great artist he was.

'I completely abandon Naturalism and Tradition' was said not in 1973 but more than half a century ago, before the First World War, in the short-lived periodical *Blast*, which was the mouthpiece of the Cubists, Futurists and Vorticists. Most of what the serious young people who frequent or live in Chelsea say today has been said before. That does not matter, nor does it mean that it is not completely sincere. No testament of belief or philosophy of living means very much until one has worked it out for oneself.

Nor does it matter – though it would have been interesting to know – what the Judge who heard the case of Whistler against Ruskin would have said to the young artist of the 1950s who, in replying to his critics, explained that he did not 'draw' horizontal lines on canvas. 'I apply polyvinyl and polythene tapes to boards which are treated with plastic emulsion paints; also of the three paintings I am exhibiting, two are horizontal with vertical readings across the plane of the painting,' he added.

The Judge may equally well have been perplexed by the work of Transmedia Exploration, a group of four men and a woman who expressed a wish to evolve a life responding to pure media and for whom, in 1970, the Arts Council's New Activities Committee granted £205. They passed their time – and perhaps still do – climbing in and out of plastic cocoons, called rain shells, or swinging upside down from scaffolding. One of them occupied himself by exploring responses to 'hornblowing, yelling, bread and food substances': but in asking for a further grant of £1,835 for the rest of the year, he complained that 'some people try to distort what we are trying to do. They try to make out that we are just a lot of layabouts.'

What really matters is that the rising generation produces men and women of talent, as the Bohemians of previous generations did, and that the drop-outs, the perpetual students and the misfits stop wasting everybody's time and are given the place in society which they merit, along with the young ruffians who have done physical damage to Chelsea. They must make room for the people of genuine gifts and purpose, who have neither the time nor the inclination for the extrovert ostentation of the inadequate and unsuccessful amateurs.

Chelsea has, of course, its own distinguished School of Art, where, before the war, both Henry Moore and Graham Sutherland were on the teaching staff. With a marked shortage of science students and a preponderance of young people studying the arts, there are fewer places available these days for art students, and admission to Colleges of Art is on a rising standard of merit.

The Chelsea School of Art, an interesting building in Manresa Road opposite the Library and the Technical College, of which it was originally a part, has an international reputation and a splendid record of achievement. It is mainly a school of painting and sculpture but has also an important department of graphic design.

Not many of its 250 full-time day students can afford to live in Chelsea and most have lodgings in Fulham, Putney or even farther afield, but within the school there is an atmosphere of calm, unhurried concentration and hard work.

The prospects of earning a living by painting or sculpture, other than by teaching, are considerably better than they were before the war and some students, on leaving college, are prepared to take any job, which will give them spare time to practise their art until they know they can live by it.

Fees are not high in comparison with the amount of money a

student will need to keep himself in food and lodging and there are one or two scholarships available, as well as a Trust Fund, from which, in addition to the public funds which can be administered by the Education Officer, grants can be made in cases of hardship.

The Chelsea College of Science and Technology at the corner of Manresa Road and the King's Road now has 1,500 students but they have a serious accommodation problem, for Lightfoot House can take only 180. Two student houses owned by the college accommodate twelve girls and twelve boys, but the rest have to rely on lodgings. First-year students are guaranteed accommodation through the lodgings office of London University, but the second- and third-year students have great difficulty in finding suitable places to live. Chelsea is too expensive and the farther afield they go, the higher the fares they must pay each day. With limited allowances and rising costs they suffer real hardship and the *Chelsea Post* for 15 October 1971 reported that some students had been reduced to sleeping on the floor of the Students' Union: but in 1973 the college plans to move to Tooting, where the situation may become easier.

Chelsea has always been a mixed society. Even when it was at its most famous as an artists' colony, the artists were never more than a small proportion of the community. Today, as a century ago, there are people from all walks of life living there and they include many who are helping to shape the contemporary thought and culture of the whole nation, authors and scientists, playwrights, actors and actresses, critics and journalists, politicians, financiers, lawyers, television personalities, film producers and directors.

Chelsea has many attractions. It is close to the heart of London, it has the river and its traditions, and an atmosphere of charm and friendliness which seems indestructible.

Only the rich can afford the large houses of Cheyne Walk and the squares and avenues. The small eighteenth-century and Regency cottages are also expensive, but for all their narrow stairs and dark basements, they are immensely popular and miracles of adaptation have been achieved, with cunningly contrived bathrooms and added windows. They are delightful, and one of their many attractions is their small but mature walled gardens.

Some of the older people have had to move away because of rising costs and a few because of repeated burglaries, but many families can claim to have lived in Chelsea for three or four generations, and among them there is still a strong community spirit, for the old village atmosphere dies very hard.

The churches still have steady and devoted congregations and are a living, active force, the centres of valuable social work as well as worship.

Chelsea does well by its old people and the incapacitated. Early in 1970 the splendid adventure playground was opened in Old Church Street for handicapped children and an important development is under way down by the World's End, where a great many wretched slum houses have been cleared and Cubitt's are building new homes for 2,500 people. Tall blocks of flats are going up, widely spaced, with gardens and playgrounds in between, as well as a church, a school, a library and shops.

Some people have overcome the problem of highly priced houses and flats by taking to the river and establishing themselves in house-boats, which are moored in Chelsea Reach at the Chelsea Yacht and Boat Club. During the 1940s the owners of these boats were mainly artists and theatre people. Today the professions of the colony are as varied as the boats themselves, including journalists and architects, editors and students.

There are some fifty boats moored here, most of them capable of being towed, though the majority have been stationary for years. They all have electricity and water laid on, and for a monthly charge the company administering the club looks after the necessary amenities, such as filling the water tanks and maintaining the gang-planks. It is a practical way of living and the community is friendly and cheerful. Here again is the village atmosphere which this part of Chelsea has never lost.

Some of the boats are luxurious conversions of roomy barges, with hulls 70 to 80 feet long, having been bought for a few hundred pounds and then transformed, at a cost of anything up to £6,000, into homes with large sitting-rooms, modern kitchens and bath-rooms and three or four bedrooms. A large number, however, have been converted from landing-craft discarded after the last war, while *Petula*, named after Petula Clark, proudly admits to having been welded from seven tons of air-raid table shelters.

The price of Chelsea studios is high and many are now used as ordinary domestic flats. There are probably no more than a hundred professional artists with studios in Chelsea today, the rest having scattered over London, to Fulham and Putney, Camden Town or Hampstead. At a recent fascinating exhibition of Artist Enamellers at the Chenil Galleries, held at the same time as the spring Antiques Fair at the Old Town Hall, it was interesting to see that, in the list of eighteen members of the group, only one had a Chelsea address.

To a great extent Chelsea and Kensington have a floating population. In the annual report of the Chelsea Society for 1969 there was an interesting note by Roland Clarke on the numbers of people moving in and out of Kensington and Chelsea. Among the thirty-two London boroughs, Kensington and Chelsea had by far the largest number of people moving into the borough. During the five years before the 1966 census, a total of 378 people per 1,000 of population had moved in, 235 from elsewhere in Great Britain and 143 from abroad. The next highest figure was Westminster, with 295 immigrants per 1,000 of population.

People move out of the borough at about the same rate as they move in, so the total population figure does not vary a great deal, but it does mean, as Mr Clarke points out: 'of a given population of the borough at any one time, three-eighths will have departed before the end of five years'.

The Chelsea Society, which has a membership of 785, was founded by Reginald Blunt in 1927, 'to protect and foster the amenities of Chelsea'. Reginald Blunt, in addition to writing his engaging and valuable histories, did much for Chelsea during his life-time. He loved it deeply and tried hard to preserve much that was being destroyed, at a time when Chelsea seemed careless of her treasures and historic buildings. Today, the Chelsea Society works valiantly to save what is left of old Chelsea and preserve it as a residential area. The floating population makes the task of the Society all the harder, for the migrants cannot be expected to be so concerned with preservation as the long-term residents. Nevertheless, though the fight is stiff and the odds heavy, the Society is doing admirable work and achieving a great deal.

They have saved Paulton's Square from demolition. They have protested against a plan to build a 405-bedroom hotel on the site of the Old Pier Hotel, on the corner of Cheyne Walk and Oakley Street, on the grounds that it would generate even more noise and traffic in a residential area and that such a massive building would be out of harmony with the surrounding houses. They have saved most of the *Pheasantry* and a number of houses and studios in Jubilee Place from demolition.

The society is not retrogressive or totally negative and is well aware that every place must develop or become moribund, but it is anxious that the world of business and entertainment should be confined to the King's Road and that the streets to the north and south should be spared as much as possible from increased traffic congestion and noise.

They worked hard for several years when it seemed that the Embankment itself was in jeopardy. There was a plan to enclose central London with a rectangular Box road, the western side of which coincided with Chelsea's western boundary. The first idea put forward by the Greater London Council was for a new bridge to be built from the Chelsea basin to Battersea, which would carry traffic bound for the east of London and the docks to the south side of the Box. This would have meant the end of the Chelsea Boat Club but would have relieved the heavy traffic along the Chelsea Embankment and the even greater amount which hurtles down Beaufort Street and over Battersea Bridge, to the mortal danger of anyone who does not use a pedestrian-crossing.

However, a new stage in the planning developed. It became known that before the new bridge was built and the construction of the south side of the Box, slip roads from Lots Road Power Station to the Chelsea Embankment were to be made, cutting across Chelsea Reach and converging at the head of Battersea Bridge. This meant that, for an indeterminate number of years, the Chelsea Embankment would have served as the south side of the Box.

An enormous volume of traffic already speeds along the Chelsea Embankment and this new diversion would have entailed widening the Embankment, presumably over the river, or perhaps destroying the gardens, which provide a small protection to the houses in Cheyne Walk.

Moreover, Battersea strongly protested against the building of the south side of the Box and, had the borough's objections been success- ful, there would have been no point in building the new bridge. Cheyne Walk was therefore in grave danger of becoming the perma- nent south side of the Box. Even though the Greater London Council had said the slip road would have been sunk, it would have been a disastrous development for Chelsea.

A later planning proposal had been to build an additional con- necting road to Wandsworth Bridge, to take north–south traffic on to the West Cross route quickly across the river, but the new Greater London Council, elected in 1973, has shelved the entire plan for the Inner Ring Road.

At a meeting of the Chelsea Society in October 1971, the chair- man, Noel Blakiston, said: 'We do not expect to be able to turn the

Embankment into a road for hay wagons and tricycles as it once was. We are not against a West Cross Route as such. But at the same time we hope to prevent the Embankment from being turned into a race-track for lorries.'

The Society is backed by the local Council in its fight to maintain the amenities of residential Chelsea, and at a by-election speech in 1970 one candidate complained that the King's Road was saturated with antique shops and boutiques, while a wide variety of old-established traders had been forced to close down. Residents are entitled to demand a balanced community, he declared, and the Council could play a part in correcting the present imbalance.

One corner of traditional Chelsea which still flourishes is the Chelsea Arts Club. The club house in Old Church Street is a conversion of two eighteenth-century cottages, and although it was remodelled in 1933 to allow for five more bedrooms for country members, the building has lost nothing of its original charm. Delightful bow windows open from the billiard-room on to about an acre of walled garden. On a raw mid-March day, with the snow only just melted and an east wind blowing down the King's Road, in the sheltered club house garden not only were the forsythia and japonica bursting into flower but a little camellia bush was in full bloom.

The membership has now reached 700 and is open to people from a variety of professions associated with the arts, including writers, journalists, dress designers, antique dealers and stage people, only a small proportion of whom live in Chelsea. Women are also admitted, with only the billiard-room remaining as a male sanctuary.

The club is essentially a friendly and informal place, and is still inexpensive, though it is hard to realise that the prices of the pre-war prospectus are well within living memory. In those days, breakfast used to cost eight old pence, luncheon, which was served at 1.20 p.m. cost from about a shilling and dinner, at 7.30 p.m. would cost from one shilling and sixpence. Four courses were served at both meals. Tea, between four and six o'clock, was six old pence and the charge for a bedroom, including bath and early morning tea, was three shillings and sixpence a night and one guinea for a week.

In the dining-room, which looks on to the garden, there is one large dining table, seating eighteen or twenty people, so that members soon get to know each other and talk freely.

In the Whistler bar there are many Whistler mementoes, including the beautifully carved pagoda cabinet, which was made in Japan during the nineteenth century from a Chinese model. This was the cabinet which William Rossetti so greatly admired at Whistler's house-warming party at 96 Cheyne Walk and which aroused his interest in Oriental art. Whistler had to part with it at the time of the White House sale and it was bought by Sydney Moss, the solicitor who had taken over 96 Cheyne Walk. In 1937 it passed to his grandson, who was still living in the Cheyne Walk house, and in 1957 it was presented to the Chelsea Library, who handed it to the Chelsea Arts Club on permanent loan.

Although there are many pictures by past members on the walls of the club, it is their policy not to hang works of contemporary artist members, for fear of making invidious distinctions.

By the same token, it would be well nigh impossible to list the present-day residents of Chelsea who are helping to shape contemporary thought and culture. John Osborne has influenced the theatre, for he was the first of the 'angry young men'. Laurie Lee and Ursula Bloom have been read and enjoyed by thousands. David Frost, Jack de Manio and Robert Robinson are among the radio and television personalities whose impact is strong. The list can never be complete for as one writes people are moving in or moving out of the borough.

It is perhaps sufficient to say that many people who have attained high distinction in their professions still choose Chelsea as a place in which to live. After the few years of the 'Swinging Chelsea' cult, when it looked for a time as though an alien intrusion were going to destroy it, Chelsea has recovered its balance and reasserted itself. Its traditions still live and its corners of quiet beauty remain.

The same can be said of Kensington. Holland House had a last-minute reprieve. By 1952 the derelict house had been taken over by the London County Council and was in danger of being totally demolished. Most of it was damaged beyond any hope of restoration and vandals had contributed to the dereliction of the ruins, but it was found that the east wing was capable of repair. The Kensington Society, backed by Lord Ilchester, petitioned for its rescue and demolition was delayed. Then the Youth Hostels Association offered to restore and adapt the east wing as part of a hostel for overseas visitors and country members. The King George VI Memorial Fund and the London County Council contributed to the cost and in 1954 the work was put in hand. The following year the remainder of the hostel, designed by Sir Hugh Casson and Neville Conder, was built adjoining it. At the same time the arcades and south front of the old house were preserved and the terrace remodelled, so that some indication of its former beauty remains.

Twenty-eight acres of woodland to the north were opened to the public in 1952 and today the orangery is a restaurant.

Close to the High Street, in the southern part of the grounds, has arisen the Commonwealth Institute, opened by Queen Elizabeth II in 1962. It has taken over the functions once undertaken by the Imperial Institute, to promote a better understanding and knowledge of the peoples of the Commonwealth. Here there are permanent displays showing the history, daily life, natural resources, industries and economy of all the Commonwealth countries, exhibitions of the work of Commonwealth artists and documentary film shows. The building, all split levels and open staircases inside, is of opaque blue glass with an undulating green roof, looking like some gigantic petrified Bedouin tent, as much out of tune with the forlorn ghost of Holland House behind it as the concrete hostel buildings adjoining the east wing, but the flags of the Commonwealth countries, planted close together on their tall flag poles, wave cheerfully enough to the Odeon cinema on the other side of the road.

Leighton House close by is now a museum. The contents of the house had been sold shortly after Lord Leighton's death but the Leighton House Association, formed by his friends, had maintained the house until 1926, when it was transferred to the Kensington Borough Council, who bought the freehold from the Ilchester Estate. The house suffered war damage and was not restored and re-opened until 1951. By 1969 a selection of late nineteenth-century paintings and sculpture was obtained, on permanent loan, from the Tate and other galleries, with furniture from the Victoria and Albert Museum, thus forming a valuable museum of High Victorian art, and adjoining the house is the British Theatre Museum.

Kensington High Street today is prosperous and trim. The teenage cult of the sixties duly arrived, with branch shops from Carnaby Street and the King's Road, Chelsea, as well as some new, independent ventures. On the north side is the vast antique Hypermarket, on the south the Kensington Market, like a huge but enclosed street market.

Pontings has moved to the basement of *Barkers* and the firm of *Derry and Toms* has gone. Changes are taking place all the time, yet the 'noble roadway' of Kensington High Street absorbs all these developments in such a way that they do not alter its essential character, just as *Harrods* in the Brompton Road has incorporated its *Way*

In floor as an intelligent and business-like salute to contemporary taste, without impairing the store's dependable Edwardian traditions.

Church Street suffered some grievous bomb damage during the Second World War but all traces of it have disappeared and the southern end has good antique shops as well as some amusing dress shops. At the northern end, round Notting Hill Gate, there has been a complete transformation of modern development.

The streets behind the High Street are little changed – a mixture of the large houses of the late Victorian developments, most of which have been turned into flats, and a few enclaves of Georgian and early Victorian terraces of cottages and small dwelling houses, such as St Albans Grove and Victoria Road, between the High Street and Gloucester Road, and Gordon Place behind St Mary Abbots, where the charming little paved gardens are full of flowering shrubs and trees. Today they are all valuable properties and are kept in impeccable order, like the houses in Edwardes Square and Kensington Square, where, not so long ago, John Richard Green, Sir Hubert Parry and Mrs Pat Campbell were living.

Kensington Palace, safe now from all thoughts of demolition, is rather overwhelmed by the mighty Royal Garden Hotel, which shoots up suddenly from the pavement of the High Street, at the edge of Kensington Gardens, but Kensington Gardens are still the best loved of the London parks, with the statues and pavilion, Queen Anne's alcove, the bird sanctuary, the children's playground, the dog's cemetery, founded by the Duke of Cambridge, the Round Pond, the beautiful flower walk and the Broad Walk which, though it has lost its famous elms is now planted with limes.

The South Kensington on to which Prince Albert gazes from his monument is a busy and vital place and the prestige of its museums and colleges has never been higher. All the museums have been reorganized since the end of the Second World War and bomb damage has been restored.

The Victoria and Albert Museum has frequent temporary exhibitions, giving the public fresh aspects of pure and applied art, old and new, as well as the wonderful permanent displays of its primary collections, 'masterpieces of all the arts, brought together by style, period or nationality'. The study collections are held in reserve for the connoisseurs.

The Science Museum is as popular as it has ever been and has over a million visitors a year.

The Imperial College of Science and Technology, with its associated buildings, fills the whole of the block from Prince Consort Road to the north and the Imperial Institute Road to the south.

From among the students of the Royal College of Art, as well as distinguished artists and sculptors, are coming many leaders of design in the applied arts, and in 1956 they undertook the commission for the stained glass in the nave of Coventry Cathedral.

In the Cromwell Road, on the other side from the Natural History Museum, is the French Institute, and a few hundred yards away is the West London Air Terminal, so that South Kensington today, with its museums and colleges, its dozens of student hostels and hotels, is as important to the intellectual and artistic life of London as Blooms-bury.

In Kensington Gore the De Vere Hotel at Hyde Park Gate, one of the oldest in Kensington, has been modernised. In the cul-de-sac be-hind it Sir Winston Churchill lived at number 28 and Epstein at number 18. Here also are more embassies, including that of Australia. In fact there are thirty-three embassies, legations and High Commis-sion residences in Kensington and twenty-eight offices of foreign countries.

In Knightsbridge, the barracks have been rebuilt yet again and at the junction with the Brompton Road now stands the vast glass and steel Bowater House, while the new Berkeley Hotel has recently opened in Wilton Place.

Yet the Brompton Road, with its antique shops and wide, stepped pavement, curving back to South Kensington, still has the air of a country town and seems oddly remote from the developments which press round it so closely.

At the first count, in 1965, after Chelsea and Kensington had been joined to become the Royal Borough, the total population was 216,800, living in an area of 2,951 acres.

The coat of arms of the new borough is a shield with an abbot's mitre on a red field, surmounted by three royal crowns. The mitre symbolises Kensington's association with the Abbey of Abingdon and Chelsea's with the Abbey of Westminster, and the three crowns are the sign of its royal status. The shield is supported by a blue boar, part of the arms of the De Veres of Kensington, and a winged ox, symbol of St Luke, the patron saint of Chelsea's ancient parish church.

And the motto is *Quam bonum in unum habitare* – 'What a good thing it is to dwell together in unity' – significant indeed for the heterogeneous population of rich and poor, artists and writers, members of the professions, office workers, artisans, shopkeepers and students living in the borough, including the large number of West Indians in North Kensington and Notting Hill.

The splendid new town hall, designed by Sir Basil Spence, is under way on the Abbey site between Hornton Street and Campden Hill, where the new Kensington Central Library, designed by E. Vincent Harris and one of the finest municipal libraries in the country, was opened in 1960.

The new town hall is a courtyard plan, which has spared some of the lovely trees of this corner of Kensington, and includes a council chamber, committee rooms, a mayoral suite, members rooms, an assembly hall seating over eight hundred people and a smaller one for about two hundred.

Here the vast work of the housing department, including clearance and redevelopment, the children's care department, the multifarious branches of the health service, the welfare services, including the 'Meals on Wheels' for the elderly and disabled, which is administered by the Kensington and Chelsea Communal Services Committee with help from the Council, the education and library services of the Royal Borough can be administered under one roof: and the building has been arranged so that access to the various departments is by way of the courtyard, creating an informal and friendly atmosphere, where people can come and go about their business without having to negotiate the sometimes daunting oppression of a formidable civic entrance hall.

Kensington and Chelsea are planning for the present and for the future, but at the same time the borough is supporting the work of the Kensington and Chelsea Societies which are concerned with preserving as far as is possible and practical the magnificent heritage of parks and gardens and beautiful old buildings which have come into being throughout the thousand years of its history.

Bibliography

ADBURGHAM, ALISON, Shops and Shopping, *Allen and Unwin, 1964.*

AUBREY, Brief Lives.

BEAVER, PATRICK, The Crystal Palace, *Hugh Evelyn, 1970.*

BLUNT, REGINALD, Handbook of Chelsea, *1900.*

BLUNT, REGINALD, Paradise Row, *Macmillan, 1906.*

BLUNT, REGINALD, Wonderful Village, *Mills and Boon, 1918.*

CAINE, HALL, Recollections of Rossetti, *Cassell, 1928.*

CECIL, DAVID, Melbourne, *Constable, 1954.*

CHEYNE BOOK OF CHELSEA, China and Pottery, *Geoffrey Bles, 1924.*

Creevey Papers.

DEAN. C. G. T., The Royal Hospital, Chelsea, *Hutchinson, 1950.*

Encyclopaedia of English Pottery and Porcelain, *André Deutsch, 1957.*

EVELYN, JOHN, Diary.

FAULKNER, THOMAS, An Historical and Topographical Description of Chelsea and Its Environs, *London, 1810.*

FAULKNER, THOMAS, History and Antiquities of Kensington, *London, 1820.*

FINBERG, A. J., Life of J. M. Turner, R.A., *Clarendon Press, 1939.*

GAUNT, WILLIAM, Chelsea, *Batsford, 1954.*

GAUNT, WILLIAM, Kensington, *Batsford, 1960.*

GAUNT, WILLIAM, The Pre-Raphaelite Tragedy, *Cape, 1942.*

Greville Diary, *Heinemann, 1927.*

HERVEY, LORD, Memoirs.

HOBHOUSE, CHRISTOPHER, 1851 and the Crystal Palace, *John Murray, 1937.*

HOLMAN HUNT, DIANA, My Grandmothers and I, *Hamish Hamilton, 1960.*

HOLME, THEA, The Carlyles At Home, *O.U.P., 1965.*

HONEY, W. B., English Pottery and Porcelain, *A. and C. Black, 1969.*

HUDSON, DEREK, Holland House in Kensington, *Peter Davies, 1967.*

HUDSON, DEREK, Kensington Palace, *Peter Davies, 1968.*

HUGHES, G. BERNARD, English Pottery and Porcelain Figures, *A. and C. Black, 1969.*

HUNT, LEIGH, The Old Court Suburb, *Freemantle and Co., 1902.*

LAVER, JAMES, Oscar Wilde, *British Council, 1954.*

LAVER, JAMES, Whistler, *Faber and Faber, 1930.*

L'ESTRANGE, A. G., The Village of Palaces, *London, 1880.*

ORPEN, WILLIAM, Outline of Art, *Newnes, n.d.*

PEPYS, SAMUEL, Diary.

POTTER, BEATRIX, Journal, *Warne and Co. Ltd.*

RICHIE, ANNE THACKERAY, Thackeray's Daughter, *Dublin, 1951.*

ROTHENSTEIN, WILLIAM, Men and Memories, *Faber and Faber, 1931.*

SANDERS, LLOYD, The Holland House Circle, *Methuen, 1908.*

SANDERS, LLOYD, Old Kew, Chiswick and Kensington, *Methuen, 1910.*

SAVAGE, GEORGE, Porcelain Through the Ages, *Cassell, 1961.*

SEMPLE, R. H., Memoirs of the Botanic Garden at Chelsea, *1878.*

WALFORD, EDWARD, Old and New London, *Cassell, 1890.*

WALLAS, ADA, Before the Blue Stockings, *Allen and Unwin, 1929.*

WALPOLE, HORACE, Memoirs and Portraits.

Chambers Encyclopaedia of English Literature.

Dictionary of National Biography.

Chelsea Old Church – 1941–50
Chelsea Old Church } Handbooks

CHELSEA PHYSIC GARDEN, Its History and Origin – Handbook, *London, 1965.*

Index

Hill, Abigail (*later Lady Masham*), 3,
  62–4
  Sir John, 95, 153
  Thomas, 19, 28, 41
Hoadley, Dr Benjamin, 115
Hockney, David, 251
Holbein, Hans, 11–12
Holland, Henry, 1st Earl of, 22–6
  Robert, 2nd Earl of, 26, 51
  Edward, 3rd Earl of, 51, 74–6
  House (*see also Cope Castle*), 2–3, 22,
    26, 51, 76, 88, 95, 157, 160–3, 166,
    177, 212, 221–2, 262
  Henry Fox, 1st Lord, 76, 88–90,
    93–4, 130
  Stephen Fox, 2nd Lord, 89, 93–4
  Henry, 3rd Lord, 94–5, 157–66
  Henry, 4th Lord, 166, 177–8
  Lady (*see Elizabeth Webster*)
Hooke, Sir Hele, 65
Howard, Catherine, 14
  of Effingham, Lord, 16, 30
  Sir Philip, 50
Hudson, George, 176
Hunt, Diana Holman, 215, 217–18
  Holman, 3, 137, 192–4, 200, 214–16
  Leigh, 2–3, 27, 133–5, 149, 175, 185
  Violet, 224
Hunter, John, 114, 155, 220
Huntingdon, Earl of, 114
Hyde Park, 17, 52
  Corner, 96

Ilchester, Lord, 89, 93
  5th Lord, 212, 221
  6th Lord, 221
Imperial College of Science and Tech-
  nology, 187–8, 264
  Institute, 187
Inchbald, Elizabeth, 168–70
Inverness, Duchess of, 152, 222
Irving, Edward, 131

Jacomb-Hood, 226, 228
James I, 19, 21–3, 29–30, 38, 152
  II, 36
  Henry, 2, 228–9, 235
  Stuart, 63–4

Jephson, William, 115
Jersey, Lady, 142
Jervoise, Richard, 13, 16, 243
John, Augustus, 235–6
Johnson, Dr, 104, 114, 117, 126
Jones, Lady, 47, 102
Jordon, Dorothy, 146–7

Katharine of Aragon, 12, 230
Kendel, Duchess of (*formerly Frau von
  Schulenberg*), 68, 70–1
Kensington
  in the 16th century, 2, 6, 19
  in the 17th century, 20–7, 49–60, 65
  in the 18th century, 2–3, 60–7, 69–99
  in the 19th century, 3, 142–89
  in the 20th century, 3, 219–24, 262–6
  the court at, 55–64, 69–72, 76–91
  early history of, 3–4, 6
Kensington Central Library, 266
Kensington Gardens, 61, 78, 95–6, 224
Kensington High Street, 168, 219, 263
Kensington House (*see also Holland
  House*), 65, 90, 154, 188
Kensington Palace (*formerly Nottingham
  House*), 2–3, 56–61, 70–1, 78, 88,
  95, 143, 147–8, 177, 222–3, 264
Kensington Square, 2, 55, 64–5, 91, 152
Kent, Duchess of (*see Victoria of Lenin-
  gen*),
  Duke of, 3, 142–3, 146–7
  House, 153
  Marina, Duchess of, 223
  William, 70–1, 118
Kielmansegge, Count Frederick, 97–8
King's Road, 40, 129, 191, 249–54
Kingsley, Rev. William, 140–1, 190
Kingston, Duke of, 97–8
  House, 98–9, 153
Kitching, Kate, 236
Knightsbridge, 3, 6, 25, 53–4, 91
Knipp, 39, 50, 53
Knowles, Admiral, 114
Koenigsmark, Count, 68

Lamb, Lady Caroline, 160–1, 165
  William (*see Lord Melbourne*)
Lang, Andrew, 224

A Map of CHELSEA, SURVEYED in the YEAR 1664 by James Hamilton. Continued to 1717.

K. HEN. VIII.th MANOR HOUSE IN CHEYNE WA

Road from Little Chelsea to Knights bridge

A-R-P
4-3-3

A-R-P
4-0-29

A-R-P
21-1-0

A.
32

A-R-P

Lord Whartons Park. 40 Acres

Lime Walk

Road to the Craße Tree

Mr Watts House

Kings Road

Dove House Close 4 Acres

Duke of Beauforts House & Garden

Church Lane

Coroner Street

Bowling Green

Mr Woodcocks Garden

al bridge Chelsea

oh's en P O

Kings Road   Worlds End

Way between the Paales

Way to Little Chelsea

Bowling Green

Priests Close

Priests and Linsey House

Lord Whartons Garden

Church

3-3-35

WEST FIELD

THE RIVER THAMES

WS

Publish'd as the Act dire